METH MANIA

Social Problems, Social Constructions

Joel Best and Scott R. Harris, series editors

METH MANIA

A History of Methamphetamine

Nicholas L. Parsons

LYNNE
RIENNER
PUBLISHERS

BOULDER
LONDON

Published in the United States of America in 2014 by
Lynne Rienner Publishers, Inc.
1800 30th Street, Boulder, Colorado 80301
www.rienner.com

and in the United Kingdom by
Lynne Rienner Publishers, Inc.
3 Henrietta Street, Covent Garden, London WC2E 8LU

Library of Congress Cataloging-in-Publication Data
Parsons, Nicholas L.
Meth mania : a history of methamphetamine / Nicholas L. Parsons.
     pages cm. — (Social problems, social constructions)
  Includes bibliographical references and index.
  ISBN 978-1-58826-983-6 (hc : alk. paper)
  1. Methamphetamine—United States. 2. Methamphetamine abuse—
United States. I. Title.
HV5822.A5P37 2014
362.29'950973—dc23
                                                    2013020812

British Cataloguing in Publication Data
A Cataloguing in Publication record for this book
is available from the British Library.

Printed and bound in the United States of America

        The paper used in this publication meets the requirements
 ∞   of the American National Standard for Permanence of
        Paper for Printed Library Materials Z39.48-1992.

  5 4 3 2 1

To Mom, Dad, and Nessie

Contents

Tables and Figures

Tables

Figures

Acknowledgments

I could not have written this book without the help and support of many individuals. I am extremely grateful for the insightful comments on early versions of my manuscript offered by Michael P. Allen, Jennifer Schwartz, Thomas Rotolo, and, especially, Clayton J. Mosher. Don A. Dillman, Alair MacLean, Bryan D. Rookey, and Michael J. Stern also provided constructive feedback on various ideas presented here. In addition to their scholarly input, I am very appreciative of the inspiration and encouragement all these individuals have extended to me throughout much of my professional career.

I am also indebted to many of my colleagues and friends at Eastern Connecticut State University. Cara Bergstrom-Lynch, Dennis Canterbury, Kimberly Dugan, Mary Kenny, William Lugo, Ricardo Pérez, James Russell, Theresa Severance, and Robert Wolf offered valuable feedback to different ideas and arguments presented in the book and served as constant sources of optimism throughout the writing process. I also thank Eastern Connecticut State University's library staff (especially Michael Gadoury, Kris Jacobi, Greg Robinson, and Tracy Sutherland); the Department of Sociology, Anthropology, and Social Work; and the larger Eastern community for their regular assistance and support.

The critiques and suggestions offered by several individuals at Lynne Rienner Publishers also helped make this book possible. Comments from Joel Best, Scott R. Harris, Andrew Berzanskis, and two anonymous reviewers proved instrumental in the revision process. In addition, I thank Karen Maye, Karen Williams, and the rest of the staff at Lynne Rienner Publishers who contributed to this project.

I also need to acknowledge the moral support of several amazing friends I've had the great fortune to know outside of my professional life, including Mike and Meg Albanese, Kevin Beaudoin, Erica Bovino, Bryson Burse, James Gaffney, Ben Hogan, Pete and Laura Montana, Paul and Gina Sasso, Brynn Simons, and Bill and Audra Walsh. Throughout and beyond the various stages of writing, their love and friendship have bettered my life immeasurably.

Finally, I am truly thankful for the encouragement and love from family, including my aunts, uncles, and cousins; my brother-in-law, Craig; and my grandmother Jean. Most significantly, I owe a mountain of appreciation to my wonderful sister and friend, Erin, and to my loving parents, Cindy and Steve, who inspired me from a young age to inquire about the world, and who have supported me in all of my personal and professional endeavors.

1

From Wonder Drug
to Public Health Menace

The drug is the stuff of nightmares, driving an Arizona father to
allegedly hack the head off his teenage son because he thought the boy
was a devil. A Fremont man who family members say is a loving son
stabbed his 76-year-old father repeatedly, police said, thinking aliens
had invaded the elderly man's body. A drug-crazed thief committed
point-blank shotgun murders of two teens he mistakenly thought
cheated him, Alameda County authorities say. He denies the killing but
said: "I can tell you that that drug makes me the evilest person in the
world." The drug is methamphetamine, but in an alarming new form
that is twice as potent and, experts say, more likely to provoke such
unbridled violence. Because it's cheaper and easier to make than in the
past, today's methamphetamine is flooding California and spreading
across the nation. —*Daniel Vasquez (1996, A1)*

These anecdotes, published in a US newspaper, provide miserable and
vile examples of human suffering, all purportedly caused by the drug
methamphetamine. These short accounts are just a few of the many horror stories written about the real-world consequences people have suffered from their association with illicit drugs. Unquestionably, methamphetamine has contributed to a variety of problems, from poor health,
violence, and property crime to family disruption, personal despair, and
community decay. But if this newspaper excerpt—and the hundreds of
similar stories communicated by US news media—were to represent
colors, brushstrokes, and figures in a painting depicting the methamphetamine problem in the United States, the portrait is unintelligible and
incomplete.

Methamphetamine, also referred to as Desoxyn, Methedrine, crystal
meth, crank, ice, glass, yaba, and Tina, among other names, is a chemical

1

stimulant, or "upper." Stimulants arouse the brain and central nervous system, generally producing wakefulness, energy, heightened awareness and concentration, and increased blood pressure and heart rate. In contrast, the large class of drugs referred to as depressants, or "downers" (e.g., alcohol, Xanax), generally instill calming feelings, decreased respiration, sedation, and sleep. Methamphetamine is one member of a broader class of stimulants—the amphetamines. Several other amphetamines include Benzedrine, dextroamphetamine, levoamphetamine, and methylenedioxymethamphetamine (MDMA, or, more popularly, ecstasy).[1] In popular culture, most amphetamines, including methamphetamine, are often collectively referred to as "speed" for their energizing effects.

From the mid-1990s through the first six or so years of the twenty-first century, media outlets, politicians, and others dedicated a considerable amount of attention to the problems wrought by methamphetamine. One of the popularly communicated messages during this time period was that meth was a "new" drug, distinctly different from other amphetamines. Such claims, however, were false (Armstrong 2007). Like cocaine, methamphetamine and other amphetamines were once widely and legally available without a doctor's prescription. A series of federal restrictions enacted during the 1950s, 1960s, and 1970s ultimately created two separate markets for the drug—a black market for "meth" and a "white market" for Desoxyn and other prescription amphetamines (DeGrandpre 2006). While amphetamines were once promoted for a multitude of physical and psychological conditions, today's synthetic stimulants are mainly prescribed for attention-deficit disorder (ADD) or attention-deficit/hyperactivity disorder (ADHD) and narcolepsy. Though nationally representative data on medically sanctioned amphetamine use are scarce, one study estimates that approximately 4.8 percent of children in the United States (about 2.7 million total) from the ages of four to seventeen were prescribed ADHD medications in 2007 (Visser et al. 2010). Table 1.1 lists the brand names and active chemical ingredients of several prescription stimulants used to treat ADD/ADHD, narcolepsy, obesity, and other conditions.

While concerns over medicinal forms of speed are occasionally raised in congressional hearings, the news media, and other domains of public discourse, white-market amphetamines are rarely met with the same degrees of fear and hysteria periodically accorded to street meth. First synthesized in the late 1800s, methamphetamine specifically, and amphetamines generally, have not always been subjects of national concern. Rather, the nation's attention toward speed has ebbed and flowed for most of the past century. In the 1940s, the Food and Drug

**Table 1.1   Brand Names and Active Ingredients
of Select Prescription Stimulants**

Brand Name	Active Ingredients
Benzedrine[a]	Amphetamine Sulfate
Dexedrine; Dextrostat	Dextroamphetamine Sulfate
Desoxyn; Methedrine[a]	Methamphetamine HCl
Adderall; Adderall XR	*Four equal parts of* Dextroamphetamine Saccharate Amphetamine Aspartate Dextroamphetamine Sulfate Amphetamine Sulfate
Biphetamine	Dextroamphetamine Sulfate and Amphetamine
Obetrol[a]	*Four equal parts of* Methamphetamine Saccharate Methamphetamine HCl Amphetamine Sulfate Dextroamphetamine Sulfate
Preludin	Phenmetrazine HCl
Prelu-2; Bontril	Phendimetrazine Tartrate
Apidex; Obe-Nix; Ionamin; Zantryl	Phentermine HCl
Vyvanse	Lisdexamfetamine Dimesylate
Ritalin; Ritalin XR; Ritalin LA; Concerta; Metadate; Methylin	Methylphenidate HCl
Focalin; Focalin XR	Dexmethylphenidate HCl
Provigil; Alertec	Modafinil
Nuvigil	Armodafinil
Strattera	Atomoxetine HCl

Sources: Drug Identification Bible (DIB) 2006; Rasmussen 2008a; McDonagh et al. 2011; DIB 2012.
   Notes: This list is by no means exhaustive.
   a. No longer in production.

Administration (FDA) expressed alarm over the abuse of amphetamine-laced inhalers sold over the counter (OTC) in pharmacies and grocery stores. In the 1960s and 1970s, speed (often called Methedrine or "crank" at the time) was linked with outlaw motorcycle gangs and working-class whites and was even despised by members of the drug-loving hippie counterculture. In 1989, during the midst of the crack cocaine problem, a mini panic erupted over "ice," a smokable form of methamphetamine.

Most recently, public health advocates, government officials, journalists, and others wholly condemned "crystal meth," the newest colloquial name for the drug. In April 1996, President Bill Clinton (1996) warned that methamphetamine was "gaining in popularity" and was poised to become "the crack of the 1990's." By 2005, *Newsweek* magazine proclaimed meth "America's Most Dangerous Drug" (Jefferson et al. 2005a). Around this time, methamphetamine arguably stole the limelight from crack cocaine as the worst mind-altering substance known to humankind. However, within a few years, meth had largely receded from public consciousness. In the early 2010s, attention toward methamphetamine slowly increased yet again, though largely in regard to its indirect connection to a seemingly new drug of concern—"bath salts."

Contrary to the majority of past and present portrayals, the connection between methamphetamine and the damage it causes cannot be understood through mere reference to the drug's chemical structure. The scope and depth of the methamphetamine problem in the United States are more complex and multidimensional than 500-word newspaper articles or thirty-second sound bites suggest. Rather, the story of methamphetamine is rife with cultural contradictions, interest groups competing for power and resources, and the unintended consequences of a century's worth of drug prohibitions. And although many news organizations, interest groups, policymakers, and members of the general public often tend to present and discuss social problems as clear-cut, black-and-white, either-or matters, the historical and contemporary realities of methamphetamine suggest the opposite is true.

In the pages that follow, I describe an assortment of cultural, historical, and social forces that have shaped the evolution of the synthetic stimulant problem in the United States since the early 1900s. Because methamphetamine hydrochloride—a drug whose chemical formula has remained unchanged since its invention in 1893—has been depicted quite differently at various points in US history, how and under what conditions such changes in public perception have occurred are worth investigating. As such, I focus largely on the shifting portrayals of methamphetamine in the news media, the many professional organizations that have sought to influence public definitions of the drug, and the variety of laws that have been enacted in an attempt to solve the meth problem.

Attention must be given to the wide range of claims made about meth over time because the content of these claims, as well as the persons making them, has helped shape and reshape the methamphetamine situation into its current form. Indeed, my primary argument throughout is that many of the contemporary problems associated with methamphetamine—the increased popularity of a relatively dangerous and addictive smokable form of the drug, the chemical contamination caused by clandestine "meth labs" where methamphetamine is often manufactured, and the high degree of violence associated with meth trafficking in the United States and along the border with Mexico—are largely due to drug policies enacted in a culture of fear perpetuated through the mass media. Before outlining the early history of drug use in the United States and examining the periodic waves of public scrutiny directed toward methamphetamine (i.e., the Methedrine, ice, and crystal meth scares), I will lay the theoretical foundation for my analysis with a discussion of two separate yet related concepts: (1) a supply-versus-demand approach to drugs and (2) a social constructionist approach to the study of social problems.

Supply-and-Demand Perspective on Drug Problems

Whether consumed for medicinal or religious purposes, for pleasure, or out of sheer curiosity, legal and illegal psychoactive drugs have been used by people in virtually every human society throughout history (Gahlinger 2004; Mosher and Akins 2007). Presumably due to the lack of vegetation, Eskimos are perhaps the only cultural group in the world without a long tradition of drug use (DeGrandpre 2006). The ubiquity of psychoactive chemicals in past and present societies suggests that the desire to alter one's consciousness is a basic human drive (Siegel 1989; Bickel and DeGrandpre 1996; Weil and Rosen 2004; Mosher and Akins 2007). Research has shown that humans are not alone—even animals seek out intoxicating foods:

> After sampling the numbing nectar of certain orchids, bees drop to the ground in a temporary stupor, then weave back for more. Birds gorge themselves on inebriating berries, then fly with reckless abandon. Cats eagerly sniff aromatic "pleasure" plants, then play with imaginary objects. Cows that browse special range weeds will twitch, shake, and stumble back to the plants for more. Elephants purposely get drunk on fermented fruits. Snacks on "magic mushrooms" cause monkeys to sit with their heads on their hands in a posture reminiscent of Rodin's *Thinker*. (Siegel 1989, 11)

Some scholars have gone so far as to posit that the human species has evolved to its present state of intelligence as a result of past psychoactive substance use. Terrence McKenna (1991) theorizes that the ingestion of psilocybin, a hallucinogenic compound found naturally in certain mushrooms that sprout from cow manure, spurred the rise of human consciousness, religion, and language. As the Sahara started to expand approximately 150,000 years ago, forest-dwelling primates began foraging grasslands and, consequently, domesticating cattle. McKenna (1991) cites archaeological evidence painted on the walls of Algerian caves to support his theory: "Here are the earliest known depictions of shamans in coincidence with large numbers of grazing animals, specifically, cattle. . . . The shamans, dancing and holding fistfuls of mushrooms, also have mushrooms sprouting out of their bodies" (147). McKenna suggests that the psychoactive properties of the psilocybin mushroom allowed early hominids to achieve levels of consciousness and conceive of the self in new and profound ways, giving them a leg up evolutionarily by facilitating the development of language and religion.

McKenna's postulation that psychedelic mushrooms spurred the earliest spiritual beliefs held by humans points to a larger connection between psychoactive substances and religion. Across time and place, people have used drugs to "transcend their sense of separateness and feel more at one with God, nature, and the supernatural" (Weil and Rosen 2004, 16). Indeed, a cursory examination of the historical record finds plentiful evidence of a relationship between mind-altering drugs and religious ceremony. For example, prehistoric Hindu and Zoroastrian texts suggest the altered states of consciousness achieved through the ingestion of psychoactive plants were central to the religious rituals of ancient India and Persia (see Shanon 2008 for a review). For thousands of years, many North American Indian tribes have used mescaline "buttons" harvested from the hallucinogenic peyote cactus to "experience God through the intermediary of nature" (Faupel, Horowitz, and Weaver 2004, 143). And while Rastafarianism is a relatively recent religion in which adherents smoke "ganja" to come to a better understanding of God (Faupel, Horowitz, and Weaver 2004), marijuana's spiritual use dates back much further (Weil and Rosen 2004).

Stimulants have also played a role in the religious institutions of some societies. By 1300 CE, coffee earned the title as the "wine of Islam" (Gahlinger 2004, 180), in part because around this time period, Muslim men would congregate weekly and chant and pray throughout the night under the influence of copious amounts of caffeine (Weil and Rosen 2004).

For millennia, indigenous peoples of modern-day Chile, Colombia, Peru, and Bolivia have chewed the leaves of the coca plant, the natural source of cocaine, to ward off fatigue and work long hours at high elevations. Coca is enjoyed during civil and religious rituals, as Andean natives regard its leaves as sacred and vital to life (Gahlinger 2004; DIB 2006). In the Incan empire, "priests and supplicants were allowed to approach the Altar of the Inca only if they had coca leaf in their mouths" (Brecher 1972, 269).

The twigs and leaves of the *Catha edulis* plant, better known as khat, have been chewed throughout areas of eastern Africa and the Arabian Peninsula for centuries (C. Brooke 1960; Halbach 1972; Warfa et al. 2007). Although it is slightly weaker in potency, khat's pharmacological effects are quite similar to the effects of amphetamines (Halbach 1972; "Catha Edulis" 1980) and many of the so-called bath salts (i.e., synthetic cathinones) that surfaced in the United States in the early 2010s (Prosser and Nelson 2012). Khat plays a central role in the daily lives of members of some Muslim Ethiopian and Yemeni cultures (C. Brooke 1960; Prosser and Nelson 2012), and its leaves are chewed to commemorate births, deaths, and religious celebrations. "Wadaja—a ceremony of group prayer performed at times of illness, death, or calamity—must have a plentiful supply of khat" (C. Brooke 1960, 52).

As this very brief overview of the history of drug use in ancient civilizations suggests, some segment of nearly every human population—including the population of the United States—possesses a demand for consciousness alteration. While some individuals fulfill this need through participation in adrenaline- and endorphin-releasing physical activities such as transcendental meditation, skydiving, extreme sports, intense exercise, or even autoerotic sexual asphyxiation, others achieve altered states of mind by ingesting psychoactive chemicals. Beyond religious motivations and the contention that the desire for altered perception is a basic animal instinct, people demand drug-induced psychoactivity for myriad other biological, psychological, and sociological reasons. Genetic predispositions, grief, hopelessness, friends, families, boredom, alienation, and economic strain are several other important factors that drive individuals to use or abuse drugs. (For a detailed discussion of theories of drug use, see chapter 2 of Mosher and Akins 2007.)

Given the widespread apparent need for consciousness alteration, it is useful to conceive of drugs as any other socially meaningful commodity subject to basic economic forces of supply and demand. When demand for a product is strong enough, enterprising groups and individuals will emerge as suppliers. For the subpopulation of drug users who desire increased levels of energy, vigor, elation, alertness, and concentration characteristic of psychomotor stimulants, caffeine and nicotine are two popular substances of choice. Others demand stronger stimulation provided by cocaine and amphetamines (Cho 1990).

A great many of the harms associated with the contemporary US drug problem generally, and methamphetamine problem specifically, stem from a history of drug policies that have primarily focused on attacking the supply of illicit drugs. Interdiction operations (e.g., the crop dusting of South American coca fields, police tactics designed to disrupt drug dealing and trafficking networks), combined with legislation prohibiting the possession of certain chemical substances, are intended to reduce the availability of drugs. The purported utility of supply interdiction measures for solving the drug problem is based on two faulty assumptions:

1. With enough persistence and determination, society can eventually eliminate the supply of illicit drugs.
2. Individuals will stop seeking drugs if society eliminates or at least severely disrupts supplies.

Over the past 100 years, millions of US citizens have been arrested and incarcerated for drug-related offenses, and billions of dollars have been spent enforcing punitive, supply-oriented policies. Although there have been temporary successes in reducing drug use through supply interdiction efforts over this time period, millions in the United States still use illicit drugs today as they have for a century. To be clear, drug interdiction is an important component of any nation's drug policy. But when institutional approaches to reducing drug use largely ignore the demand side of the equation, efforts at lessening drug harms are futile.

With stimulants, the story is no different. In short, the scores of past policies enacted to remove the supply of illicit stimulants have mostly ignored the "need for speed" felt by millions of Americans. Demand has persisted, and users, traffickers, and producers have adapted accordingly, often creating new, worse harms than previously existed. Many of these harms (e.g., territorial violence, adulteration, increased potency of product) stem from the nature of the black market for illegal drugs that serves to satisfy user demand.

How could this happen? How could a nation continuously call for drug policies that, in the long run, actually create more harm than good? And when new harms spawn from supply-side policies, why do lawmakers and the public at large call for more of the same? While these questions have no easy answers, much less no single answer, I believe much of the explanation lies in the ways in which drugs and drug problems are defined and discussed in public discourse. In order to more fully understand the many injuries associated with the contemporary methamphetamine situation, considering the ways in which individuals and groups have helped shape public understandings of the drug becomes imperative.

The Social Construction of Drugs and Drug Problems

I utilize a social constructionist approach to social problems in my inquiry into the history and evolution of methamphetamine in the United States. Social constructionists are interested in how, why, and when certain phenomena are brought to the public's attention and defined as social problems (Best 1990). At any given moment in time, individuals and society face a virtually limitless array of threats and harms, from child abuse, gun violence, and homelessness to unemployment, white-collar crime, and terrorism. Yet public concern with these and other social problems is not constant over time, nor is the level of concern always consistent with the actual extent of the threat posed by the phenomenon receiving heavy consideration.

In 2005, national news media and politicians devoted considerable attention to methamphetamine, more than in any year prior or since. Meth was undoubtedly directly or indirectly responsible for innumerable personal and social injuries that year, but available empirical data on the scope of methamphetamine use and harms tell a slightly different story. Nationally representative survey data on adolescent schoolchildren indicate that methamphetamine use among this population had steadily declined since the turn of the century (Johnston et al. 2012). Data on the broader population of US residents age twelve and older estimate that 0.2 percent (about 512,000 people) were "current" methamphetamine users (defined as having used the drug at least once in the past month) in 2005—a statistic that had remained stable since 2002 (SAMHSA 2009a). Perhaps more interesting is the fact that cocaine consumption was much more prevalent than meth among both youths and adults in 2005, and virtually every year for which data are available. The same is true when data on drug-related visits to hospital emergency rooms are examined: 30 percent of such visits in 2005 were cocaine related, whereas only 6.8 percent involved methamphetamine (DAWN 2012). In spite of the empirical indicators, mass media were not proclaiming a cocaine "epidemic" in the early 2000s.

The social constructionist is interested in why meth—and not cocaine, white-collar crime, or homelessness—received such a high level of public scrutiny during this time period. From this perspective, the "process of calling attention to a troubling condition, not the condition itself, . . . [is what] makes something a social problem" (Best and Harris 2013, 3). Central to this process are claims and claims makers. In order for any phenomenon to be defined as a problem deserving of public attention, it must be constructed and communicated to an audience by claims makers. Claims makers take the form of interest groups and moral entrepreneurs. Their primary goal in drawing public attention to some issue is usually to obtain support—economic, moral, or otherwise—to deal with the phenomenon in a particular way. In the public arena, claims makers seek ownership of social problems, endeavoring to define them in ways specific to their needs and goals (Best 1990).

In the social construction of drugs and drug problems, law enforcement groups (e.g., the Drug Enforcement Administration [DEA]), the medical community (e.g., drug treatment providers), politicians, lobbyists (e.g., pharmaceutical industry representatives), community groups, religious leaders, academic researchers, and individual citizens are common primary claims makers. In the social problems marketplace, primary claims makers involved in attempts to socially define drug issues compete with each other as well as claims makers involved in the social construction of other (i.e., nondrug) issues, seeking recognition, resources, and public awareness (Best 1990).

Mass Media's Role in the Social Construction of Reality

The news media occupy a central position in the social construction of drugs and drug problems.[2] Though sometimes themselves primary claims makers, the media usually play the role of secondary claims makers by selecting and transmitting the messages of others. Primary claims makers often seek to communicate their concerns through the mass media in order to influence public opinion and policy (Best 1990). The relationship among media, public opinion, and policymaking is often complex and multidirectional, but as Jack Doppelt and Peter Manikas (1990) point out, news organizations often play a fundamental role in public policy and the decisions made by criminal justice officials. Gladys Lang and Kurt Lang (1983) describe public opinion as a basic form of social control that can be influenced by mass media and can influence the decisions of policymakers. Media attention toward a social problem can lead to an increase in public awareness and, consequently, increased support for the claims maker's cause and increased pressure on policymakers or criminal justice officials to act (Best 1990, 2008; Loseke 2003).

The relationship between primary claims makers and mass media has been discerned through studies of news production. Press coverage of crime or any other social phenomenon is not "objective," but rather the result of struggles by competing interest groups (Molotch and Lester 1975). In order for any occurrence (e.g., homicide, corporate crime, adulterous act) to receive press coverage, it must be promoted by individuals who know about the occurrence, assembled by news agencies who learn of the occurrence, and consumed by an interested public (Molotch and Lester 1974). Harvey Molotch and Marilyn Lester (1975) explain that news organizations tend to report on public events drawing from a "hierarchy of credibility" (257), in which groups with the highest levels of social power (e.g., governmental officials, corporations) tend to have more routine access to news production than those who are less powerful (e.g., individual citizens, grassroots protest groups). As a result, news presentations of crime or any other social phenomena are often framed according to the viewpoints and perspectives of those placed atop this hierarchy. Thus, the "knowledge" consumed by television viewers, newspaper subscribers, or weblog readers is filtered by biases built into the social organization of news production, a process that "cannot be understood apart from the political economy of the society in which it occurs" (Molotch and Lester 1975, 255).

The knowledge news consumers obtain about crime, including drugs, is distorted by the news-making process (Barak 1994). According to Steven Chermak (1994), this process entails "condensing a significant amount of crime into a limited amount of news space" (97). Since an abundant number of crimes can be chosen from on any given day, news organizations strategically place themselves in close proximity to source organizations (e.g., police departments, political offices) in order to maximize accessibility of crime news (Chermak 1994). Journalists share a symbiotic relationship with source organizations. Not only do the media depend on source organizations for news stories, but source organizations depend on the media for positive publicity and the shaping of public agendas (Lavrakas, Rosenbaum, and Lurigio 1990; Chermak 1994; Kasinsky 1994). News reporters are well aware that portraying criminal justice agencies or other source organizations in a negative light could potentially strain their relationships. Hence, journalists are sometimes hesitant to cover stories that might jeopardize their future access to privileged information (Chermak 1994).

Because of the close relationship between source organizations and news companies, crime news is heavily predisposed to represent official perspectives. Thus, unsurprisingly, content analyses of crime stories find that governmental officials are most often cited as sources of information. In one study, Chermak (1994) learned that almost 30 percent of the sources mentioned in crime stories were police, and 25 percent were court officials. By contrast, defendants made up only 8.9 percent of sources cited, citizens made up 2.6 percent, and "experts" constituted only 0.9 percent. In a content analysis of feature articles about crime published in major US newspapers from 1992 to 1995, Michael Welch, Melissa Fenwick, and Meredith Roberts (1997) found that 34.6 percent of sources quoted were members of law enforcement organizations. State managers (i.e., law enforcement, politicians, prosecutors, and so forth) accounted for almost 63 percent of all those quoted in crime stories. Thirty-two percent of those cited were professors, and 5 percent were nonacademic researchers.

Though the news media have the final say over which crime stories make the news, their knowledge of criminal events depends heavily on information provided by source organizations. Once satisfactory information on specific crimes has been acquired, the news organization must decide which crimes become news, how they are covered, and so forth. Market forces influence organizational decisions, and individual reporters are allowed discretion on a variety of decisions (Chermak 1994). As secondary claims makers, mass media do not simply repeat the claims of law enforcement, interest groups, or other primary claims makers. Rather, news organizations translate and transform initial claims in an effort to attract and persuade audiences (Best 1990, 2008).

News presentations deserve scrutiny because the media are often the principal avenue through which many people learn about the existence and scope of social problems (Best 1990; Loseke 2003). Several studies have found, perhaps unsurprisingly, that mass media serve as individuals' main source of information about crime and crime problems (Graber 1980; Skogan and Maxfield 1981; Chermak 1994; Dowler 2003), especially for those persons with little to no direct personal experience with crime (Surette 1990). Robert Blendon and John Young (1998) conducted a study more specific to the epistemology of drugs by analyzing results from a 1996 poll taken by the Roper Center. Among their findings was the discovery that 68 percent of Americans "report getting most of their information about the seriousness of illicit drug problems from the news media" (828).

An annual survey by Gallup and other polling organizations asks respondents, "What do you think is the most important problem facing this country today?" The question is open ended, and interviewees are asked to list up to three issues and rank them according to importance (Soroka 2002). Blendon and Young (1998) provide data on Gallup poll results for select years from 1979 to 1996, contrasted with data from the National Survey on Drug Use and Health (NSDUH) showing the percentage of US residents age twelve and over who were "current" illicit drug users. In short, they found no consistent relationship between drug use and public opinion of drug problems. For instance, illicit drug problems were ranked lowest in importance in 1979 and 1985, the two years with the highest percentage of past-month drug use (14.1 percent and 12.1 percent, respectively). In 1990, Americans rated drugs as the second most important problem, even though less than 7 percent of the population had engaged in past-month drug use (Blendon and Young 1998). See Nicholas Parsons (2012) for a more detailed discussion of these data.[3]

Moral Panics and Drug Scares

If, as the above observations suggest, people's misperceptions about drugs are related to press coverage of the subject, it is worth examining how and why the media often succeed in capturing the public's imagination with news presentations of drugs. Throughout much of US history, primary claims makers have strategically used the news media to engage in "moral crusades" against drugs. Typically (though not always) coordinated by members of privileged classes, moral crusades are "special campaigns which highlight the dangers of a particular type of deviance" or social problem (Best and Luckenbill 1994, 210). In campaigning to prohibit the use of certain drugs, crusaders participate in an act of "moral enterprise," endeavoring to create "a new fragment of the moral constitution of society, its code of right and wrong" (Becker 1963, 145).

The efforts of moral crusaders may lead to a state of "moral panic" (Goode and Ben-Yehuda 1994a, 1994b; Adler and Adler 2012). After studying public reactions to delinquent British youth, Stanley Cohen ([1972] 1980) formally defined a moral panic as occurring when

> a condition, episode, person or group of persons emerges to become defined as a threat to societal values and interests; its nature is presented in a stylized and stereotypical fashion by the mass media; . . . socially accredited experts pronounce their diagnoses and solutions;

ways of coping are evolved or (more often) resorted to; the condition then disappears, submerges or deteriorates and becomes more visible. Sometimes the object of the panic is quite novel and at other times it is something which has been in existence long enough, but suddenly appears in the limelight. Sometimes the panic passes over and is forgotten, except in folklore and collective memory; at other times it has more serious and long-lasting repercussions and might produce such changes as those in legal and social policy or even in the way the society conceives itself. (9)

Moral panics are characterized by a heightened level of concern over a problem, hostility toward those thought to be responsible for the problem, consensus (i.e., agreement by a sizable proportion of the population that a problem exists), and volatility. As suggested by the word *panic,* the final key element of a moral panic is disproportionality (i.e., the notion that the extent of the problem is exaggerated by claims makers; Goode and Ben-Yehuda 1994a, 1994b).

Though Cohen is often credited with coining the term *moral panic,* British sociologist Jock Young used the phrase one year earlier when writing about societal reactions to drug use. Emphasizing the role of the press in the social construction of drugs, Young (1971) observed that the news media tend to present drug issues

dramatically, . . . overwhelmingly, and . . . suddenly. . . . [T]he media can fan up very quickly and effectively public indignation concerning a particular deviant group. It is possible for them to engineer rapidly what one might call "a moral panic" about a certain type of deviancy. . . . There is institutionalized into the media the need to create moral panics and issues which will seize the imagination of the public. (182)

Several researchers have characterized the contemporary outcry over methamphetamine as a moral panic. For example, Edward Armstrong (2007) argues that news coverage of meth has been hostile in its presentation of users, volatile in its rapid eruption and disappearance from the public spotlight over time, and disproportionate to empirical data on drug-related harms. The alarmist and hysterical nature of media portrayals of meth has made it difficult for a news-consuming public to fully understand and appreciate the extent to which methamphetamine use in the United States is a consequence of the declining agricultural and manufacturing industries once central to rural economies (Armstrong 2007). This concern is echoed by Robert Weidner (2009), who found some evidence that methamphetamine coverage by three midwestern newspapers was disproportionate to data on meth-related admissions to drug treatment facilities. In a study specifically focused on gendered portrayals of meth users, Travis Linnemann (2010) argues that frenetic media constructions of the methamphetamine problem encourage news consumers "to conclude that the phenomenon of the female meth user is a symptom of decay of the core American social life: motherhood, childhood, and family" (98).

Referring to the periodic waves of moral outrage toward drugs as "drug scares," Craig Reinarman (2012) asserts that panics over drugs are often characterized by several features, including the involvement of politico-moral entrepreneurs and interest groups (i.e., claims makers), scapegoating, and the linking of drug problems to "dangerous" marginalized social groups (e.g., racial minorities, the poor). Reinarman also stresses the importance of historical context. Specifically, drug scares stand a better chance to proliferate during times of "cultural anxiety" (e.g., economic depression) (164). For example, various interest groups and representatives of the moral order campaigned for decades to outlaw alcohol in the United States. But not until the early 1900s, when tensions heightened over the mass influx of European immigrants, did crusaders finally earn enough public support for Prohibition. The social, ethnic, and class conflicts of the early twentieth century provided a historical context highly conducive to widespread panic over alcohol (Levine and Reinarman 1991; Gusfield 1996; Reinarman 2012).

Claims makers involved in the majority of moral crusades against psychoactive substances have employed the "dope fiend mythology" (Lindesmith 1940a, 1940b) by defining drug use as immoral behavior that results from the bad character traits and moral weaknesses of individual users. According to Charles Reasons (1976), the dope fiend mythology consists of the following beliefs:

- "The drug addict is a violent criminal . . . [and] moral degenerate" (136).
- People become addicted to drugs because they possess "inferior and abnormal" personality traits (137).
- Both drug dealers and users seek "to convert nonusers into addicts" (137).

Like the common street criminal, the dope fiend is constructed as a careless, unfeeling scourge on society. An uncontrollable, self-chosen addiction to chemicals propels the dope fiend to commit violent, atrocious acts of inhumanity. Under the influence of drugs, the addict is unpredictable in behavior and indiscriminate when choosing victims.

The dope fiend serves as the prototypical folk devil in public discourse of drugs. Folk devils personify evil and exist as a central feature of moral panics (David et al. 2011). "All moral panics, by their very nature, identify, denounce, and attempt to root out folk devils" (Goode and Ben-Yehuda 1994a, 29). Like all folk devils, the dope fiend is portrayed as a threat to social stability and thus must be dealt with using any means necessary. A cursory examination of past drug scares in the United States finds that the typical proposed solution to the dope fiend menace entails drug policies that call for harsher punishments and stricter controls on drug supplies. These solutions tend to benefit formal agents of social control, who are so often called upon to solve the problems that they have helped construct (Altheide and Michalowski 1999). Reasons (1976) points out this tendency when he writes that the dope fiend's danger to society serves to "frighten the public into appropriating increased funds to combat the 'dope menace'" (134). In addition to increasing the power of criminal justice agencies, punitive, supply-oriented policies help to single out the dope fiend (or dope pusher) for symbolic exorcism, which functions as a form of social catharsis. Like most moral panics, drug scares often subside upon the enactment of new legislation that symbolizes an end to the threat and leaves new definitions of deviance in its wake (Cohen [1972] 1980; Goode and Ben-Yehuda 1994a, 1994b; Adler and Adler 2012).

A mainstay of US drug discourse, the popular depiction of the drug-addicted dope fiend suggests the existence of a widely held cultural belief in what Craig Reinarman and Harry Levine (1997a) call "pharmacological determinism," the notion that a drug's chemical properties are solely responsible for its effect on human beings. The image of the innocent, calm citizen transforming into a drug-crazed lunatic upon immediate ingestion of a prohibited substance epitomizes this ideology. Cocaine, heroin, methamphetamine, and other taboo substances are understood to contain a sort of magical power believed to universally take hold of every user. Claims that a drug is "instantly addicting" or provokes "uncontrollable violence" embody this perspective. Yet if drugs affected every user in this manner, the estimated 9.8 million persons in the United States who have used methamphetamine at least once in their lifetimes would be violent addicts. Since roughly 798,000 US residents used methamphetamine at least once in 2011 (SAMHSA 2012a), and since fewer than 15,000 known homicides were committed in the United States that year (FBI 2013a), claims of immediate addiction and mandatory violence are clearly gross exaggerations.

The ideology of pharmacological determinism "invests the substances themselves with more power than they actually have" (Reinarman and Levine 1997a, 8). In actuality, when psychoactive drugs enter the body, they produce their effects through the release or reuptake of brain chemicals called neurotransmitters. That is, drugs work by stimulating substances already present in the human brain. The fact that "psychoactive drugs produce their effects by neurotransmitters points out their true secret: *All drug sensations, feelings, awareness, or hallucinations can also be achieved without drugs*" (Gahlinger 2004, 159; emphasis in original). Though many find this idea controversial, people can and do achieve altered states of mind through non–drug related activities such as religious fervor, gambling, long-distance running, roller coaster riding, dreaming during sleep, and other behaviors that affect the flow of brain chemicals.[4]

My point is that drugs do not produce feelings that the body and brain are incapable of producing by themselves. "All the thoughts, perceptions, and behaviors [resulting from drug use] already exist" (Gahlinger 2004, 159). By themselves, drugs are inert substances—they do not cause harm or relief until people choose to consume them (Reinarman and Levine 1997a). But by placing heavy emphasis on "the sphere of molecules" (DeGrandpre 2006, 27), a cultural acceptance of pharmacological determinism fails to consider the social, cultural, and historical contexts of drug use. And contexts (i.e., the conditions under which people take drugs) are often more important than molecular structures for understanding consequences and patterns of use (Zinberg 1984).

Richard DeGrandpre (2006) debunks pharmacological determinism by providing a detailed description of a study on the worldwide use of cocaine conducted jointly by the World Health Organization (WHO) and the UN Interregional Crime and Justice Research Institute (UNICRI) from 1992 to 1994. The study was exceptional not just because of its scale (nineteen countries across six continents) but also for its depth. Its investigators sought to examine the variety of contexts—historical, market, economic, and cultural—in which cocaine use occurs. In Brazil, researchers found heavy cocaine use among impoverished São Paulo children. Mexican researchers found the drug was confined mostly to homeless males from the ages of twenty to twenty-four. In Cairo, wealthy adults made up the majority of the cocaine-using population. Researchers also discovered that methods of cocaine administration differed across populations. Upper-class Nigerians smoked the drug in rock form (crack). As they have for centuries, Bolivian and Peruvian users obtained the effects of cocaine by chewing the leaves of the coca plant. Prostitutes in Colombia smoked cocaine paste (created during an intermediary stage of cocaine powder production). In Mexico City, homeless users injected the drug, and in Sydney, gay club-goers generally snorted it. In addition, researchers learned that people use cocaine for different reasons—to stay awake, celebrate, accomplish work-related tasks, and cope with hopelessness and socioeconomic blight (DeGrandpre 2006).

One basic conclusion derived from the study was that no "typical" cocaine user exists. According to DeGrandpre (2006), US political leaders did not find this conclusion amenable since it did not reaffirm popular stereotypes about cocaine and cocaine users. To be sure, both powder cocaine and crack are demonized in the United States, though the former has often been associated with the upper and middle classes and glamorized as one of the nation's more prestigious illicit drugs. Crack, on the other hand, is associated with urban blacks, gangs, violence, and irrepressible addiction. Since the mid-1980s, political and media rhetoric "have consistently attributed devastating consequences to crack, as if these consequences flowed directly from its molecular structure. Such rhetoric squeezes out of public discourse any serious consideration of the social, cultural, economic, and psychological variables that are essential for understanding drug use and its behavioral consequences" (Reinarman and Levine 1997a, 13).

The WHO/UNICRI study's finding that attitudes toward and reasons for using cocaine vary markedly across societies does not support the theory of pharmacological determinism, or the myth that crack and powder cocaine are disparate substances. While smoking or injecting cocaine produces a much quicker onset of effects than snorting or swallowing it, the pharmacological properties of cocaine are identical regardless of the physical form it takes (Hatsukami and Fischman 1996; Reinarman and Levine 1997a; Morgan and Zimmer 1997; DeGrandpre 2006; "Federal Crack Cocaine Sentencing" 2010). Rather than embracing pharmacological determinism, researchers and policymakers alike might consider viewing drugs as "socially defined commodities" (DeGrandpre 2006, 25).

One of the greatest insights DeGrandpre (2006) draws from his analysis is that cocaine is "not one thing—neither an angel nor a demon, neither good nor evil—but rather different things to different peoples" (26). The same line of reasoning can be applied to methamphetamine or the large majority of other mind-altering substances referred to as "drugs" and "medicines" in American culture. Consider these accounts of methamphetamine use, taken from a variety of US media sources:

- "You don't want to mess with it. . . . They say people [who smoke meth] walk around like zombies" (homeless person, cited by Terry 1989, A1).
- "It affects not merely the user, but it's the leading cause of property crime, it's the leading reason why children are removed from their homes. . . . [I]t's very hard to go to any part of Oregon and not experience the effects of methamphetamine" (journalist, cited by Byker 2006).
- "I see walking death" (police officer describing meth users in his community, cited by Jefferson et al. 2005a, 48).

Next, consider these descriptions of a prescription medicine, advertised in two issues of *The American Journal of Nursing:*

- "An effective curb for the appetite" (1951, 29).
- "An effective morale booster with minimum side effects" (1951, 29).
- "Effective in depressive states associated with menopause, prolonged illness, and convalescence as well as in treatment of alcoholism and narcolepsy" (1952, 23).

These latter three remarks describe the indications and effects of Desoxyn, an early trade name for methamphetamine hydrochloride, the pharmaceutical version of meth. Though not as commonly prescribed as Adderall and Ritalin, Desoxyn has been available via prescription since the early 1950s and was sold OTC beginning in 1944.

Both sets of quotations describe the same chemical substance, yet "meth" is constructed as a dangerous and destructive drug, whereas Desoxyn is described as a medicinal panacea. To be sure, important differences exist between illicit and licit methamphetamine in terms of purity, dosage, and routes of administration (e.g., oral, intravenous). But these differences have nothing to do with pharmacology; rather, they result largely from the existence of separate black (illicit) and white (pharmaceutical) markets for the drug (DeGrandpre 2006).

Despite the fact that meth (the drug) and Desoxyn (the medicine) are chemically identical, political and media discourse about methamphetamine almost always concerns the illicit version. Thus, when President Clinton (1997) proclaimed, "Meth has a devastating effect on those who use it," he certainly was not referring to the cure-all medicine manufactured by Abbott Laboratories, nor to the scores of chemically similar amphetamines or amphetamine-like preparations (e.g., Ritalin) consumed legally and daily by millions in the United States. This contradiction—"of meth as a demon drug and methamphetamine as a prescription angel"—cannot be resolved by any amount of pharmacological determinism (DeGrandpre 2006, 33). Under some circumstances, methamphetamine use has devastating consequences. In other contexts, the drug helps people to function and lead more fulfilling lives. But as Reinarman and Levine (1997a) note, "American culture lacks a vocabulary with which people can speak about drugs in this more complicated, qualified way" (9). Thus, in the either-or arena of drug war discourse, meth is notoriously "the world's most dangerous drug" (Crowley 2006).

The simultaneous existence of methamphetamine as a drug and a medicine is made possible in part through differences in the language used to describe them. In popular culture, *drug* and *medicine* are oppositional terms. The former leads to sickness and disease, while the latter is a *cure for* sickness and disease. As a consequence of this terminology, those who consume meth illegally are perceived as dangerous drug addicts deserving of arrest and imprisonment, while persons who obtain Desoxyn or other prescription amphetamines through institutionalized medical channels are generally considered patients seeking treatment.

Thomas Szasz (1974) argues that contemporary attitudes toward drugs are based more on ceremony than on actual chemistry. He likens the public unease and trepidation accorded to illicit chemicals, and the public acceptance and relief attributed to licit chemicals, to the ways in which some Christian denominations treat holy water. Both holy water and drugs are seen to possess special, supernatural qualities. But the mystical properties of both cannot be discerned under a microscope. "To understand holy water, we must examine priests and parishioners, not water; and to understand abused and addictive drugs, we must examine doctors and addicts, politicians and populations, not drugs" (Szasz 1974, 17).

In this spirit, I will focus much of this book on the variety of claims and claims makers involved in episodic social constructions of speed in its many forms. A superficial glimpse of the history of public discourse about drugs might lead the uninterested observer to infer the existence of a 100-year-long moral panic over drugs. Yet upon closer examination, US drug scares have been considerably time delimited (Goode and Ben-Yehuda 1994a). Indeed, my analysis of national media trends identifies three separate moral panics over methamphetamine: (1) the Methedrine scare of the late 1960s and early 1970s, (2) the ice panic of 1989 and 1990, and (3) the crystal meth "epidemic" of the late 1990s and early 2000s.

Though they shared several commonalities, each of the three methamphetamine scares was unique in its own right, and each differed in terms of its volatility, participatory claims makers, depiction of users, and so forth. And while my constructionist approach entails asking how, when, and why meth has been periodically brought to the forefront of public attention as an urgent social problem in need of repair, I also address why methamphetamine was *not* at times defined as a national emergency. For example, epidemiological data indicate that rates of methamphetamine use were highest from the mid-1970s until the mid-1980s, a span during which the drug was rarely mentioned by major news sources. Why? As a related question, considering it has been used and misused since the 1940s, why did it take sixty years for full-blown meth hysteria to erupt, as it did during the third scare?

As I attempt to answer these and other questions, my historical analysis of the many social, economic, and cultural contexts of the American methamphetamine experience reveals several characteristics that uniquely set meth apart from other extensively scorned drugs. These characteristics indicate that methamphetamine has perhaps been more closely connected to the power structure and culture of the United States than any other drug (besides alcohol) subject to sustained periods of moral panic. Specifically:

- For much of its US history, methamphetamine was "homemade" (i.e., domestically produced).
- Methamphetamine is deeply rooted in the social institutions of medicine and pharmacy.
- Methamphetamine has been traditionally portrayed as the illicit drug of choice among poor whites.
- Methamphetamine has a history of being promoted and used for instrumental purposes (e.g., to enhance job performance).

At the risk of oversimplification, these themes often manifest in the content of claims makers' answers to three basic questions: (1) Who is providing methamphetamine? (2) Who is using it? and (3) Why are they using it? These questions are important to audience members, because the answers help diagnose the existence of a social problem, ascribe meaning to it, and assign blame to those responsible (Loseke 2003).

To borrow a term from Paul Manning (2006), the unique aspects of methamphetamine's US history in terms of the drug's providers, users, and user motivations have informed various "symbolic frameworks" through which the drug has been socially constructed and reconstructed

(49). In other words, anti-meth crusaders have described methamphetamine differently at different points in time. The nature or *quality* of claims makers' explanations of who is providing, who is using, and why people are using methamphetamine has influenced temporal variations in the *quantity* of public concern. Claims makers tended to be most successful when they challenged images of domestic production, impoverished white addicts, and medicinal and instrumental motivations for use. An examination of the changing frames through which the scope and source of meth problems have been communicated helps explain not only the genesis, duration, and intensity of the three methamphetamine scares in the United States, but also the periodic lulls in meth-related moral outrage *and* the initial widespread social acceptance of speed.

Finally, while claims makers are directly responsible for the many historical changes in social constructions of methamphetamine, they must also be credited with indirectly transforming the US stimulant market. Beginning with an examination of the inception and aftermath of cocaine prohibition, I unearth a cyclical pattern whereby public hysteria over a chemical substance culminates in supply-side solutions, which in turn foster newer forms of stimulant abuse, which in turn lead to another round of hysteria. Indeed, in many respects, the most recent wave of attention to the synthetic class of stimulants referred to by the popular press as bath salts appears to be merely the next phase in this cycle.

Organization of the Book

As much of this introduction indicates, the contemporary US stimulant problem cannot be fully appreciated without an understanding of the past. For this reason, Chapter 2 examines early drug use in the United States. Once widely and legally available, cocaine and opium were the subjects of the country's first drug scares. The resulting Public Law 63-223, often referred to today as the Harrison Act,[5] marked the nation's first major federal drug prohibition and led to the creation of the black market for illicit drugs. Public demand for consciousness alteration persisted after the Harrison Act, prompting a pharmaceutical revolution in which new drugs (or "medicines") were synthesized.

Chapter 3 investigates the introduction of amphetamines, including methamphetamine, into US society. Initially proclaimed as panaceas, amphetamines were consumed by athletes, housewives, movie stars, militaries, and others. Throughout the mid-twentieth century, speed was periodically subject to scorn from politicians and the press, especially when it became associated with black jazz musicians, prisoners, and other groups with relatively low levels of social power. During this time period, amphetamine users and abusers proved very innovative in their responses to a series of government and industry restrictions designed to control licitly manufactured and distributed stimulants.

In Chapter 4, I discuss the first US drug scare specifically focused on methamphetamine. The 1960s saw the emergence of the menacing "speed freak" in pop culture. Hysteria over intravenous use of Methedrine signified the cultural dichotomization of meth from the other amphetamines, a distinction that remains to this day. Although Methedrine abuse was initially portrayed as a problem affecting socially marginalized "others," the widely publicized rape and murder of an eighteen-year-old woman from an elite upbringing served to recast Methedrine as a threat to innocent members of mainstream society. The media frenzy over methamphetamine subsided following the Controlled Substances Act (CSA) of 1970, and meth would remain relatively absent from public discourse until the short-lived ice panic of 1989.

Because disproportionality is a primary characteristic of moral panics, in Chapter 5 I assess the extent to which patterns in media coverage correlate with empirical data on early methamphetamine use. In Chapter 5, I also examine how the black market for meth emerged and evolved in response to strictly imposed quotas on pharmaceutically manufactured speed. Smokable methamphetamine was one of the eventual consequences of a series of legislative acts that began in the 1970s and ultimately became the subject of the second (and most fleeting) methamphetamine scare in the United States. Drawing on the imagery of the crack cocaine frenzy of the late 1980s, claims makers warned that the use of ice in Hawaii was poised to spread to the US mainland. An examination of the social problems marketplace and the various political interest groups who worked to construct the threat helps explain why ice disappeared from public discourse almost as hastily as it had arrived.

In the next two chapters, I cover "crystal meth," the third and most dynamic methamphetamine scare. In Chapter 6, I trace the evolution of meth media discourse from 1995 up through the first decade of the 2000s. As with the Methedrine panic of many years prior, initial portrayals of crystal meth framed the drug as geographically and socioeconomically isolated. The increase in national news attention during the first few years of the 2000s coincided with revised depictions of meth use spreading across the country into all social classes. Around this time, domestic meth problems became more frequently attributed to foreign producers and traffickers. The crystal meth scare diminished following implementation of the Combat Methamphetamine Epidemic Act (CMEA) in 2006.

The discussion of crystal meth continues in Chapter 7. After placing the third scare in the context of several national indicators of methamphetamine use and associated problems, I argue that the crystal meth panic thrived in the early 2000s partly because claims makers successfully connected methamphetamine with other topics prevalent in the social problems marketplace at that time. In this chapter, I also examine more recent changes in the black market, as it evolved in response to a series of precursor regulations implemented from the late 1980s into the early twenty-first century. I find that the victories resulting from the more contemporary supply interdiction efforts have been momentary, as the continual demand for stimulation has led to a plethora of unintended harms.

In the final chapter, I situate methamphetamine as a bridge between cocaine use of the late 1800s and early 1900s and the "bath salts" phenomenon of the early 2010s. Because all of these substances have the same general physiological effects, I argue that bath salts may be seen as a logical consequence of historical and contemporary policies designed to criminalize and limit the supply of other stimulants. I conclude by advocating respect for the valuable lessons of history, and by making the case for an approach to drug problems based less on hysteria and more on concerns for public health.

Research Methodology

I consulted a variety of news sources when researching and writing this manuscript. Several electronic databases—ProQuest, LexisNexis, *Time* magazine's website, NewspaperARCHIVE, and Vanderbilt Television News Archive—were used to gather quantitative and qualitative information on media portrayals of methamphetamine and other amphetamines. While most of my focus is on coverage by major national news sources (i.e., *Time, Newsweek, US News and World Report, New York Times, Washington Post, Wall Street Journal, Los Angeles Times, USA Today,* and prime-time television news reports broadcast by ABC, NBC, and CBS), I occasionally include information from secondary national news sources and local news media. See the Appendix for a detailed description of specific search parameters utilized to locate news literature and compile data presented in many of the figures.

Notes

1. While MDMA is chemically classified as an amphetamine, it is not considered a typical stimulant due to its hallucinogenic effects (Mosher and Akins 2007).

2. Some of the text in this section previously appeared in Nicholas Parsons's "Fear of Crime and Fear of Drugs: The Role of Mass Media," in *Local Issues, Global Impact: Perspectives on Contemporary Social Issues*, edited by Michael J. Stern (San Diego: Cognella, 2012), pp. 157–173.

3. The limitations of these data need to be noted. Since Blendon and Young (1998) do not provide data for several years between 1980 and 1995, one should not assume that public opinion or illicit drug use followed a linear pattern during these interim years. For example, Reinarman and Levine (1997b) note that the percentage of Americans who cited drugs as the country's most important problem fluctuated greatly in the mid- to late 1980s, corresponding to election cycles. Also, these data are subject to general errors inherent in survey methodology (e.g., social desirability, sampling error, question wording effects).

4. Dimethyltryptamine (DMT) provides an excellent example of the curious connection among psychoactive drugs, neurotransmitters, and nondrug activities. DMT is an intensely powerful but short-acting hallucinogen that exists naturally in various plants and animals, including the *Bufo* toad (Weil and Rosen 2004; Mosher and Akins 2007). Terrence McKenna—a man who dedicated much of his life to trying to unlock the existential, shamanic, and cosmic mysteries of myriad psychedelic drugs—recounted being exposed to alien life forms, black holes, and talking elves during DMT smoking sessions. Upon coming down from one out-of-body experience, McKenna (1991) described DMT by exulting, "I cannot believe this; this is impossible, this is completely impossible" (38). Also of note: DMT is virtually identical in molecular structure to a hormone produced by the brain's pineal gland (McKenna 1991; Weil and Rosen 2004). Research indicates that the human brain significantly increases its production of DMT (or DMT-like molecules) during "sexual ecstasy, childbirth, extreme physical stress, . . . meditation . . . dream consciousness," near-death experiences, and in the moments immediately prior to death (I. Miller 2013, 217–218). In other words, one does not need to smoke toad venom (or introduce any other foreign psychoactive substance into the body) in order to "trip" on DMT.

5. In both the popular and scholarly literature, Public Law 63-223 is also sometimes referred to as the Harrison Narcotics Act, the Harrison Narcotics Tax Act, and the Harrison Narcotic Control Act, among other names.

2

Early Drug Use

I believe that most drug addiction today is due to the Harrison Anti-Narcotic Act, which forbids the sale of narcotics without a physician's prescription. . . . Addicts who are broke act as "agent provocateurs" for the peddlers, being rewarded by gifts of heroin or credit for supplies. The Harrison Act made the drug peddler, and the drug peddler makes drug addicts. —*Robert Schless, Philadelphia physician, February 1925, as cited by Thomas Szasz (1974, 211)*

Although amphetamines were not introduced into the United States until the 1930s, a selection of other drugs satisfied American desires for consciousness alteration centuries prior. According to Edward Brecher (1972), the nineteenth-century United States could accurately be termed a "dope fiend's paradise" (3). People were generally free to ingest whatever chemicals they could get their hands on (e.g., marijuana, opiates, cocaine), and obtaining chemicals was as easy as visiting the doctor or local store.

From the late 1700s to the early 1900s, Dover's Powder and other opium-based medicines designed to relieve pain, colds, fevers, athlete's foot, alcoholism, diarrhea, hiccups, and other ailments were sold in US pharmacies and grocery stores (Ashton 1906; Inciardi 2002; DIB 2006). In 1898, the semisynthetic opiate diacetylmorphine was introduced to consumers after a series of experiments found it effective in treating common discomforts associated with pneumonia and tuberculosis. Bayer Laboratories marketed this drug under the trade name Heroin, and it soon became an ingredient in many medications and tonics. Two years later, articles published by physicians in leading medical journals extolled heroin's benefits and asserted it was not addictive (Manges 1900; Inciardi 2002; DIB 2006; Mosher and Akins 2007).[1]

In the late 1800s, products such as Ryno's Hay Fever and Catarrh Remedy, Pemberton's French Wine Cola (later renamed Coca-Cola), and other cocaine-containing products were used to treat nasal congestion, toothaches, chronic fatigue, and depression (Inciardi 2002; Mosher and Akins 2007) and "almost any [other] illness" (Gahlinger 2004, 242). Dr. Nathan Tucker's Asthma Specific contained nearly one half of one gram of cocaine per ounce, and was one of the most popular medications used to treat hay fever and asthma. Pharmaceutical companies manufactured cocaine-laced cigarettes and cigars to provide "increased vigor" and to medically "cure" lethargy (DIB 2006, 253). Cocaine was even enjoyed by elites, including President William McKinley and psychoanalyst Sigmund Freud. Though he warned that cocaine could produce physical and "moral" problems if used excessively, Freud argued its benefits outweighed its risks. Freud used cocaine throughout much of his life to treat depression and fatigue and endorsed cocaine as a remedy for morphine addiction (Mosher and Akins 2007).

Marijuana was also quite popular in the nineteenth-century United States. Hundreds of articles appeared in European and US medical journals from 1840 to 1900, promoting its therapeutic benefits and recommending it as an anticonvulsant, analgesic, muscle relaxant, and appetite stimulator. At one point, marijuana was available in twenty-eight different preparations in the form of pills, elixirs, and tablets sold OTC in the United States (Gahlinger 2004). In addition to its medicinal uses, marijuana was cultivated for its fibers (i.e., hemp) from 1629 until the end of the Civil War.[2] During this time period, hemp was a major North American crop and played a significant role in colonial and national economic policy. Marijuana production was important enough to colonial Virginia that in 1762 its government levied penalties on landowners who did not cultivate hemp (Brecher 1972).

The legal means and relative ease through which US residents could obtain substances that are now classified as dangerous drugs suggest that support for prohibition laws during the 1800s and early 1900s was scarce. Brecher (1972) argues that little demand existed for outlawing opiates during this time period because they "were not viewed as a menace to society and . . . they were not in fact a menace" (7). While the nonmedical use of opiates was not always respected in many social circles, users were not ostracized from society and did not lose their jobs or families as a consequence of their habit (Brecher 1972). Although Brecher's comments are specific to attitudes toward opiate use in the 1800s and early 1900s, the same sentiments held true for cocaine and marijuana. Generally speaking, most nineteenth-century users of "narcotics" were law-abiding, productive members of society (Musto 1987; Inciardi 2002).[3]

But substances touted as medicinal cure-alls long ago have been redefined as today's poisons and demon drugs (DeGrandpre 2006), as evidenced by the remarkable shift in public and official sentiment toward the use of cocaine, opiates, and marijuana, beginning roughly 100 years ago. Cocaine went from being "a wonderful alleviator of pain" that any "true scientist would. . . . [freely] give to suffering mankind" ("The Aim and Future" 1890, 239) to "a dangerous, addictive drug . . . [that] can kill" (Reagan 1986). Opiates, referred to by physicians as "God's own medicine" during the late 1800s (Brecher 1972, 8), were alleged by President Richard Nixon to be casting the nation into "the hell of addiction" in 1971 (Epstein 1990, 173). And marijuana, the moderate use of which was once said to produce "no injurious effects on the mind" (Indian Hemp Drugs Commission 1893, as cited in Mosher and Akins 2007, 7), was deemed a "loco narcotic [that] destroys the body, soul and mind" less than twenty years later ("The Loco Weed" 1912, 183).

As national definitions of drugs and medicines changed, so too has government involvement in drug control, as measured by exponential increases in federal expenditures and legal consequences for illicit drug use. In 1967, decades after the enactment of the nation's first drug prohibition, the federal budget for drug enforcement totaled $3 million (Epstein 1990), equal to roughly $20.6 million in 2012 currency.[4] The Office of National Drug Control Policy's (ONDCP) budget request for fiscal year 2014 totaled $25.4 billion. Of this amount, $14.7 billion was proposed for spending on drug enforcement efforts (i.e., domestic law enforcement, interdiction, and international drug control) (ONDCP 2013). Adjusting for inflation, the amount of federal money allocated for drug enforcement in 1967 was 0.14 percent of the expenditures projected for 2014. These figures do not include funds distributed at state and local levels, estimated to be roughly $33 billion in 1996 alone (Blumenson and Nilsen 1998), or money spent to imprison persons convicted of drug offenses. In 1980, approximately 41,000 people were incarcerated in prisons or jails across the United States for drug offenses. By 2010, that number reached 507,000, representing 31.7 percent of the roughly 1.6 million people constituting the nation's jail and prison population ("Trends in US Corrections" 2012). Arrests for drug violations totaled 581,000 in 1980 (Mauer and King 2007). Of the 1.53 million drug arrests made in 2011, 81.8 percent were for possession, and 49.5 percent were for marijuana offenses (FBI 2013b). Indeed, the United States' war on drugs is alive and well.

How did therapeutic panaceas come to be seen as deadly toxins in such a relatively short time period? Why are so many public resources dedicated to punishing consciousness-modifying behaviors? Why do many Americans generally accept their government's dictation of what chemicals they can and cannot put into their bodies, a concept that was seen as wholly un-American only 100 years ago? In order to begin to address these questions, we need to ask others: Who is responsible for current definitions of both illicit and licit drugs? How have messages about drugs been conveyed and received over time? Who benefits from the social and legal structure of drugs in contemporary society?

A historical examination of the enactment and evolution of multiple narcotics laws, the growth of various claims-making interest groups and moral entrepreneurs, and media portrayals of drug use and drug users may help elucidate this marked shift in perception. The remainder of this chapter contains an overview of the developments leading up to the United States' first federal drug prohibition. While the Harrison Act targeted cocaine and opiates, an understanding of the history is particularly important because it sheds light on the genesis of methamphetamine use in the United States.

Drug Scares and Early Federal Drug Legislation

Before the twentieth century, cocaine, opium, morphine, heroin, and marijuana were made available to consumers in two ways: from physicians and from the marketplace. Generally speaking, doctors were their own pharmacists, preparing and mixing medicines in accordance with their patients' individual ailments and needs. Alternatively, people could purchase these drugs OTC at local pharmacies, grocery stores, or even through the mail (Brecher 1972; DeGrandpre 2006). These so-called patent medicines were manufactured by early pharmaceutical companies, many of which are still in business today (Musto 1987).

No restrictions were placed on the kinds of drugs that could be sold by both the patent medicine industry and doctors. Additionally, no laws required a list of ingredients to accompany the medicines dispensed by either source (DeGrandpre 2006). Consequently, likely many parents who administered Mrs. Winslow's Soothing Syrup to quiet their teething infants were completely ignorant of the fact that the product contained morphine. The public was also largely unaware that patent medicines marketed as "cures" for opium habits often contained large quantities of opiates. Throughout the 1800s, patent medicine manufacturers were quite effective in preventing Congress from passing laws requiring the disclosure of ingredients in commercial drug preparations (S. H. Adams 1905; Musto 1987).

Many citizens and interest groups grew weary of the patent medicine industry as its products started having negative effects on some consumers. Claims that opiates and other drugs found in patent medicines were harmless began to be questioned and reevaluated as some people became sick or died, and others developed addictions. David Musto (1987) estimates that by 1900, the United States was home to approximately 250,000 narcotics addicts. Around this time, public concerns about drug use increased (Bertram et al. 1996), and, plausibly, some of the concern was based on real increases in narcotic drug use and the subsequent harms it caused.

The growing concerns over cocaine and opiate abuse culminated with the passage of the Harrison Act of 1914. But cocaine, heroin, morphine, and opium did not become prohibited simply because they caused users and society harm. If US drug policies and public attitudes toward drugs were strongly correlated with levels of objective harm, tobacco and alcohol would surely be off limits (as would many prescription drugs). Rather, the present legal status of various mind-altering substances can be viewed as a consequence of the successes and failures of various interest groups and moral entrepreneurs who have contested public meanings of drugs over time.[5]

Contrary to common belief, most drug prohibitions do not completely ban the use of drugs, including many of those that have come to be regarded as illicit. For example, to say that cocaine is illegal really means that its use is illegal under most circumstances. With a proper license, dentists and other medical specialists can administer cocaine as an anesthetic during surgery. Similarly, many prescription painkillers contain opiates or opioids. So while heroin and raw opium are illegal to possess, with a doctor's prescription pharmacologically similar, opiate-based substances (e.g., OxyContin, Vicodin) can be used lawfully. Thus, when history claims, for example, that cocaine and opiates were prohibited by the federal government with the passage of the Harrison Act, what this statement really means is that tighter restrictions were placed on who can sell them, who can use them, and in what context they can be obtained.

In the late 1800s, when cocaine, opiates, and other narcotics were widely and legally available, physicians (and to a lesser extent, pharmacists) and the makers of patent medicines were in direct competition with one another (DeGrandpre 2006). Since OTC preparations were less costly than a visit to the doctor, the patent medicine industry dominated the drug market. Beyond the fact that patent medicine manufacturers rarely provided information on the ingredients contained in their wares, they also were not required to demonstrate that their products were safe and effective (Inciardi 2002; Mosher and Akins 2007). Manufacturers capitalized on the lack of regulation by making misleading claims (e.g., portraying their medicines as panaceas). During this time period, public definitions of opiate and cocaine use as social problems in need of solutions gained popularity, due to a combination of a crooked patent medicine industry and the claims-making activities of doctors, pharmacists, and others. One popular strategy used by demonizers of these drugs was to associate their use with racial and ethnic minorities.

In the nineteenth-century United States, many citizens considered federal control and prohibition of drugs unconstitutional (Musto 1987). At the time, decisions to impose legal restrictions on drugs and the prescription practices of physicians were left up to individual states. Although no federal laws put prohibitions on opiates throughout most of the 1800s, a series of local and state laws were enacted, mostly on the West Coast, to ban the smoking of opium in smoke houses or opium "dens." Opium smoking had been a traditional pastime in China and other Asian countries for centuries. Political leaders in some Asian countries would socialize by smoking opium much in the same way that Western elites enjoy cocktails and cigars. Opium smoking in the United States began during the 1850s and 1860s with the influx of tens of thousands of Chinese immigrants who mined gold and helped construct parts of the vast railroad system that still functions today (Brecher 1972; Szasz 1974; Inciardi 2002).

The roots of the first local and state ordinances banning the smoking of opium were "racist rather than health-oriented" (Brecher 1972, 42). They sought to drive out or at least isolate Chinese immigrants, particularly when economic depression resulted in a labor surplus (Musto 1987). As immigrant numbers grew, much of the US citizenry feared competition for jobs and resented the Chinese for agreeing to work for very low wages (Brecher 1972; Szasz 1974). The Chinese were "actively persecuted" throughout the latter half of the nineteenth century (Musto 1987, 3), and many Americans came to associate opium smoking with criminality and a Chinese plan to undermine US society (Musto 1987; Inciardi 2002).

Under intense pressure from labor unions, the Chinese Exclusion Act, barring Chinese immigration, was passed in 1882. About 100,000 immigrants of Chinese descent were already in the United States by this time, so opium smoking "became the focal point of attack and . . . the leading symbol of the Chinese people's 'dangerousness'" (Szasz 1974, 76). This trend was evident in 1887 when Congress passed a ban on opium importation by Chinese immigrants but not by other US residents. In 1890, a federal law was created that limited the manufacturing of opium in smokable form to American citizens only (Szasz 1974). The importation of smokable opium was barred altogether at the federal level in 1909 with the passage of the Smoking Opium Exclusion Act (Brecher 1972; Szasz 1974; Musto 1987). This act, as well as the series of local, state, and federal opium-related laws that came before it, was a response to public hysteria over the "filthy Oriental habit" (Gahlinger 2004, 58). The fact that these laws only addressed the product and practice of smoking opium, both of which were favored by the Chinese, points to their racist and xenophobic origin.

The gradual prohibition of cocaine exhibited many similarities to the outlawing of opium. As with the opiates, few restrictions could be found on cocaine during the 1800s. Cocaine powder was cheaper than alcohol. For this reason, poor people, many of whom were black, often used cocaine in place of alcohol to achieve altered states of mind (Gahlinger 2004). It is probably not a historical coincidence that cocaine use became associated with southern blacks shortly after the Civil War. Musto (1987) notes that fears of "the cocainized black coincided with the peak of lynchings, legal segregation, and voting laws all designed to remove political and social power" from the African American community (7). The growing condemnation of cocaine was not due to its chemical properties but rather to its association with black people. Southern whites feared that blacks would use cocaine and "attack white society" (Gahlinger 2004, 42). Myths about cocaine's effects (e.g., it made blacks impenetrable to .32-caliber bullets, thus prompting some southern police departments to adopt .38-caliber bullets) typified whites' fears, not reality. The evidence suggests cocaine did not cause an increase in crime. Instead, the expectation of cocaine-induced black rebellion created alarm among whites (Musto 1987).

In addition to linking drug problems to socially disempowered groups, the challenge to publicly redefine the use of opiates and cocaine as evil succeeded in part because of the professional activities of claims makers. Well before the passage of the Volstead Act, crusaders from the Progressive and Temperance movements helped lead the push for the national narcotic prohibitions (Bertram et al. 1996). Members of the medical establishment of the day can also be considered moral crusaders because of their moral opposition to the casual use of opiates and cocaine. Generally speaking, by the late 1800s, many had grown weary with the accepted practice of self-medication made possible by the ease with which opiate- and cocaine-containing elixirs and tonics could be obtained. The American Medical Association (AMA) and the American Pharmaceutical Association (APhA, later renamed the American Pharmacists Association) argued that these substances should only be used for medicinal purposes (Musto 1987), partly because of deep-seated beliefs that taking mind-altering substances for recreation or experimentation was immoral. Beyond their moral reservations, the AMA, APhA, and other professional medical organizations had economic interests in changing the definitions of drugs and reconfiguring the power structures through which they were made available to the public. Thus, first and foremost, these organizations can be considered professional interest groups.

In 1900, the AMA was one of many splinter groups contending for legitimacy and domination over public definitions of drugs (Musto 1987; Hogshire 1999), but five years into the twentieth century it had emerged as an authority on drugs and medicine, and its word still reigns supreme today. The AMA earned much of its legitimacy through an organized attack against the patent medicine industry. First, the AMA removed from its journals misleading advertisements printed by patent medicine manufacturers (Inciardi 2002). Then, in 1905, the AMA established the Council on Pharmacy and Chemistry in order to evaluate patent medicines. The council's publication, *New and Nonofficial Remedies,* rapidly gained influence over public and legal definitions of drugs and painted the patent medicine industry as negligent and deceptive (DeGrandpre 2006). The AMA successfully constructed a new categorization of drugs, distinguishing between "'ethical" and "patent" medicines. The former were "defined as preparations of known composition advertised exclusively to physicians," while the latter were deemed "preparations of unknown or secret composition advertised, usually in a shamelessly deceitful manner, directly to the public" (DeGrandpre 2006, 141). Essentially, this bifurcation created a new set of public meanings regarding the moral nature of using drugs. By definition, taking "ethical" drugs (i.e., those provided by doctors) for medicinal purposes was deemed acceptable, whereas the use of patent medicines came to be seen as nonmedical, dangerous, and immoral (DeGrandpre 2006).

The AMA's newly proposed definitions of drugs entered the public sphere when the council passed on the findings of its evaluation of the patent medicine industry to journalists. At this point, news media began to play a crucial role in the magnification of the drug problem. Articles decrying the fraudulent activities of patent medicine makers began appearing in newspapers and magazines, arousing public antidrug sentiments (Inciardi 2002). Chief among these media reports was a series of articles titled "The Great American Fraud" published in *Collier's* magazine. The scathing critique of the patent medicine industry opened as follows:

> Gullible America will spend this year some seventy-five millions of dollars in the purchase of patent medicines. In consideration of this sum it will swallow huge quantities of alcohol, an appalling amount of opiates and narcotics, a wide assortment of varied drugs ranging from powerful and dangerous heart depressants to insidious liver stimulants; and, in excess of all other ingredients, undiluted fraud. For fraud, exploited by the skilfulest [sic] of advertising bunco men, is the basis of the trade. (S. H. Adams 1905, 14)

The article also stated that while opium and cocaine were effective analgesics, they were "not the safest drugs to put into the hands of the ignorant, particularly when their presence is concealed in the 'cough remedies,' 'soothing syrups,' and 'catarrhal powders' of which they are the basis" (S. H. Adams 1905, 14). This exposé, along with Upton Sinclair's *The Jungle,* which revealed in sickening detail the disturbing and unhealthy conditions at Chicago's meatpacking plants,[6] was arguably the tipping point for the first federal piece of drug legislation, the Pure Food and Drug Act of 1906 (Inciardi 2002; Mosher and Akins 2007).

As a professional interest group, the AMA stood to directly benefit from federal laws designed to clamp down on the patent medicine industry. If the AMA's distinctions between "ethical" and "unethical" drugs were codified into law, people would come to rely less on the patent medicine industry and more on doctors and pharmacists. The Pure Food and Drug Act marked the beginning of this codification. Though the act did not prohibit the use of opiates, cocaine, and other drugs available as patent medicines, it required manufacturers to list the ingredients in their products. This law significantly weakened the patent medicine industry's stranglehold on the drug market and greatly increased the strength and legitimization of the medical establishment, especially the AMA (Musto 1987; DeGrandpre 2006).

The climate of fear over drugs slightly waned following the passage of the Pure Food and Drug Act, but the public soon again became "increasingly receptive" (Bertram et al. 1996, 66) to the claims made by antidrug crusaders, and a belief in expanded governmental control of drugs gained widespread legitimacy. Some of these newer calls for reform came after a series of international opium conferences held at The Hague, during which US diplomats pressured foreign suppliers to curtail their production and exportation of the drug. For its part, the United States vowed to rein in its residents' consumption of opium and other narcotic drugs by implementing stricter controls on the medicinal channels of its domestic supply network (Musto 1987; Bertram et al. 1996; Gieringer 2006). In order to fulfill treaty obligations and avoid international embarrassment for failing to control its domestic narcotics problem, US political leaders urged more national legislation (Musto 1987). While estimates of national levels of opium use were hotly debated, drawing on a report of a threefold increase between 1870 and 1909, Representative Francis Burton Harrison of New York contended,

> This enormous increase in the importation . . . and consumption of opium in the United States is startling and is directly due to the facility with which opium may be imported, manufactured . . . and placed within the reach of the individual. There has been in this country an almost shameless traffic in these drugs. Criminal classes have been created, and the use of the drugs with much accompanying moral and economic degradation is widespread among the upper classes of society. We are an opium-consuming nation today. (quoted in Bertram et al. 1996, 67)

In addition to concerns of uncontrollable opiate abuse, also around this time, moral crusaders heightened the link between cocaine use and the freed black slave (Reinarman 2012). Fears that the African American would "rise above his place" intensified (Gahlinger 2004, 42), perhaps exemplified in the following medical journal excerpt authored in early 1914 by an accomplished US physician and professor:

> Once the negro has reached the stage of being a "dope taker"—and a very few experimental sniffs of [cocaine] make him an habitué—he is a constant menace to his community until he is eliminated. For his whole nature is changed for the worse by the habit. Sexual desires are increased and perverted, peaceful negroes become quarrelsome, and timid negroes develop a degree of "Dutch courage" that is sometimes almost incredible. (Williams 1914, 13–14)

Clearly, the conditions were ideal for the first federal drug prohibition. Despite modest declines in domestic opiate and cocaine use since the Pure Food and Drug Act (Brecher 1972; Musto 1987; Inciardi 2002; DeGrandpre 2006), an increasing fear of drugs among the public, coupled with the US government's international promise to effect domestic controls, meant that a national law was imminent. However, early drafts of an antinarcotics bill were vehemently opposed by professional interest groups, including the AMA.

By 1913, the AMA had grown to 36,000 members, up from 8,500 in 1900, and "was well on its way to consolidation of American medical practitioners" (Musto 1987, 56). The AMA sought to institutionally legitimize physicians by increasing and standardizing the educational requisites for doctors in the United States. They knew engaging in political activity would help them accomplish this goal. Their earlier support of the Pure Food and Drug Act helped provide them with institutional access to the legislative activities involved in the writing of the Harrison Act. The AMA's primary reservation over early versions of the Harrison Act was that it would give the government too much control over physician dispensing of drugs and thus hinder their trade. The AMA was also concerned that physicians might face charges for prescribing soon-to-be restricted drugs to their addicted patients (Musto 1987; DeGrandpre 2006).

While Representative Harrison and many other prohibitionists favored a complete ban on opiates and cocaine, the final version of the Harrison Act, signed by President Woodrow Wilson on December 17, 1914, represented a compromise (Musto 1987; Bertram et al. 1996). Its enactment symbolically demonstrated to the world that the United States was serious in its plan to curb narcotics, and that it could be counted on to uphold its end of the recent international drug control agreements. On the other hand, the bill seemed to protect the professional and financial interests of the medical community. Physicians would be allowed to continue to dispense opiates and cocaine, but only "in the course of [their] professional practice" (Harrison Act 1914, Sec. 2a), and pharmacists could continue selling narcotics so long as purchasers had a doctor's prescription (Harrison Act 1914, Sec. 2b). Thus, "on its face . . . the Harrison bill did not appear to be a prohibition law at all. . . . [Rather, it] was merely a law for the orderly marketing of opium, morphine, heroin, and other drugs" (Brecher 1972, 49). The law required physicians and pharmacists to maintain records of drugs they prescribed or distributed. It also imposed taxes on opiates and cocaine, requiring importers, pharmacists, physicians, and manufacturers to obtain a license from the federal government in order to legally continue their practices (Brecher 1972). From this point forward, the unlicensed dealing of these drugs was illegal (DeGrandpre 2006).

In short, the terms of the Harrison Act illuminated the institutional legitimacy of the medical profession. The "enforcement mechanisms—

registration, taxes, penalties—were designed to keep drugs under the control of the medical community" (Bertram et al. 1996, 68). The law also appeared to support a treatment model of drug control. Drug users—both addicts and nonaddicts—were not criminalized. They were merely obliged to obtain a physician's prescription in order to acquire the drugs they sought (Bertram et al. 1996).

Although antidrug crusaders failed to achieve their ultimate goal of complete prohibition, they saw the Harrison Act as an effective step toward inhibiting addiction, curtailing the perceived overuse of narcotics (Gahlinger 2004), and thereby treating immorality. However, the medical community defined addiction more as a disease and less as an immoral character defect. Hence, they treated addicts as patients and prescribed them drugs to avoid the suffering associated with withdrawal (Inciardi 2002). This difference in perspective became a crucial point of contention between the medical establishment and the federal government. Shortly after the Harrison Act was passed, physicians were arrested and imprisoned for dispensing opiates and other drugs to addicts (Brecher 1972). The act's provision that allowed a doctor to prescribe narcotics "in the course of his professional practice only" was construed by legal and justice officials "to mean that a doctor could not prescribe opiates to an addict to maintain his addiction" (Brecher 1972, 49).

In the end, the strict interpretation held. Moral objections to drug use became codified into law, and prohibitionists transformed the mostly medical model of controlling drug addiction into a punitive model that banned drug use through force (Bertram et al. 1996). A series of Supreme Court decisions handed down in the first few years after the Harrison Act upheld that physicians who prescribed drugs to addicts were in violation of the law (Inciardi 2002). Musto (1987) suggests that events surrounding World War I influenced the Court's interpretation of the Harrison Act, as propaganda framed drug addiction as an unpatriotic "threat to the national war effort" (133). Narcotics-using African Americans and Chinese immigrants were not the only folk devils by this time. During the war, American drug users became associated with Bolsheviks, anarchists, Wobblies, and other despised groups (Musto 1987).[7]

Long-Term Consequences of the Harrison Act

In terms of its eventual effects on the present methamphetamine problem in the United States, the Harrison Act is noteworthy for several reasons. As the first federal drug prohibition, it would serve as a blueprint to define US drug policy up to the present. The Harrison Act and many other subsequent federal drug laws embody a punitive approach to drugs. Such laws are designed to solve drug problems by punishing offenders with fines, prison terms, asset seizures, and other penalties. When people continued to use cocaine and opiates after the passage of the Harrison Act, legislators and the public at large presumed penalties were too lenient. Historically, the typical solution has been to enact more punitive laws, including the Jones-Miller Act of 1922, which imposed hefty fines and prison sentences on violators; the Boggs Amendment of 1951, which set up mandatory minimum prison sentences for opium, cocaine, and marijuana violations; and the Narcotic Drug Control Act of 1956, which raised these mandatory minimums and defined the sale of heroin to a minor as a capital offense (DeGrandpre 2006). Orchestrated with the Harrison Act of 1914, a primarily punitive method of drug control has served as the business-as-usual approach to drug problems ever since, despite the fact that increases in the retributive nature of drug prohibitions over the past hundred or so years have not done much to deter use (Brecher 1972; Dai 2012).

The second important consequence of the Harrison Act is that it spawned the creation of the black market for illegal drugs. The black market is probably the greatest cause of modern drug-related problems and is responsible for many more harms than the actual chemical properties of prohibited drugs. Several previously nonexistent drug harms that stem from the black market include haphazard drug-manufacturing operations, trafficking-related violence, inconsistent drug purity levels (including the use of adulterants), and the invoking of the Iron Law of Prohibition (i.e., the transition of users to more potent drugs or more harmful methods of use in response to increased law enforcement scrutiny). On a national level, the black market's damages to society are immeasurable. More locally, its injurious effects are most acutely experienced by law-abiding members of poor, urban communities where black-market activities tend to thrive (Nadelmann 1989; Thornton 1998; Fish 2006).

The third significant outcome of the Harrison Act was the heightening of the bifurcation (i.e., "differential prohibition") between "ethical" medicines and dangerous drugs. Although many physicians lost their careers due to the government's refusal to adopt a disease model of addiction, the fact that certain opiates and other narcotic drugs could be used (and can still be used) for many medical purposes attests to the medical community's strength. By invoking the power of the physician's pen, drug prohibitions have facilitated the institutionalization of the cultural dichotomies of medicine/drug, licit/illicit, moral/immoral, and angel/demon that underpin many popular constructions of drugs. The current distinctions between Desoxyn and meth, between OxyContin and heroin, are present-day manifestations of this dichotomy (DeGrandpre 2006). At the risk of sounding cynical, I must point out that persons in the United States can legally use and sell most mind-altering drugs if they do so through legitimate channels. Interest group definitions of "good" and "bad" drugs have allowed for analogous definitions of "good" and "bad" people, decided in terms of whether or not they employ institutionally sanctioned means to acquire or distribute chemical substances (DeGrandpre 2006).

The fourth important result of the Harrison Act was its promotion of the discovery and synthesis of new drugs. Like illicit drug users and black-market distributors, the pharmaceutical industry overcame the challenge of fulfilling the widespread and continued demand for consciousness-altering drugs by inventing new ones. The industry adapted to the Harrison Act's restrictions on nature-based drugs (e.g., coca, opium) by "synthesizing new, artificial angels" that would allow for the continued maintenance and expansion of a "parallel, legal drug market" (DeGrandpre 2006, 144). Starting in the 1930s, opioids (i.e., synthetic opiates), such as Demerol (meperidine) and, a little later, Darvon (propoxyphene), were created in chemistry laboratories and marketed by drug companies to alleviate pain. Creating new drugs similar in their effects and chemical structures to the natural opiates, the discovery and synthesis of opioids were both industry adaptations to newly enacted drug laws and legal means to meet the continuing demand for potent analgesics (Gahlinger 2004; DeGrandpre 2006).

Parallel discoveries were made with other classes of drugs. Though first sold to the US public in 1903, barbiturates gained a great deal of scientific attention shortly after the Harrison Act. Chemists working for pharmaceutical companies developed "new and improved" barbiturates in the 1920s and early 1930s, including Amytal (amobarbital), Nembutal (pentobarbital), and Seconal (secobarbital) (DeGrandpre 2006).[8] Barbiturates are used as sedatives, sleep aids, anticonvulsants, and anesthetics. Like opiates, barbiturates are downers. Unlike opiates, this entire class of drugs (over 2,500 total kinds) is purely synthetic. By the 1950s, barbiturates had reached their pinnacle of popularity in US society, especially among movie stars and other entertainers (Gahlinger 2004).[9] Eventually barbiturates would be succeeded in popularity with the synthesis of the "minor tranquilizers," including benzodiazepines (e.g., Valium, Halcion, Xanax), which were also created during the 1950s.[10] Millions of prescriptions have been written for these drugs, and drug companies have made billions of dollars promoting them as antianxiety cures (Weil and Rosen 2004).

Because, technically, the Harrison Act and subsequent early drug prohibitions outlawed "narcotics" and not "drugs," control of synthetic substances would come to fall under the jurisdiction of the FDA, a civil regulatory agency whose enforcement powers were much weaker than those of the Federal Bureau of Narcotics (FBN). Pharmaceutical companies flourished as industry chemists synthesized new cures, while the federal government focused its attention and resources on the evils of cocaine, opium, and, by the 1930s, marijuana (Jenkins 1999).

Enter Amphetamines

Generally speaking, synthetic barbiturates, minor tranquilizers, and opioids can all be considered depressants since they reduce the nervous system's activity (Weil and Rosen 2004). Another class of synthetic drugs that was discovered and popularized during the first decades of federal drug prohibition was the amphetamines. Unlike synthetic depressants, amphetamines are considered stimulants because they function to increase the activity of the nervous system, promoting sensations of increased energy and wakefulness.

Whereas synthetic depressants filled much of the void created by the criminalization of opiates, amphetamines were the medicine industry's solution to the prohibition of cocaine. Both amphetamines and cocaine are stimulants, and as such, their effects on users are quite comparable. Despite their similarities, amphetamines were initially seen as superior to cocaine in at least two respects. First, amphetamines are much more effective than cocaine when taken orally in tablet form. Second, the feelings of alertness and energy produced by a standard dose of amphetamines persist anywhere from two to ten hours, whereas cocaine's stimulating effects dissipate much more quickly (Brecher 1972).

Following the criminalization of cocaine, the race to develop and market a synthetic stimulant was under way. The first amphetamine became available to the public less than twenty years after the passage of the Harrison Act. Benzedrine was for sale OTC by 1932, and a host of other amphetamines, including methamphetamine, shortly followed. By 1971, fifteen pharmaceutical companies manufactured and distributed at least thirty-one preparations of speed (Brecher 1972).

The invention and popularization of speed can be seen as a demand-side consequence of the Harrison Act and other early punitive, supply-restrictive drug laws. "Cocaine would not be allowed back into the kingdom of ethical drugs" but its departure was overcome when the amphetamines were discovered (DeGrandpre 2006, 144). And although the amphetamines were initially touted as wonder drugs, much like their natural predecessors, speed too would ultimately be the subject of crusading interest groups and moral entrepreneurs. The seeds for the United States' next stimulant panic, as well as the subsequent round of prohibitionist policies, had been planted.

Notes

1. Milan Korcok (1978) discusses some of heroin's therapeutic benefits, such as its effectiveness in the treatment of pain and dyspnea in cancer patients and its superiority to morphine.

2. George Washington grew hemp at Mount Vernon circa 1765 (Brecher 1972) and Queen Victoria of England used it for relieving menstrual cramps (Mosher and Akins 2007). Hemp production became sanctioned again in World War II, as imports were not sufficient to satisfy the war effort's demand for rope (Brecher 1972).

3. In this context, *narcotics* refers to opiates and cocaine. When discussed in legal and public discourse, the term *narcotic* encompasses this very broad definition. However, medically, *narcotic* "refers specifically to drugs related to opium or its synthetic forms. The word comes from the Greek *narkotikos,* meaning 'to numb'" (Gahlinger 2004, 14). Opiates were the first drugs controlled through international laws, but the term *narcotics* has subsequently been redefined in popular vernacular and legalese to include all illegal drugs (Gahlinger 2004).

4. This figure was estimated on July 25, 2013, using the "Purchasing Power Calculator" for the United States at www.measuringworth.com.

5. Indeed, the remarkable shift in pro-marijuana attitudes in the 2010s (as evidenced by public opinion polls and the 2012 voter referendums to legalize recreational use in Colorado and Washington State) is also due in part to the successes and failures of claims makers.

6. For example, plant workers controlled rat infestations by "baiting the unsuspecting rodents with poisoned bread. Then, dead rats (poisoned bread and all) typically went into the hoppers of oddments used in sausages and other processed meats used for human consumption" (Inciardi 2002, 28).

7. *Wobblies* is the slang term for members of the International Workers of the World, a labor union founded in Chicago in 1905. During the early 1900s,

sensationalist media accounts of the union portrayed its existence as a grave threat to capitalism (Hoxie 1913). While the International Workers of the World hoped for an overthrow of capitalist society, the organization never posed a real revolutionary threat. President Wilson ordered raids on local chapters after labor protests took place in areas vital to the war effort. In the end, 101 members were indicted on charges of undermining the war effort. They were quickly demonized as an unpatriotic "American version of bolshevism" (Renshaw 1968, 67).

8. The first barbiturates were so long acting that users were sometimes sedated well after taking them. The "new and improved" barbiturates were shorter acting (DeGrandpre 2006).

9. An autopsy conducted after the sudden death of Marilyn Monroe in 1962 revealed she had ingested forty-seven Nembutal pills (Gahlinger 2004).

10. According to one source, the use of the word *minor* to describe these drugs is misleading. They were called "minor" in an attempt to "distinguish these drugs from the 'major' tranquilizers . . . used to manage psychotic patients. . . . There is nothing minor about their effects, the problems they can cause, or their potential for abuse" (Weil and Rosen 2004, 86).

3

The Emergence
of Amphetamines

One day by mistake, I picked up the Benzedrine thinking it was my calci-
um lactate. . . . All day I had the most marvelous feeling of exultation
(not knowing the cause). Whereas I am ordinarily inactive and without
ambition to do things, that day I painted the porch furniture, caught up on
garden work long neglected, rearranged the furniture in the living room,
altogether feeling for the first time in years like a colt. . . . One or two
daily rations of it apparently changes me in spirit from a forlorn old lady
to a cheerful young woman. —*"Doctor Brady's Health Talks"* (1939, 8)

Before we delve into the early history of amphetamines in the United
States, a brief chemistry lesson is in order. Specifically, I am referring to
the difference between isolating and synthesizing a drug. Chemists isolate a drug by taking a substance (e.g., plant) with a known or suspected
effect (e.g., psychoactive, therapeutic) and determining which chemical
or chemicals in that substance produce the desired effect.[1] For example,
green tea (*Camellia sinensis*) has been enjoyed for its health benefits in
the Far East since ancient times. It contains a variety of chemical compounds, some of which are therapeutic and some of which are inert.
Scientists isolated the antioxidant epigallocatechin gallate (or EGCG)
from green tea and determined it was one of the "active" chemicals that
improves health (Weil and Rosen 2004).

Once scientists have mapped out the structure of an active chemical
from a plant or other substance (i.e., once they have isolated it), efforts
are often made to synthesize it. Synthesizing a drug is producing it
through artificial means. Synthesis usually involves mixing together
laboratory chemicals to force reactions, the end result of which is a drug
with the same chemical structure achieved through isolation. Synthesis
is often preferred over isolation because the former method does not

require a steady and healthy supply of trees, plants, or other cumbersome (and sometimes scarce) natural products that contain the desired chemical.[2] In some cases, synthetic drugs are discovered by accident in a chemistry lab. In other instances, scientists intentionally synthesize a drug based on information known about other chemicals (Weil and Rosen 2004).[3]

Unlike cocaine, purely synthetic drugs, like the amphetamines, are not derived from a natural source. No amphetamine plant grows in the wild or otherwise from which chemists can isolate amphetamine (cf. Clement, Goff, and Forbes 1998). Amphetamines did not exist until 1887, when European pharmacologist Lazar Edeleano became the first person to synthesize phenylisopropylamine. The AMA renamed this substance *amphetamine* in the early 1930s (Grinspoon and Bakalar 1979). In strict chemical terms, *amphetamine* refers to beta-phenyliso-propylamine sulfate, the specific type of amphetamine more commonly known as Benzedrine (Berggren and Soderberg 1938; Shulgin 1976; J. P. Morgan 1979). However, I use the term *amphetamine* to refer more broadly to the many variations of the amphetamine molecule, all of which have similar stimulating properties (Gahlinger 2004). Included in this class of stimulant drugs is methamphetamine, first synthesized in 1893 by Nagayoshi Nagai, a Japanese pharmacologist (Suwaki, Fukui, and Konuma 1997).

In this chapter, I trace the early use of amphetamines in the United States, examine media portrayals of amphetamines up to about 1965, and discuss a series of industry restrictions and federal laws aimed at curtailing supplies of the drug. Synthetic stimulants, including methamphetamine, entered US society under opportune historical circumstances. As such, they were initially embraced by actors, artists, athletes, politicians, and the public alike. These factors, combined with a powerfully burgeoning medical and pharmaceutical community, explain why it would take several decades for crusaders to mount even a partially successful anti-amphetamine campaign. And while I do not discuss the details of the United States' first methamphetamine scare until the next chapter, the following section provides a brief genealogy of methamphetamine as it sociologically evolved from cocaine, epinephrine, ephedrine, and amphetamine.

Pharmacological Enlightenment

In addition to inventing methamphetamine, Nagayoshi Nagai is credited as the first person to isolate ephedrine, the psychoactive ingredient in the ephedra plant (*ma huang,* in Chinese) that has been used medicinally for millennia (Joseph 2000).[4] Ephedrine and amphetamines are similar in that both stimulate the central nervous system, affecting respiration and energy levels. When the nervous system is stimulated, the muscular walls of the bronchial tubes relax, opening respiratory tract airways and allowing asthma sufferers to breathe more easily (J. P. Morgan 1979; Weil and Rosen 2004).[5] The stimulation produced by amphetamines often leads to mood elevation, decreased fatigue, and increased alertness, initiative, confidence, and elation (J. P. Morgan 1979). Though milder in its impact, ephedrine produces similar effects on psychoactivity and the nervous system (Iversen 2006). Indeed, of all known naturally occurring substances, ephedrine is probably closest in chemical structure to amphetamine. Due to their chemical similarities, ephedrine and pseudoephedrine (e.g., Sudafed) are often used as chemical precursors in illicit methamphetamine synthesis.

Until Nagai isolated ephedrine in 1887, the scientific community could not pinpoint precisely what chemical in the ma huang plant soothed asthmatics and produced psychomotor stimulation (Joseph 2000). Popular in Japan for the treatment of asthma during the 1910s, ephedrine was relatively unknown to the Western world until the following decade when the AMA endorsed its use in the United States (Chen and Schmidt 1930). During the mid- to late 1920s, ephedrine was promoted as an antiasthmatic, an anesthetic, and a treatment for colds, low blood pressure, hay fever, and "shock and accidents" ("Psychic Treatment" 1931, 18; see also "Ancient Drug" 1926; Chen and Schmidt 1930). In less than five years after its introduction in the United States, ephedrine rose "from obscurity to . . . [a] state of widespread popularity" (Chen and Schmidt 1930, 2), was produced by several manufacturers, and was "quite generally obtainable" (Chen and Schmidt 1930, 7).

Many of these ailments, including asthma, pain, and, especially, low blood pressure, were treated with epinephrine prior to the introduction of ephedrine (Hartung 1931) and after the demonization of cocaine (Rasmussen 2008a). Norepinephrine (also known as noradrenaline) is a neurotransmitter manufactured by the adrenal gland. Whether triggered by a physical experience (e.g., bungee jumping, fighting, having a medical emergency) or through the introduction of epinephrine or epinephrine-like drugs, the result is the body's preparation for "fight or flight: the heart rate increases, blood is moved away from the digestive organs to the muscles, and the lungs open up to breathe faster" (Gahlinger 2004, 139). The heightened senses and occasional distortions in time accompanying the "adrenaline rush" reported by daredevils or persons in dire situations occur from the brain's rapid release of norepinephrine during survival mode. Epinephrine, ephedrine, and amphetamines mimic the effects of endogenous chemicals, causing the brain to release stockpiles of norepinephrine (Gahlinger 2004; Weil and Rosen 2004).

After its discovery, ephedrine became medically preferable to epinephrine because of the former's longer duration and effectiveness when taken orally (J. Peterson 1928; Chen and Schmidt 1930; Hartung 1931). As a result of the rapid increase in medical use of ephedrine, "demand quickly outstripped supply . . . creating an incentive for chemists to develop substitute drugs" (Rasmussen 2008a, 14). If chemists could successfully synthesize ephedrine, they would no longer have to rely on foreign *ma huang* imports, which had become inconsistent and unreliable due to political developments in the Far East (Osborne 2005).

In 1940, Ernest H. Volwiler of Abbott Laboratories (one of the first companies to market methamphetamine in the United States) expressed the disadvantages of depending on transcontinental sources for natural drugs and herbs:

> When the world is at peace, commerce flows almost effortlessly and industry itself gives relatively little thought to the degree of its dependence upon supplies which must come from foreign sources. When widespread war occurs, pinching needs may develop; this was painfully evident during World War I, when a considerable number of essential drugs became scarce or even unobtainable. Fortunately the American pharmaceutical manufacturing industry took those lessons to heart, and largely by its own industrial and inventive contributions, it has removed the danger of shortages of the great majority of drug items. Even in cases of certain raw or finished drugs which heretofore have still been imported, adequate products for the same purposes are or can be made available in the United States. (Volwiler 1940, 1179)

The pharmaceutical industry did not fully master the chemical synthesis of ephedrine until the late 1930s, but by that time, amphetamines were widely available (Osborne 2005).

As drug companies struggled from a combination of prohibition-induced revenue losses and increased risks involved in relying on foreign sources for legal drugs, the age of pharmacological enlightenment brought amphetamines to the United States. Forty years after amphetamines' invention, US scientists began to explore speed's therapeutic potential as an ephedrine substitute, especially in the treatment of asthma (Rasmussen 2006, 2008a). Gordon Alles, a Los Angeles chemist, discovered Edeleano's research from the 1880s and successfully reproduced amphetamine in 1927 (Grinspoon and Bakalar 1979; Joseph 2000). After trying the drug himself, Alles proclaimed that amphetamine could serve as an ephedrine substitute in treating not only respiratory problems but fatigue, lack of confidence, and poor concentration (Grinspoon and Bakalar 1979). Amphetamine's promise in relieving asthma, as well as its psycho-stimulating side effects, appealed greatly to a pharmaceutical industry searching for a legal cocaine substitute.

Amphetamines offered many benefits over similar drugs. Like ephedrine, amphetamine could be administered orally, boost blood pressure for a longer duration than epinephrine, and was not especially toxic (Rasmussen 2006). Best of all, the drug could be produced synthetically, releasing the US medical industry from its dependence on foreign ephedra supplies. "The discovery of a cheap synthetic drug [i.e., amphetamine] with a known and controllable composition, that was not vulnerable to the variable quality and availability of a natural herb from a faraway foreign land, was a major step forward" (Joseph 2000, 20).

When the chief chemist at Smith, Kline, and French (SKF, now GlaxoSmithKline) discovered Alles's work, his firm began to explore various commercial applications of amphetamine. SKF executives "realized the potential bonanza this 'new' class of synthetic 'ephedrine substitutes' represented, and persuaded Alles to sell them all his patent rights" (Grinspoon and Bakalar 1979, 19). By 1932, SKF released the first amphetamine available to the public, in the form of Benzedrine inhalers. Like cocaine and opiates pre-1914, Benzedrine and other amphetamine inhalers were available OTC in drug and grocery stores throughout the United States (Anglin et al. 2000; DeGrandpre 2006). Amphetamine tablets, also accessible OTC, became publicly available in 1937 (Grinspoon and Bakalar 1979; Gahlinger 2004).

Methamphetamine's introduction into US society was actually quite unremarkable. Upon witnessing SKF's earnings from Benzedrine sales skyrocket, other drug companies sought a stake in the market. However, a series of court rulings in the early 1940s upheld sole patent rights to SKF, granting them a monopoly over Benzedrine. Other companies responded by developing and promoting a structurally similar product (Rasmussen 2008a). In 1944, the FDA approved public sales of d-phenyl-isopropyl-methylamine. Called Methedrine by its manufacturer and deoxyephedrine by others, methamphetamine, as it is better known today, was provided in injectable and pill forms by Burroughs Wellcome when it first entered the consumer market (Jenkins 1999; Osborne 2005). Abbott Laboratories released methamphetamine under the trade name Desoxyn shortly thereafter (Joseph 2000). Other, less popular brand names of methamphetamine sold in various preparations in the decades following World War II included Clark-O-Tabs Modified,

Gerilets Filmtab, Oesoxyn, Meditussin, Methampex, Amerital, Span-RD, Amphaplex, Obetrol, Obestat Ty-Med, Carrtussin Syrup, Opidice, Desefedrin, Norodin, Secodrin, and Syndrox (Seevers 1968; Iversen 2006; Owen 2007; Rasmussen 2008a). Like other pharmaceutically produced amphetamines sold in the 1940s and 1950s, methamphetamine was marketed to treat asthma and a host of other ailments. Thus, in the beginning, methamphetamine was understood as just another amphetamine, a perception markedly different from the one held today.

Another similarity shared between meth and other amphetamines was their popularity. Indeed, SKF's suspicions of a speed "bonanza" were confirmed less than ten years after the introduction of Benzedrine. From 1937 to 1939, over 50 million dosage units of Benzedrine tablets were sold in the United States (Grinspoon and Bakalar 1979), and amphetamine sales would increase exponentially over the next thirty years. In the following section, I describe and offer explanations for this surge in popularity.

Amphetamines in American Culture, 1932–1960

With cocaine off limits and ephedra supplies unpredictable, stimulant-seeking residents of the United States welcomed the arrival of amphetamines with open arms. Much of the country's initial infatuation with speed was driven by the medical profession. Soon after Benzedrine was marketed for asthma, researchers and pharmaceutical companies announced a variety of other conditions that could be remedied with amphetamines, including narcolepsy ("Find Drug" 1935), boredom (Barmack 1938), weight gain (J. P. Morgan 1979), and alcoholism (Osborne 2005). As early as 1937, amphetamines were found to treat children with hyperkinesis (Bradley 1937), a condition characterized by hyperactivity and inattentiveness that is better known today as ADHD.[6] Nicolas Rasmussen (2006, 2008a) argues that amphetamine should be considered the first pharmaceutical antidepressant, since it was used widely in therapy for neurotic depression, beginning in the late 1930s. Throughout the late 1930s and early 1940s, the utility of amphetamines seemed endless (Joseph 2000). Physicians and psychiatrists recommended speed to treat schizophrenia, morphine addiction, tobacco smoking, low blood pressure, radiation sickness, Parkinson's disease, epilepsy, "caffeine mania," and even persistent hiccups (Lukas 1985, 20; see also Anglin et al. 2000; Joseph 2000). By 1946, the pharmaceutical industry listed thirty-nine separate clinical uses for amphetamines (Lukas 1985).

Initially, amphetamines were touted as nonaddictive, safe, and effective (Stuart 1962; C. Jackson 1979; Lukas 1985; Jenkins 1999; Joseph 2000; Osborne 2005).

The medical community's influence on public perceptions of amphetamines extended beyond scientific journals and into the mass media. A *Time* magazine article described a doctor reporting that Benzedrine had "very interesting and favorable results in a good many of those normal and quasi-normal [such as hangover] states where the individual has not had sufficient rest or is depressed in the morning" ("Trial and Error" 1936). An article in the *New York Times* likened amphetamine to "high octane . . . gasoline" that would allow the brain to more effectively "hit on all cylinders." Quoting from a doctor's lecture at the New York Academy of Medicine, the article proclaimed, "The extraordinary energy-stimulating powers of Benzedrine . . . appear to prove that the potential of brain cells is far from being fully realized under ordinary conditions" ("Efficiency of Brain" 1937, 6). Other *Times* articles published during the 1930s relayed results from medical studies supporting the use of Benzedrine in reducing depression and curbing suicide ("New Drug" 1936), curing alcoholism ("Drug Held" 1938), and treating colds ("New Gain" 1939). Smaller-market newspapers also extolled the virtues of amphetamines, as communicated by medical professionals. For example, a headline appearing in the *Lima News* (Ohio) read, "Harmless Drug Will Make You Life of Party." The article begins:

> An apparently harmless and non-habit forming drug which can convert a tired individual into the life of a party for only two cents a day was described today by Dr. Henry B. Gwynn of Georgetown University's medical school. The drug is known as Benzedrine sulfate. Dr. Gwynn said the drug has been tested by 147 Georgetown medical students. . . . Students who took the drug were able to obtain better grades. Grouchy personalities were converted into charming, considerate persons. ("Harmless Drug" 1937, 5)

Beyond the fact that Benzedrine and other amphetamines were manufactured by pharmaceutical companies, the heavy media representation of physicians as primary claims makers helped frame speed as a medicine rather than a drug. The mostly positive sentiments expressed early on, combined with the array of conditions amphetamines were being used to treat, led to their widespread acceptance among a variety of people motivated to use for a variety of reasons. Truck drivers used amphetamines to travel long distances without rest. Blue-collar workers utilized speed to work long hours at factories and plants and to counteract abnormalities in biorhythms experienced in the "shift system" (Jenkins 1999, 31). Under normative pressures to maintain a thin figure, amphetamines appealed to middle-aged women trying to lose or keep off weight (Jenkins 1999). Dozens of amphetamine preparations were advertised to housewives for depression and diet (Gahlinger 2004). Speed was also adopted by high school and college students trying to handle the ins and outs of term papers, exams, and the like (Jenkins 1999). As early as 1940, business executives were reported to use amphetamines (Brecher 1972), presumably to increase their work capacity. Athletes took amphetamines to heighten endurance and aggression (Plumb 1959; Jenkins 1999). Even animals were given speed, as several horse owners and jockeys were found to have injected their racehorses with the drug (e.g., Field 1941).[7]

Starting in the 1940s, amphetamines became more fully integrated into pop culture as their use began to be associated with musicians, artists, actors, and others in the entertainment industry. Speed became a key element of the sociability and community of the Beat subculture and was enjoyed by Jack Kerouac, Allen Ginsberg, and other beatnik poets of the 1940s and 1950s (Rasmussen 2008a). According to Miriam Joseph (2000), "speed stood at the crossroads of early rock 'n' roll and country music, consumed by the performers, roadies and audiences alike" (40–41). Jerry Lee Lewis, Hank Williams, Elvis Presley, Mick Jagger, the Everly Brothers, and Johnny Cash were popular musicians of the middle twentieth century who used amphetamines when playing music and managing long concert tours across the country (Hogshire 1999; Joseph 2000). The Beatles "got by with a little help from their friends," enjoying generous amounts of amphetamines when performing many hours per day, seven days per week, at various venues across Europe (Joseph 2000). Royston Ellis, a British poet, taught John Lennon how to crack open Benzedrine inhalers in order to ingest "the amphetamine-laced wads inside" (Rasmussen 2008a, 104). Film producer Cecil B. DeMille, comedian Lenny Bruce, composer Leonard Bernstein, writer Truman Capote, playwright Tennessee Williams, pop artist Andy Warhol, and movie star Judy Garland were several other distinguished entertainers who frequently used speed (Iversen 2006). According to Jim Hogshire (1999), David O. Selznick, the producer of the classic film *Gone with the Wind,* "constantly ate Benzedrine tablets to fuel consistent 22-hour days" on the movie set (105). Several prominent cast members in *Dr. Zhivago, Lawrence of Arabia,* and *Ciao! Manhattan* took speed throughout filming (Hogshire 1999).

Numerous powerful world leaders also used amphetamines from time to time. Adolf Hitler took amphetamine tablets and, at one point during World War II, injected himself with methamphetamine on a daily basis (Joseph 2000). Winston Churchill used both amphetamines and barbiturates during the war (Gahlinger 2004). Prime Minister Sir Anthony Eden of Great Britain admitted to taking Benzedrine daily throughout the Suez crisis with Egypt in 1956 (Joseph 2000). John F. Kennedy received amphetamine injections twice per week during various parts of his political career. Max Jacobson (the notorious "Dr. Feelgood") injected Kennedy the night of his first televised debate with Richard Nixon, before his first summit talk with Nikita Khrushchev, and throughout the Cuban missile crisis (Rasmussen 2008a).[8]

Amphetamines have also been used as "performance enhancers" by militaries since the Spanish Civil War (Iversen 2006, 71). During World War II, amphetamines were rationed to US, Japanese, German, and British soldiers to combat fatigue and increase endurance (Rawlin 1968; Brecher 1972). Several news reports printed during the 1940s suggest that the United States considered giving its troops amphetamines after hearing of their use by German armed forces. For example, a 1940 story published in the *New York Times* quoted a doctor who suggested German infantry seized France, Belgium, and Holland with the aid of a "powerful stimulant." The speed with which Nazi troops advanced into Allied territory "probably meant [they experienced] 48 continuous hours of action and tension, no sleep and an imperative need for unbroken alertness" ("Thinks Nazis" 1940, 21). Another *New York Times* article, published in 1942, claimed Benzedrine spurred Hitler's troops to "superhuman assignments" ("Pep Pills" 1942, 7).[9]

Although the United States did not "officially" sanction amphetamine use among its troops during World War II, tablets were supplied in army-issued first-aid kits and given to weary pilots on long bombing missions (C. Jackson 1979; Rasmussen 2008a, 2011).[10] In a letter written from Guam in 1945, First Lieutenant Wilfred N. Lind described his experiences flying B-29 bombers over Japan with the aid of Benzedrine. On the perils of air warfare, he wrote,

> To begin with, you're flying in combat, which fact alone adds to the obstacles in a man's mind. You're flying long drawn-out flights at altitudes ranging all the way up to 30,000 feet . . . , and being the navigator of one of these sky wagons means that you must work every minute of the flight. The pilot and co-pilot can get a bit of shut-eye every so often. Automatic pilot is a great help to everyone but the nav-

igator. He just rubs his tired eyes, takes some more Benzedrine and
goes to work again. (Lind 1945, SM3)

World War II was the first but certainly not the last time speed would be
utilized by the US military.[11]

Benzedrine Backlash

The United States' love affair with amphetamines did not go unchallenged. Throughout the middle half of the twentieth century, speed was
periodically subject to negative media coverage. During this time period, one common theme in the sporadic news reports was the association
of amphetamines with groups of relatively low social power.

The first major instance of bad press came from a series of reports
linking Benzedrine use with college students. *Time* magazine warned
about "Pep-Pill Poisoning" (1937) among students at three major midwestern universities, claiming that "a new, powerful, but poisonous
brain stimulant called Benzedrine kept college directors in dithers of
worry" (53). Small quantities of the drug were said to "maintain [the
student's] intelligence. Overdoses, such as uninformed college students
seem to be using, bring on dangerous after effects" (53). In a June 1937
article, the *El Paso Herald-Post* cited an AMA warning to college students not to use Benzedrine when cramming for final exams. Physicians
reported "collapse, fainting, and insomnia following" the use of pep
pills to study and avoid sleep. One doctor described these methods of
use as "about as efficient as whipping a tired horse" ("Students Warned"
1937, 9). Similar stories appeared in several other regional newspapers,
including the *Wisconsin State Journal* ("Use of Drug" 1937) and the
Brainerd Daily Dispatch (Minnesota) ("Warn Students" 1937).

Negative public perceptions of speed grew when its users began to
be portrayed as living on the margins of society. In the early 1940s, the
use of Benzedrine became associated with black jazz ("bebop") musicians like Charlie Parker and other subversive members of the entertainment industry (DeGrandpre 2006). Around that time, columnist Earl
Wilson reported that amphetamine pills were being used recreationally
by "less sophisticated" segments of society, including "New York's
Benzedrine Set" (as cited in C. Jackson 1979, 36). An article in *Time*
magazine discussed the pro-amphetamine lyrics of the bebop music
scene, quoting an outraged director of a Los Angeles radio station who

said, "Bebop . . . tends to make degenerates, out of our young listeners" ("Be-bop Be-bopped" 1946, 54).

Of particular concern during this time period was the misuse of Benzedrine inhalers. By the 1940s it was well-known that the inhalers could be broken open in order to access the entire drug at once, rather than in the small doses attained by following SKF's instructions. The wads of paper contained within the inhalers were saturated with 250 milligrams of amphetamine (approximately twenty-five tablets' worth). Thrill seekers would remove the paper and either soak it in water, coffee, or some other drinkable solution or chew it with gum. Anecdotal accounts of users breaking open inhalers and ingesting their contents whole spread throughout the speed-using subculture (C. Jackson 1979; DeGrandpre 2006).

By the mid-1940s, some members of the medical establishment began to express opposition to the nonmedical use of amphetamines. In an article published in the prestigious *Journal of the American Medical Association,* Russell Monroe and Hyman Drell (1947) issued a warning to the medical community:

> Amphetamine ("Benzedrine") has become a popular drug among the laity as evidenced by its mention in songs, magazines, and commercial advertisements. The song, "Who Put the Benzedrine in Mrs. Murphy's Ovaltine?" has been popular recently. A newspaper advertisement featuring a charm bracelet with a pill box attached states the following: "For 'Benzedrine', if you're having fun and going on forever; 'aspirin' if it's all a headache." An article entitled, "On a Bender with Benzedrine" appeared in the September 1946 issue of *Everybody's Digest*. The anonymous author discussed the oral use of the volatile base from inhalers by those in the entertainment field, its availability and its effect. (909)

In addition to media reports of amphetamine abuse by irresponsible young college students and "undesirables" within the entertainment industry, accounts of Benzedrine misuse among members of the prison population circulated. Generalizing findings from methodologically questionable research, Monroe and Drell (1947) estimated that 25 percent of inmates in US prisons abused amphetamine inhalers. Citing Monroe and Drell's study, a 1947 *New York Times* article warned that abuse of Benzedrine inhalers by prisoners was "apparently widespread," and that the drug caused "poisoning, hallucinations, other mental disturbances, and even death" ("Notes on Science" 1947, 127). Media coverage linking the abuse of Benzedrine inhalers to criminal groups was repeated by US newspapers the next year (e.g., F. Carey 1948; "Convicts Use" 1948).

Associations between amphetamines and crime continued to appear intermittently in the press throughout the 1950s. The unpredictably violent dope fiend emerged as a common theme in these reports. For example, in June 1954, *Time* magazine reported that Benzedrine led to the kidnap and murder of Bobby Greenlease, a six-year-old from Missouri. The article claimed that doctors were overprescribing the drug and associated amphetamine use with "neurotics," convicts, dieters, and truck drivers ("Bennies the Menace" 1954). Another news story linked illicit use of amphetamine "thrill pills" with delinquent teenagers and quoted a doctor as saying, "Excessive use of the drugs causes a breakdown of social and moral barriers and produces anxiety, confusion, hallucinations, delirium, and depression" (Morriss 1955, 25). In 1959, *Time* related amphetamine use to prostitution, burglary, robbery, and other crimes, cautioning that the "abuse of amphetamine was growing so fast that it had the Kansas City police, Missouri legislators, federal officials, even the US Congress seriously concerned." The news story also described amphetamine injecting among youth from "the most expensive neighborhoods and the poorest" ("Amphetamine Kicks" 1959).

In spite of the negative media portrayals of amphetamines from about 1940 to 1960, the periodic press attention toward speed during this time period was relatively minor in intensity and duration compared with the methamphetamine panics that unfolded over the next several decades. Edward Brecher (1972) notes that "enormous quantities of amphetamines were consumed" throughout the 1950s "apparently with little misuse" (281). While he disagrees with Brecher's contention that few people abused speed during the 1950s, Rasmussen (2008b) acknowledges that up until the early 1960s, amphetamine was perceived as a relatively innocuous drug. In the following section, I suggest various aspects of the social, cultural, and economic milieus of this time period that helped limit endemic, sustained hysteria over speed. I also discuss several seemingly ineffective legislative attempts to stem the perceived amphetamine problem.

Historical Context of Early Amphetamines, 1929–1960

One of the main ingredients of a bona fide drug scare is a historical context of conflict (Reinarman 2012). Interest groups, mass media, and moral entrepreneurs may work diligently to construct a particular chemical substance as a threat to morality and social stability. However, if not compatible with historical conditions unique to the larger society, the efforts and messages of claims makers are less likely to be taken seriously by audiences. In other words, the public is more receptive when claims are "made at the right time" (Loseke 2003, 58).

If historical timing is important in the escalation of a drug scare, a logical presumption would be that it may also be inhibitory. In this light, I offer three important sociohistorical phenomena present around the time amphetamines were introduced into the United States—the Great Depression, the anti-marijuana campaign, and the US involvement in World War II—that may be partly responsible for the sluggishness with which claims makers mounted a respectable crusade against speed.

In 1929, the US stock market crashed, sending the economy into a depression that would last until World War II. Unemployment rates reached 25 percent in 1933, bankruptcies skyrocketed, and income levels plummeted (Romer 1992). Joseph (2000) suggests that amphetamines were an appealing coping mechanism for many of those hit hard by economic catastrophe. "In the absence of other effective pharmaceutical remedies for depression, doctors were relieved to be able to offer speed to their patients" (22). The fact that the US medical community was the original primary advocator of amphetamines—as evidenced in both research literature and the popular press—meant that these drugs were not likely to be perceived as dangerous (H. W. Morgan 1981).

The Great Depression was intimately connected to the "reefer madness" crusade that was in full force during the 1930s. With a surplus of Mexican laborers, claims coupling Mexicans with marijuana resonated with an economically struggling white majority (Bertram et al. 1996). Newspaper and magazine coverage of marijuana was rife with assertions that marijuana-smoking Mexicans were violent and sexual deviants and a grave threat to children (Mosher 1985). Harry Anslinger, the first director of the FBN, led the campaign. Anslinger whipped the public into a frenzy by providing "media sources with 'information' on the effects of marijuana that was widely reported and served to demonize the substance" (Mosher and Akins 2007, 7). The Marihuana Tax Act, the culmination of the FBN's anti-pot crusade, was passed in 1937.

Amphetamines entered the consumer market precisely during this period of heightened concerned with marijuana. David Musto (1987) notes that despite the fact that amphetamines began to receive negative publicity shortly after their arrival in US stores, Anslinger and the FBN were hesitant to address the new drug. The FBN was small, understaffed, and invested heavily in the anti-marijuana campaign. Speed's white-market status and the potential bureaucratic difficulties inherent in going after an FDA-monitored substance did not appeal to an organization that had spread itself thin. Furthermore, Anslinger did not "wish to tread on the toes of politically powerful pharmaceutical firms like Parke-Davis and Smith Kline French, with which he had a congenial relationship" (Jenkins 1999, 36).

A sociohistorical factor that may have dampened early attempts to demonize amphetamines was their widespread use by the US military during World War II for purposes of enhancing combat. Advertisements appearing in medical journals steeped amphetamine use by American troops in images of patriotism, accomplishment, and victory (Owen 2007; Rasmussen 2008a, 2011). During the war, US civilians learned of the increased energy and confidence troops gained from amphetamines. When servicemen returned home, many helped popularize and legitimize speed for these purposes, ensuring its "cult status . . . as a good-time drug on the street scene" (Joseph 2000, 22). While amphetamines were used for a variety of purposes, including recreation, people also took them as a means to an end. Some of the postwar social and economic boom was plausibly due in part to people using speed to work long hours, drive long distances, and handle multiple jobs.[12]

Images of patriotic and instrumental amphetamine use illuminate one of the unique aspects of early portrayals of amphetamines (including methamphetamine). Because they alter consciousness and, consequently, detract one's attention from a life of asceticism, most intoxicants have historically been perceived as antithetical to self-control, individualism, and utilitarianism (Becker 1963; Levine and Reinarman 1991; Gusfield 1996; Thornton 1998; Reinarman 2012). These widely cherished values are deeply rooted in the religious tenets of early Protestant groups (Weber [1920] 2002) and help explain traditional widespread moral opposition to the use of opiates, cocaine, and many other mind-altering chemicals in US society (Becker 1963; Levine and Reinarman 1991; Gusfield 1996; Reinarman 2012).

This distinction of amphetamines from most other psychoactive drugs is important because claims makers are more likely to succeed if they portray social problems as violating deeply held values, or what Donileen Loseke (2003) calls "cultural themes," defined as taken-for-granted, collectively shared "beliefs about how the world should work" (63). Individualism, nationalism (i.e., patriotism), and capitalism are three cultural themes salient in the United States (Loseke 2003). Especially prominent during the 1930s, 1940s, and 1950s, constructions of amphetamines as workplace performance enhancers to be taken in pursuit of the

American Dream were *congruent* with these cultural themes, as evidenced by speed's popularity among students, truckers, laborers, housewives, athletes, and others seeking to maximize their occupational and work output. Thus, the inability of early claims makers to convince audiences that these cultural ideals were under siege from amphetamine use must partly explain why full-blown moral panic never developed.

Playing Cat and Mouse

Even if the historical context of the first twenty or so years of amphetamine use in the United States accounts for the relative lack of ensuing panic over the drug, the fact remains that claims makers succeeded in generating some public concern, especially with regard to inhaler abuse. Such concerns periodically elicited the federal government's attention. Whether informally exerting pressure on manufacturers or formally passing legislation to limit amphetamine availability, governmental efforts to deal with the early speed problem shared one common denominator: their focus on restricting supply.

Rasmussen (2008a) provides a detailed historical analysis of the early supply-side efforts to curb amphetamine misuse. What emerges from his examination of legislative hearings and pharmaceutical trade archives is a perpetually evolving cat-and-mouse game in which new restrictions on amphetamine supplies were met with innovative adaptations by those who demanded the drug. For instance, after the Elixir Sulfanilamide Incident[13] generated a new wave of skepticism over the pharmaceutical industry, SKF voluntarily labeled its Benzedrine tablets as prescription only in January 1940. As this change made Benzedrine in pill form more difficult to procure, users switched to amphetamine tablets marketed by other companies, which were still available OTC (C. Jackson 1979; Swann 1994; Marks 1995; Rasmussen 2008a). Additionally, the Benzedrine inhaler was still widely and legally available OTC at this time, as SKF elected not to restrict it as a prescription drug (Rasmussen 2008a). Thus, when state pressures and industry self-regulation made amphetamine pills more difficult to obtain, abuse of Benzedrine inhalers tended to increase (C. Jackson 1979).

In the face of alarmist news coverage and pressure from the FDA and Congress to cease its sales of Benzedrine inhalers, SKF removed them from the market in 1949 ("Notes on Science" 1949; C. Jackson 1979; Rasmussen 2008a).[14] SKF's voluntary withdrawal of the Benzedrine inhaler did not matter much for users and misusers since other pharmaceutical firms had been marketing their own amphetamine inhalers as early as 1944 (Rasmussen 2008a). By 1947, Vonedrine, Drinalfa, and Tuamine were three other brand-name, amphetamine-containing inhalers available OTC (Monroe and Drell 1947).

When public outcry over amphetamine-laced inhaler misuse persisted into the next decade, many manufacturers attempted to package their products with tamper-proof devices. As the FDA continued to receive reports of inhaler abuse, in 1953 S. (or St. Louis) Pfeiffer Company added denaturants to its Valo inhaler, and Wyeth to its Wyamine inhaler. People surmounted these antiabuse efforts by boiling down the inhaler wick into a fluid that could be administered intravenously (C. Jackson 1979), a practice that became increasingly common by the late 1950s (Rasmussen 2008a).

In response to users successfully tampering with tamper-proof inhalers, the FDA banned amphetamine inhalers in 1959, except as prescription items (Grinspoon and Bakalar 1979; Owen 2007). However, this ban was "almost totally ineffective" since it only covered inhalers containing Benzedrine and Dexedrine (Grinspoon and Bakalar 1979, 21). Companies seized upon this major loophole by producing inhalers laced with methamphetamine and mephentermine (Grinspoon and Hedblom 1975), which could be purchased OTC until 1965 (Rasmussen 2008a) and 1971 (Grinspoon and Bakalar 1979), respectively.

Well before the government mandated prescriptions for amphetamine inhalers, OTC sales of amphetamine tablets were prohibited with the 1951 Durham-Humphrey Amendment (Fort 1964). Overall, this law did little to slow amphetamine consumption. Estimates of the actual number of users during the 1950s are difficult to come by, since the first national surveys of stimulant use were not conducted until the 1970s. Analyzing market data, Rasmussen (2008a) estimates that "several million Americans" consumed amphetamines on a daily basis in 1951 (199). Several billion pills were produced annually by US manufacturers throughout the 1950s. By 1958, legal production of amphetamines in the United States numbered approximately 3.5 billion pills, enough to supply every resident with twenty standard doses (Cox and Smart 1970; Grinspoon and Hedblom 1975; Owen 2007). This figure does not include amphetamine-containing inhalers. Paul Gahlinger (2004) reports that of all the prescriptions written during that decade, 20 percent were for amphetamines.

Macro-Level Demand for Amphetamines in the 1950s

An obvious interpretation of the cat-and-mouse game and licit production figures outlined above is that a sizable proportion of the US populace sought synthetic stimulation during the mid-1900s. Beyond traditional theories of drug use that purport to explain the general demand for drugs (e.g., nature theory, strain theory), I offer three macro-level explanations for the relatively high need for speed specific to this time period.

From a structural perspective, the United States experienced the arrival of the "teenager class" in the 1950s (Joseph 2000). Child labor laws enacted in the first half of the twentieth century, the extension of schooling, and the decline of the family farm combined to foster a sense of "rolelessness" among children (Coontz 1999). The rapid social change accompanying the postwar United States extended the transition from child to adult, solidifying a new class of teenagers segregated into a separate peer culture (Coontz 1999; Joseph 2000). When kids lack socially meaningful duties and relationships with adults, and when they are given "fewer opportunities . . . for gradual initiation into productive activities" (Coontz 1999, 25), they may become alienated and defiant (Joseph 2000).

The creation of the teenager class ultimately spawned "a new generation of disaffected . . . youth" (Joseph 2000, 38). Though conformist to anti-Communist excitement of the 1950s, US teenagers sought "safe rebellion—weekend unconventionality, crossing on to the wild side every so often" (Joseph 2000, 38). While structurally prohibited from adulthood status, white adolescents identified much more with 1950s pop culture—specifically James Dean, Elvis Presley, and other idols venerated by the white working class—than they did with the black jazz musicians of the previous decade. "The sneer, the curling lip, the cynicism and the black leather jacket" of these icons, infused with speed, resonated with many alienated youth (Joseph 2000, 40).

A more cultural explanation for the high amphetamine demand during the 1950s is the birth of frenzied consumerism. Following the Allied victory in World War II, US society underwent a period of rapid social change (Joseph 2000). The "white flight" to the suburbs was under way, and more Americans were striving for their own homes, cars, and other "domestic conveniences" (Rasmussen 2008a, 180). Leisure, achievement, and enjoyment of consumption became as morally imperative as the Protestant work ethic. As these new social norms were increasingly promoted in a postwar United States, individuals who failed to adopt these values came to be seen as "depressed" and in need of a boost afforded by speed. Also, dieting became increasingly popular in the 1950s (Joseph 2000). Accordingly, amphetamines became a new "technology of the self" for healthy postwar consumers, as speed was pushed on overweight persons to remedy their purported lack of self-control

(Rasmussen 2008a, 181). The initial construction of speed as a pro-capitalist, workplace performance enhancer aligned well with the growing culture of consumerism that proliferated in the 1950s.

Related to the emergence of the consumer culture, another demand-side explanation for the high rate of midcentury amphetamine use was the intense marketing activities of licit speed manufacturers. Given the 1951 Durham-Humphrey Amendment's prescription provision, one might presume that drug companies anticipated a decrease in amphetamine-based revenues. To the contrary, profits soared. For example, SKF doubled its Dexedrine sales from about $5.5 million in 1952 to $11 million by 1954 (Rasmussen 2008a). Throughout the 1950s and 1960s, a host of manufacturers heavily marketed speed, especially to women, for both depression and obesity (Gahlinger 2004; Weil and Rosen 2004). Rasmussen (2006, 2008a) argues that World War II helped institutionalize the field of psychiatry as a legitimate profession, largely because its practitioners played a significant role in the screening and mental health treatment of members of the armed forces. After the war, Americans were more accepting of a psychiatric diagnosis (and psychiatric medication) than ever before. New socially constructed definitions of mental illness and beauty reflected an increasingly materialistic and consumer-oriented public. Thus, in some respects, the pharmaceutical industry helped manufacture some of the demand for amphetamines by marketing its products in ways that resonated with the evolving norms and ideals of the larger culture.

Beyond a vigorous marketing campaign that promised "patients" happiness and good looks, drug companies also maintained consumer demand through the promotion of seemingly novel drugs (Rasmussen 2008a). Repackaging old medicines into "new and improved" formulas is one of the least talked-about practices of the pharmaceutical industry. Since purely synthetic drugs do not exist in nature, by law they are considered inventions. As inventors of pharmaceutical, manufacturers receive patent protection on their products. When a drug's patent expires, other companies are allowed to offer generic versions. The introduction of market competition drives prices down and severely diminishes the original manufacturer's profits. In today's multibillion-dollar pharmaceutical industry, patent expirations are often seen as a death sentence by stockholders and potential investors, especially when a company's revenue stream is heavily dependent on a single patented drug.

One of several clever responses to a drug's pending patent expiration is to tweak a molecule in a protected chemical to "invent" a new chemical substance. In 2012, Cephalon's patent ran out on Provigil, a nonamphetamine stimulant FDA approved for treating excessive sleepiness in persons diagnosed with narcolepsy, "shift work disorder," and sleep apnea ("Mylan and Teva" 2012). Company executives planned ahead. From 2005 to 2010, Cephalon nearly tripled the wholesale price of Provigil from $5.50 to $13.60 per pill. By November 2010, Provigil was 50 percent more expensive than its more recently invented, chemically fraternal twin, Nuvigil. Raising the price of Provigil over this time period encouraged many users to switch to Nuvigil. Cephalon hoped that this maneuver would keep converted Nuvigil users from opting for generic formulations of Provigil when its patent expired in 2012. Conveniently, the company's patent on Nuvigil does not expire until 2024 (Pollack 2010; "Mylan and Teva" 2012).

Though arguably crooked, Cephalon's business tactics are not new. SKF used this strategy in the 1940s and 1950s, as its patents on Benzedrine and Dexedrine neared expiration. As generic competition from other firms loomed, SKF created a new type of capsule dubbed the "Spansule." Introduced in 1952, the Dexedrine Spansule contained the same old Dexedrine but in time-release form. A second SKF amphetamine innovation of the 1950s was a product called Dexamyl, which combined Dexedrine with Amytal, a sedative barbiturate that was popular at the time. Marketed as a "remarkable new preparation for relieving mental and emotional distress," Dexamyl burst onto the medical landscape and remained virtually unchallenged for five years (Rasmussen 2008a, 130).

Macro-Level Supply of Amphetamines During the 1950s

The macro-level explanations for the widespread demand for amphetamines during the 1950s—the emergence of an alienated teenager class, the increase in frenzied consumerism, and the ingenious marketing strategies of licit speed manufacturers—cannot be fully appreciated without a complementary examination of why amphetamines were so widely available at this time. On the supply side of the equation, the practices of physicians and pharmacists were one reason for the easy obtainability of speed. Doctors continued to eagerly recommend amphetamines for weight loss, depression, and other physical and psychological ailments after the enactment of the 1951 Durham-Humphrey Amendment. Members of the medical profession were fairly liberal in doling out prescriptions to patients at the time (Owen 2007), and most users could easily obtain amphetamine tablets from physicians until at least 1966 (Grinspoon and Hedblom 1975). According to Rasmussen

(2008a), professional ties with drug manufacturers partly explain why some doctors were reluctant to curb their support for amphetamines. But beyond professional interests, many physicians continued to tout synthetic stimulants because they seemed to genuinely help people, particularly those suffering from depression.

Faced with the newly legislated prescription status of amphetamine pills, individuals who did not seek a doctor's signature had other opportunities to acquire speed. While many types of amphetamine inhalers did not require a prescription until 1971, some stores and pharmacies continued to sell amphetamine tablets OTC, in blatant defiance of the Durham-Humphrey Amendment (Rawlin 1968; Rufus King 1972). In 1954, over half of all US pharmacists who were convicted of illegally selling prescription drugs dealt in amphetamine (Owen 2007). If speed seekers could not obtain amphetamines illicitly from pharmacists, some stole them from supply warehouses or ordered them from pharmaceutical companies under the guise of "scientific research" (Rawlin 1968, 60).

The birth of the black market for stimulants is a major supply-side factor that explains the abundance of amphetamines during the 1950s. As with previous prohibitions, such as those against alcohol and cocaine, anti-speed legislation that ignored the demand for stimulation inevitably resulted in the creation of an underground supply. Though it mandated that users obtain a prescription, the Durham-Humphrey Amendment did nothing to control licit amphetamine production or reduce amphetamine demand. With legal production rates in the billions of doses by the late 1950s, a sizable proportion was redirected into the black market for non-medical use (Iversen 2006). Testifying before Congress in 1962, Lewis Lasher of the FDA estimated that 50 to 67 percent of legally produced speed was annually diverted into illicit channels (Byles 1968). Although determining the accuracy of Lasher's estimate is impossible, a considerable amount of the amphetamines manufactured by drug companies clearly ended up on the black market. "Some was bought from manufacturers by bogus drug wholesalers for resale on the street, some disappeared during shipment, and some simply could not be accounted for" (Rasmussen 2008a, 171).

Black-market diversion of licitly produced amphetamines continued well into the 1960s. Media coverage of this issue increased, prompting more attention by powerful politicians and, consequently, more legislation. In the concluding section of this chapter, I examine media and political discourse over amphetamines from 1960 to 1965. By connecting amphetamine use to a larger social problem (i.e., crime), claims makers garnered support for more supply-side controls in the form of the Drug Abuse Control Amendments of 1965.

Speed Diversion and the State's Response, 1960–1965

It is important to point out the unique status of amphetamines as prescription drugs, when contrasted with purely illicit drugs such as heroin, lysergic acid diethylamide (LSD, i.e., acid), and phencyclidine (PCP, i.e., angel dust).[15] Amphetamine's prescription status made it rather difficult for the government to impose availability restrictions, due in large part to the powerful lobbying efforts of the pharmaceutical industry and professional organizations such as the AMA and National Association of Retail Druggists. While the patent medicine industry and other interest groups fought legal controls in the early 1900s, once the federal government enacted prohibitions on certain opiates, cocaine, and other drugs legally defined as narcotics, opponents eventually gave up the fight to relegitimize them. During the 1960s, many interest groups sought to maintain amphetamine's classification as a prescription drug, much as organizations of the late nineteenth and early twentieth centuries lobbied to keep cocaine and opiates legal. Since amphetamines are still available via prescription, it may be presumed that these interest groups succeeded. However, some of their power was wrested away by the government in a series of battles fought throughout the 1960s.

Although it became clear in the 1950s that a significant proportion of amphetamines were being diverted into the black market, concerns did not escalate significantly until the next decade, in part due to claims made by the most powerful members of the federal government. In spite of his personal use of amphetamines, President John F. Kennedy declared "thrill pills" a looming menace to society in 1962 (Jenkins 1999).[16] Kennedy and his successor, President Lyndon Johnson, along with many federal legislators, expressed serious interest in curtailing the diversion of amphetamines into illicit channels (Byles 1968). Senator Thomas Dodd of Connecticut was the most vocal federal legislator opposed to amphetamines during this time period (Jenkins 1999). Dodd headed several congressional inquiries into street crime and used thrill pills as a scapegoat for juvenile delinquency, a topic that had become an "obsession" in the 1950s (Rasmussen 2008a). In 1962, Dodd penned an article about a "growing teen-age menace" that appeared in *Family Weekly,* an insert in many newspapers circulated throughout the country.

Dodd (1962) warned of the "epidemic-like" consumption of "pep pills" by teenagers and wrote that some drug-seduced youngsters had been led "into ultimate drug addiction, murderous fights, and fatal automobile accidents" (59).

Intermittent during the 1950s, media coverage of the relationship between amphetamines and crime—especially juvenile crime—amplified in the 1960s. In the first half of that decade, the *New York Times* published stories decrying the misuse of amphetamines by athletes (Hyman 1960), announcing the increases in amphetamine-related crime ("Narcotics Addicts Hunted" 1962), exposing the nonprescription sale of amphetamine pills by pharmacists (Lelyveld 1964), and warning of the increased use of amphetamines by youngsters involved in criminal activities (Bigart 1964). A 1963 article quoted FDA commissioner George Larrick as saying, "The illegal sale and misuse of amphetamines and barbiturates have become serious social and police problems" ("Controls on Abuse" 1963, 46).

Notably, the subjects of crime and delinquency came to the forefront of national attention in the 1960s. Barry Goldwater's 1964 campaign for presidency raised street crime as a major political issue (Chambliss 1994). Although the 1960s experienced an actual rise in rates of street crime, especially among youth (Simon 2007), public opinion polls taken at that time suggest that the public was more concerned with war, unemployment, poverty, and civil rights than with crime. Goldwater lost the election to Lyndon Johnson, but the seeds had been planted for a moral panic (Chambliss 1994; Barlow 1998). Upon taking office, Johnson quickly launched a national "war on crime" that has been supported, in principle, by virtually every presidential candidate since (Simon 2007).[17]

From this larger perspective, news-consuming residents came to perceive street crime as a new and untamed social problem facing the United States. Though claims makers offered many reasons for the growing crime problem, drugs certainly became a major talking point in public discourse.[18] The increasingly publicized connection between drugs and crime is well illustrated in a 1965 article published in *Time* magazine. The article quotes President Johnson's calls for new laws to protect society from a rampant crime wave purportedly sweeping the nation: "Our streets must be safe. Our homes and businesses must be secure." One way in which Johnson proposed to reduce crime was to tighten controls over barbiturates and amphetamines and impose stricter penalties on those who engaged in illicit drug sales ("The Malignant Enemy" 1965).

All of these factors—increasing concerns of illicit amphetamine use expressed by governmental officials, heightened media coverage of the relationship between amphetamines and crime (especially among youth), an actual increase in crime rates, and a proliferation of fear among the US public about drugs and crime in general—formed the tinder for the Drug Abuse Control Amendments of 1965. When a bill proposed by Senator Dodd appeared to have been defeated by the actions of powerful governmental lobbyists, CBS's *McMullen Report* seems to have been the tipping point that ignited Congress to enact Public Law 89-74 (Rufus King 1972; Jenkins 1999; Rasmussen 2008a). News reporter Jay McMullen documented the ease with which one could obtain amphetamines and barbiturates without a prescription. He created the phony "McMullen Services" and procured speed from nine separate companies with little resistance. For only $600, McMullen purchased over 1 million amphetamine and barbiturate pills, valued up to $500,000 on the black market (Grinspoon and Hedblom 1975; Jenkins 1999; Rasmussen 2008a). "Public excitement seethed and members of Congress crowded forward once again to call for tighter controls and a tough new federal law" shortly after the CBS documentary aired (Rufus King 1972). Around this time, Dodd proclaimed that there were "more than 100,000 seriously addicted pill-heads in the United States" and up to "three million other Americans who take the drugs indiscriminately and without medical control" (as cited by Davidson 1965, 24).

The Drug Abuse Control Amendments of 1965 required manufacturers, distributors, physicians, and pharmacists to keep more accurate records of amphetamines and barbiturates that passed through their hands (Grinspoon and Hedblom 1975). It placed tighter restrictions on the types of people who could produce, deliver, and possess these drugs and gave the FDA increased authority by creating the police-like Bureau of Drug Abuse Control (Byles 1968; Jenkins 1999). According to Philip Jenkins (1999), the armed agents of the new bureau "made it look more like the FBI and FBN than the FDA" (38). This law marked a fundamental shift in US drug control policy by transferring enforcement powers from taxation to interstate commerce (Musto 1987).

To the chagrin of the pharmaceutical industry, AMA, and other interest groups who opposed the bill, the Drug Abuse Control Amendments appeared, on their face, to be a victory for the federal government. Shortly after the law passed, one narcotics agent from California wrote that the amendment would "without a doubt, help curb illicit manufacturing and distribution of" amphetamines (O'Connor 1968, 88). While Brecher (1972) says that the law made the diversion of legally produced amphetamines more difficult, others argue it was wholly ineffective. Lester Grinspoon and Peter Hedblom (1975) point out that the amendments set no production quotas and thus did nothing to reduce industry profits. Indeed, toward the end of the 1960s, 8 billion amphetamine tablets—more than double the amount produced in 1958—were being legally manufactured on an annual basis. In 1970, pharmaceutical companies produced over 10 billion amphetamine tablets (Grinspoon and Hedblom 1975).

The Drug Abuse Control Amendments were also rather lax about controlling prescription-filling practices, and the law's record-keeping protocols could not easily be enforced, leading to continued black-market diversion (Grinspoon and Hedblom 1975; Rasmussen 2008a). "Essentially, the Drug Abuse Control Amendments did nothing to control the major source of abused drugs, pharmaceutical firms" (Rasmussen 2008a, 212). In 1967, consumers spent an estimated $692 million on 178 million amphetamine prescriptions, representing about 16 percent of all prescriptions written that year. By 1969, about 6,100 separate amphetamine products made up the "amphetamine family" (Graham 1972).[19]

In instances in which the newly enacted legislation at least temporarily interrupted the flow of legally produced amphetamines to illicit domestic markets, speed seekers and peddlers responded in at least one of two ways. First, large amounts of amphetamines were shipped by US manufacturers to nonexistent Mexican drugstores, where smugglers picked them up and brought them back into the United States (Iversen 2006). Second, in some areas, clandestine amphetamine and methamphetamine laboratories sprouted up to meet demand (Brecher 1972; Jenkins 1999; Gahlinger 2004; Rasmussen 2008a). Through word of mouth and underground chemistry handbooks, people learned how to synthesize amphetamines for black-market distribution and their own personal use.

In short, the Drug Abuse Control Amendments of 1965, like many of the supply-focused measures before, failed to stop amphetamine use and black-market diversion. Federal control of amphetamines finally got serious in 1971, when the Bureau of Narcotics and Dangerous Drugs (BNDD, a predecessor of the DEA) enforced production quotas. In 1972, the year quotas took effect, legal production was restricted to 400 million standard doses (Rasmussen 2008a), only 3.3 percent of the estimated 12 billion tablets produced the year before. This remarkable decrease in the licit manufacturing of amphetamines put a major dent in illicit diversion. However, the black market for speed did not cease to exist. Rather, it evolved to accommodate the demand for psychomotor stimulation by more completely shifting to illicit production operations. In fact, much of the illicitly produced speed following the implementation of production quotas was in the form of methamphetamine.

Notes

1. Tyler Biggs, e-mail messages to the author, July 7, 2008, and July 8, 2008; Randall Contento, personal communication to the author, July 13, 2008.

2. Tyler Biggs, e-mail messages to the author, July 7, 2008, and July 8, 2008; Randall Contento, personal communication to the author, July 13, 2008.

3. Not all drugs can be synthesized. For example, no method has been found to produce morphine or cocaine synthetically. All the morphine and cocaine in the world are derived from their natural sources, the opium poppy and coca plant, respectively (Weil and Rosen 2004).

4. The date on which ephedrine was isolated from the ephedra plant is debated. Hartung and Munch (1929) claim that Nagai isolated ephedrine in 1885. However, Chen and Schmidt (1930) note that an impure form of ephedrine was isolated from ma huang in 1885 by G. Yamanashi. Chen and Schmidt report that, continuing Yamanashi's research, Nagai obtained ephedrine in its pure form two years later.

5. John P. Morgan's (1979) claim that "amphetamine has not been useful therapeutically for asthma" (7) is curious given the fact that asthma was one of the drug's first indications. Even today, the Vicks inhaler, available without a prescription, contains fifty milligrams of the L-isomer of methamphetamine. While the L-isomer has no psychoactive properties, it does mimic central nervous system stimulation (Iversen 2006).

6. Besides *hyperkinesis, minimal brain dysfunction* is another outdated term that was once used to describe a condition similar to what is known today as ADD/ADHD.

7. In one amusing tale, the medical superintendent of the Cook County, Illinois, hospital reported using amphetamine-covered crabs to catch fish. "I was tired of waiting for bites, so I dipped a crab in Benzedrine. When the crab hit the water on the end of the line, he dived down, grabbed a bass by the nose with his claws. From then on, fishing was good. I got fifty-six bass" ("Doctor-Angler" 1949, 15).

8. JFK also used Librium and Miltown for anxiety, methadone and Demerol for pain, and barbiturates to help him sleep (DeGrandpre 2006).

9. It was later discovered that German armed forces had actually been using Pervitin (a European brand name for methamphetamine), not Benzedrine ("Benzedrine Alerts" 1944; Rasmussen 2008a).

10. A full-text search of old articles from the *New York Times* using the word *amphetamine* returns several classified advertisements from the 1940s for military survival and first-aid kits. For example, one ad published December 2, 1945, lists 13,973 first-aid kits for sale, with "1 vial containing 5 amphetamine tablets" in each kit ("Offerings to Buyers" 1945, F6).

11. By the Korean War, amphetamines were standard issue to army soldiers (Iversen 2006). In Vietnam, amphetamine pills were distributed in great quantities to servicemen on long patrols (Jenkins 1999). Though temporarily banned by the air force in 1992, amphetamines were reintroduced during the Second Gulf War and used routinely in long flights by bomber crews (Iversen 2006).

12. Grinspoon and Bakalar (1979) note that after World War II, "military stockpiles of amphetamines flooded an exceedingly depressed and disillusioned but determined and growth-oriented [Japanese] civilian population" (23). While the surplus of leftover speed created many problems for Japanese society, some scholars (e.g., Klee 2001) have argued that amphetamines played a crucial role in helping Japan rebuild economically in the postwar era.

13. Bacterial infections are often treated with a drug called sulfanilamide. In the early part of the twentieth century, the S. E. Massengill Company sold tablet and powder versions of this product. Prompted by a rising demand for the drug in liquid form, the company's head chemist learned that sulfanilamide dissolved well in a substance called ethylene glycol. Soon after the experiment, in 1937, the Massengill Company packaged and shipped the liquid solution to doctors and pharmacists throughout the United States. Within two months, over 100 people had died from using the product. Massengill later learned that ethylene glycol, better known today as antifreeze, is extremely toxic when ingested by humans. Supporters of the 1938 Food, Drug, and Cosmetic Act that was passed as a direct consequence of the Elixir Sulfanilamide Incident argued that this tragedy could have been prevented if drug companies were required to test the safety of their products before making them available for public sale. The 1938 act codified this requirement into law. While Massengill's president denied responsibility for the deaths, the chemist who formulated the deadly liquid poison killed himself after learning of his error (Ballentine 1981).

14. While C. Jackson (1979) notes that one additional reason SKF removed the inhaler was that they were "a reputable old Quaker company" (38) whose executives were personally distressed about the misuse of their product, Rasmussen (2008a) points out that SKF conveniently revoked its product from store shelves when its "amphetamine patents . . . were about to expire" (104).

15. Surely, amphetamines were not the only drugs to occupy a prescription status during this time period, nor were they the only pharmaceuticals that government officials sought to moderate.

16. Politicians used the term *thrill pills* to refer to both amphetamines and barbiturates, seldom differentiating their largely opposing effects on the mind and body (Rasmussen 2008a).

17. The early phases of Johnson's war on crime attempted to address criminogenic social conditions. Starting in 1968 with Richard Nixon, many candidates for president have generally rejected sociological causes of crime in favor of individual-level factors such as bad character traits or immorality (Simon 2007). Thus, virtually all politicians support anticrime measures, but most favor "get-tough" policies that focus on individual punishment while ignoring social factors that influence criminal behavior (including drug use).

18. While it is difficult to determine if the increased coverage of the link between street crimes and drugs, as purported by the media during the 1960s, was a result of a concentrated campaign to garner support for punitive legislation, it is

also possible that the apparent increase in the "drugs-cause-crime" theme repeated by the media was due to a real increase in drug-related crimes. Notably, the restrictions enacted during the 1950s and 1960s slowly made pharmaceutical drugs more difficult to obtain legally, which likely contributed to more street crimes as the black market took over more and more of the distribution.

19. This number does not refer to individual amphetamine-like chemicals, but rather the total number of preparations and brand names produced by different drug companies.

4

The First Scare:
Speed Freaks

> The first time I rushed I thought it was nirvana. I was tired and suddenly
> my head was light. All the heaviness and dust in my brains were cleared
> out. Everything was empty. Anything that was to happen was fine,
> because it was so easy to do anything. —*self-report of a Methedrine
> injector, as quoted by James Carey and Jerry Mandel (1968, 167)*

As mentioned briefly in Chapter 3, over the first fifteen years of its availability in US pharmacies and stores, methamphetamine was perceived as
merely one of the many types of amphetamines used by asthmatics, the
obese, and persons in need of a pick-me-up. This construction of methamphetamine is quite dissimilar from contemporary discourse, which most
definitely dichotomizes "meth" from "amphetamine," where the latter
usually refers to a host of amphetamines often framed in a medical context, such as Adderall, Dexedrine, and Benzedrine (J. P. Morgan 1979;
DIB 2006; Iversen 2006; Armstrong 2007). An article from *Scientific
American* provides a subtle yet sober example of the contemporary distinction of methamphetamine from other varieties of speed. In discussing
methamphetamine problems in Thailand, journalist Gary Stix (2011)
writes, "efforts to stem meth use have gone as far as banning all amphetamines, a class of drug that is used medically for the treatment of ADHD
and other conditions."

Research by some scholars suggests that meth's original portrayal as
just another amphetamine may in fact be more accurate than modern
depictions. According to Nicolas Rasmussen (2008a), "the subjective
effects [of amphetamine and methamphetamine] are virtually indistin-
guishable" to users (19). Clinical studies investigating addiction liability
have found that when methamphetamine is compared with other

amphetamines, animals and humans prefer similar amounts and cannot distinguish between equal doses of each (see Shoblock et al. [2003, 359–360] for a short review). Commenting on the methamphetamine media frenzy during the early 2000s, Edward Armstrong (2007) argues, "The vision that meth is something new, different from other drugs, is fundamentally flawed" (429).

In this chapter, I identify the roots of methamphetamine's cultural split from the other amphetamines in the United States' first meth scare, which began in the early to mid-1960s and lasted until about 1971. During this time period, methamphetamine was usually referred to as Methedrine, the most popular brand name of the "medicine" available in the United States since the mid-1940s. Though all amphetamines came under the scrutiny of the mass media, polity, and general public during the 1960s, by the end of the decade Methedrine emerged as the particularly evil form of speed. To trace the development and proliferation of the Methedrine panic, I examine media depictions of users and meth-related crime. I argue that claims makers ultimately succeeded in generating a sustained campaign against Methedrine by attacking the medical and pharmaceutical fields, and by portraying the drug as a threat to the middle and upper classes. The symbolic and legal recasting of methamphetamine from medicine to drug was finalized with the passage of the Controlled Substances Act (CSA) of 1970.

Intravenous Use by Korean War Veterans

Perhaps the first public event that began methamphetamine's cultural divergence from other amphetamines was its intravenous use by US soldiers during the Korean War. While stationed in Korea, some American servicemen substituted army-issued amphetamine for cocaine when they injected "splash," the street name given to a combination of amphetamines and heroin (Brecher 1972; Grinspoon and Hedblom 1975). The effects of splash are similar to the "speedball" effects achieved from mainlining cocaine and heroin, a practice dating back as far as 1918 (Inciardi 2002). Soldiers who experimented with splash found that amphetamine was superior to cocaine, as the former produced longer-lasting effects and was often available at no cost from army medics (Grinspoon and Hedblom 1975). Upon their return to the United States in the 1950s, many of the addicted veterans visited doctors for amphetamine and heroin dependence. Injectable methamphetamine became one popular method of treating ex-servicemen and other addicts, especially in the San Francisco Bay Area (Brecher 1972; Grinspoon and Hedbloom 1975; Asnis and Smith 1979; Iversen 2006). Besides doctors, several pharmacies in San Francisco sold injectable amphetamines either "without a prescription or on the basis of crudely forged prescriptions" (Brecher 1972, 282).

San Francisco Bay Area pharmacies sold only a few hundred Methedrine ampoules in 1959. In less than three years, sales increased drastically from 280,000 ampoules in 1960, to 580,000 in 1961, and to 550,000 over the first seven months of 1962 (Rawlin 1968). Soon thereafter, the "Bay area became home to a large and growing number of intravenous methamphetamine users" (Iversen 2006, 96). In the Haight-Ashbury section of San Francisco, methamphetamine seemed to replace LSD in popularity (Iversen 2006). While the injectable speed market in California seemed to prefer methamphetamine, midwestern users tended to favor amphetamine (Rasmussen 2008a). By 1965, intravenous use of amphetamine and methamphetamine was occurring in many urban areas throughout the country (DeGrandpre 2006), a practice that did not go unnoticed by the popular press.

Mass Media and Methedrine

In the early 1960s, California newspapers began devoting attention to what appeared to be an emergence of intravenous methamphetamine use among the local population. An article in the *Oakland Tribune* dubbed Methedrine "the first drug prepared in [a liquid] solution to appear on the list of off-limits favorites" ("Juvenile Thrill Seekers" 1962, 12). The same article provided separate anecdotes on the alarming experiences of two users. One mainliner was quoted as follows: "Recently I took 40 ampoules in 48 hours and stayed awake for eight days. I had hallucinations. I was afraid and climbed a four-story fire escape to a rooftop. I jumped from one roof to another but didn't feel safe until I got into a phone booth. Later I slept for 40 straight hours" ("Juvenile Thrill Seekers" 1962, 12). The article concluded with an informal plea from a local narcotics officer for more resources to combat the "growing and illegal drug traffic" ("Juvenile Thrill Seekers" 1962, 12). Other San Francisco Bay Area newspapers printed stories describing arrests for illegal possession of liquid methamphetamine ("'Hypo' Party" 1962; "Police Arrest" 1962; "Typist Jailed" 1962). At least two separate regional newspapers published a request from California attorney general Stanley Mosk to modify the legal definition of "addict" in order to incorporate Methedrine users. Mosk's proposal was an effort to exert more punitive sanctions upon users ("Mosk Urges Addicts" 1962; "Mosk Urges Changes" 1962).

The medical community also faced criticism and scrutiny by California print media during the early 1960s. Though inexplicably describing the effects of Methedrine as "heroin-like," the *San Mateo Times* conveyed results from a police investigation that uncovered illegal sales of the drug by four area pharmacies ("Drug Ring" 1962). Another news source reported on a San Francisco nurse arrested for giving patients Methedrine ("Prescribing S.F. Nurse" 1962). The arrest of an osteopathic doctor for overprescribing methamphetamine was particularly sensationalized in area newspapers. Sixty-three-year-old Dr. Kenneth Blaylock was described by Attorney General Mosk as "a major source of illicit drugs in California" ("Agents Crack Drug Source" 1963, 1). Undercover police officers purchased "over 5,000 vials of Methedrine" from Blaylock and claimed that methamphetamine users throughout California would visit him for prescriptions ("S.S.F. Woman Cracks Ring" 1963, 15).

As local elected officials, law enforcement, and journalists converged to decry the seemingly ample supply of injectable methamphetamine available through quasi-illicit means, pressure mounted on legitimate suppliers to curtail transactions. Abbott Laboratories agreed to pull Desoxyn ampoules from store shelves in late 1962 (M. Miller 1997). The following year other liquid meth providers, including Burroughs Wellcome (manufacturer of Methedrine), followed suit, after a request by the California State Board of Pharmacy and the Attorney General's Office to discontinue sales to retail pharmacies in the state (Grinspoon and Hedblom 1975). At least in the state of California, from 1963 forward, legal distribution of injectable methamphetamine would be limited to hospitals only (Rawlin 1968).

For several reasons, intravenous injection of methamphetamine continued in California and elsewhere after pharmaceutical companies restricted sales. First of all, companies continued providing methamphetamine ampoules to pharmacies in other states until about 1968 (Karch 2001, 2002). Second, when liquid methamphetamine was scarce, people dissolved tablets for injection (Grinspoon and Hedblom 1975). Most significantly, as all forms of legally produced amphetamines came under tighter controls during the 1960s, another way in which demand was met through the illicit manufacture of methamphetamine in clandestine laboratories. The first "meth labs" in the United States sprung up in

California in 1962 (Smith 1969a; Brecher 1972; Anglin et al. 2000; DeGrandpre 2006). Philip Jenkins (1999) traces their origin to "a group of ex-servicemen . . . [who] led the move to create an illicit manufacturing industry . . . in the San Francisco Bay area around 1962" (39).

One of the earliest newspaper accounts of illicit methamphetamine manufacturing was published on the front page of the *Oakland Tribune* on January 13, 1963. Four men, including a university-trained bio-chemist, were arrested by a team of narcotics agents for operating "a crude [methamphetamine] home laboratory" out of a San Francisco apartment. The arrest was announced by law enforcement as "the first . . . ever . . . in the Bay Area for actually producing black market narcotics and drugs" ("4 Seized" 1963, 1).

This discovery was the first of tens of thousands that followed. The genesis of clandestine methamphetamine labs was a direct consequence of controls on legally available supplies, as evidenced by the timing of California restrictions and the first lab seizures. The intermittent disruption of the diversion of legally manufactured speed to the black market resulting, first, from manufacturers' decisions to stop selling to California pharmacies and, then, from restrictions imposed by the Drug Abuse Control Amendments of 1965 brought about an increase in clandestine laboratories, especially on the West Coast (Brecher 1972; Gahlinger 2004). According to Lester Grinspoon and Peter Hedblom (1975), five to ten meth labs were in operation in the Bay Area alone by 1968. Each was estimated to produce between 25 and 100 pounds of powder or liquid speed on a weekly basis. "An unknown number of smaller 'bathroom' or 'kitchen labs', most in Haight-Ashbury, contributed an equal amount" (25).

The Speed Freak Icon

As suggested by Figure 4.1, by the late 1960s, the public had become more aware of methamphetamine abuse with the aid of increased media coverage of the speed scene (Jenkins 1999). Also around this time period, the term *speed freak* entered the popular vernacular as a way to describe someone who mainlines methamphetamine (Iversen 2006). An article in *Time* magazine warned that "plastic flower people" of the Haight-Ashbury district had turned into "speed freaks . . . who shoot drugs with hypodermics . . . [and] are passing hepatitis around on dirty needles" ("Where Have All" 1967). The meaning of the term was soon expanded to incorporate persons who used moderate to heavy amounts of any amphetamine through any route of administration. Helen Bottel authored the nationally syndicated column "Helen Help Us!" which regularly appeared in newspapers throughout the country. In a piece published in October 1967, a writer asked Bottel, "What is a 'speed freak'?" Bottel's answer is telling:

> A Speed Freak is one who has taken so many pep pills (Speed, "A," uppies, bennies, methedrine, amphetamines) that he is "freaked out." He is irritable, confused, tense, highly nervous, often aggressive and sometimes a real psycho. He suffers from nausea, loss of weight and, if he continues his overdoses, the pills may kill him. . . . While marijuana gets the headlines these days, it's my belief that MISUSE of pep (or diet) and tranquilizer (or barbiturate) pills is our big drug problem. In my files are letters from teenagers—housewives too—so hung up on pills they are almost incoherent, yet they can't stop. They don't even dare confide in a doctor, for often they get their doses illegally. If they become dangerously ill, they may be treated for other ailments—and some of them will die. (Bottel 1967, 15)

Figure 4.1 Coverage of Methamphetamine in *Time* Magazine, *New York Times*, and *Oakland Tribune*, 1961–1977

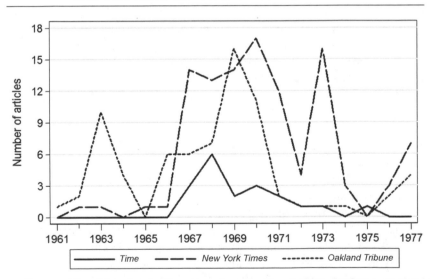

Sources: *Time* Magazine Archive, www.time.com/time/archive; ProQuest, www.pro quest.com; NewspaperARCHIVE, www.newspaperarchive.com.

Another *Time* article warned that the number of "'speed freaks,' 'meth freaks,' 'meth monsters,' or 'meth heads'" in Greenwich Village, New York, had, "according to the hippies, increased enormously within recent months" ("Unsafe at Any Speed" 1967). In 1968, a story of a man who planted dynamite sticks in mailboxes throughout San Francisco was published in at least four California newspapers. According to one article, an eyewitness described the suspect "as a 'speed freak' who appeared to be high on methedrine" ("S.F. Police Hunt" 1968, 17). One newspaper in Wisconsin quoted a former meth user as saying, "The speed freak—that's a good word, freak . . . he looks like something out of a concentration camp. One speed freak I've worked with, a girl, makes Twiggy look like Santa Claus" (W. Gould 1969, 43).[1] In another story, a Maryland state trooper taught members of a local community that "a 'speed freak' can be identified by their physical appearance; thin and exhausted, irritable, with dark bands under their eyes" (O'Brien 1969, B14).

As early as the mid-1960s, media coverage of the methamphetamine subculture was declaring that speed freaks were scorned by the drug-loving hippies of Haight-Ashbury and elsewhere (Jenkins 1999). Allen Ginsberg, the beloved poet who had enjoyed Benzedrine with Jack Kerouac and other members of the beatnik community during the 1940s and 1950s, was particularly outspoken in his hatred of speed. In 1965, Kerouac complained to a reporter from the alternative *Los Angeles Free Press* that speed freaks, which he described as "horror monster Frankenstein[s]," were ruining the local street scene (as cited by Rasmussen 2008a, 183). Other newspapers marveled over the fact that members of a subculture so emphatic about the use of marijuana and LSD despised methamphetamine. For example, one headline in the *Albuquerque Tribune* read, "Even Hippies Worried About Methadrine [sic] Use" (Kifner 1967a, A4). The *Bridgeport Sunday Post* (Connecticut) proclaimed "'Speed' Drugs Bring Hate, Horror to Hippies' Haight-Ashbury Mecca" (Strand 1968, C19), and the *Kingsport Times* (Tennessee) stated, "Haight-Ashbury Now a City of Fear" (1968), largely because of "violence-producing methamphetamine" (5C).

As the above media excerpts suggest, the speed freak epitomized the dope fiend mythology and served as the primary folk devil of the Methedrine scare. Media coverage at that time, and during subsequent meth scares, has portrayed the typical user as dirty, immoral, sick, violent, weak minded, and erratic. As in other drug scares—where marijuana smokers are delegitimized as "stoners," heroin injectors as "junkies," and cocaine smokers as "crack heads"—the speed freak image serves to represent all that is evil and reprehensible with methamphetamine. These labels function to dehumanize drug users, absolving nonusers of any desire for empathic understanding. Such labels also help to simplify drug problems by tracing their causes to chemicals ingested by individuals.

Methedrine-Related Crime and Violence

The depiction of the speed freak as ruthlessly violent and criminal illustrates what Alfred Lindesmith (1940a) and Charles Reasons (1976) identify as a central theme of the dope fiend mythology: the distorted relationship between drugs and violence. One of the biggest falsehoods in popular depictions of drugs is that their use frequently leads to violent behavior. This myth is rarely questioned by news organizations, politicians, and media consumers. For example, Sam Staley (1992) notes that in some cities, "drug-related murders" account for 50 to 80 percent of all homicides. When newspapers or televised news programs present statistics of this nature, little to no attempt is made to explain their meaning. As a result, news consumers are often left with the impression that 50 to 80 percent of murders are directly a result of chemically induced maniacs.

The more general phrase "drug-related crime" is referred to by criminologists as "offenses committed while the perpetrator is using drugs or criminal acts related to the use, purchase or sale of drugs" (Staley 1992, 107). While many drugs, including alcohol, can trigger violent and aggressive behavior in users, media portrayals of the drugs-violence relationship tend to be misleading. For example, motivated by the barrage of reports by New York media purporting that heightened levels of violence in New York City were a result of increased crack cocaine use, Henry Brownstein (2000) analyzed the circumstances surrounding every murder that occurred in the city during 1986 and determined that the psychopharmacological effects of crack use explained five of the 414 homicides that year. "Before anyone really knew much about the drug or what it was actually doing to people and their communities, crack became the demon drug, and programs and policies were made to respond to it" (Brownstein 2000, 30).

The majority of the drug-violence relationship can be explained by the illicit nature of the prohibition-produced black market, rather than pharmacological effects of drugs themselves (Staley 1992; Thornton 1998; Brownstein 2000). The "economic compulsive violence" model proposed by Paul Goldstein (1985) acknowledges violence resulting from drug users engaged in financially motivated violent crimes (e.g., robbery) to acquire money for drugs. The drugs-violence relationship explained by the "systemic model" encourages an examination of the "traditionally aggressive patterns of interaction within the system of drug distribution and use" (Goldstein 1985, 497). Unlike legitimate businesses, black markets do not have the comfort of legal recourse and enforcement. Thus, for example, if an illicit drug theft takes place, if a user is in debt to a dealer, or if rival dealers are in competition for the same customers, violence is often used as a means to administer sanctions, uphold informal contracts, secure business, or assert market territory (Goldstein 1985; Nadelmann 1989; Reinarman et al. 1997; Thornton 1998; Brownstein 2000).

Donileen Loseke (2003) argues that overlooking the complexity inherent in the social world through the construction of very one-dimensional diagnostic frames is a particularly effective claims-making strategy. As with coverage of many social problems, most media reports of the relationship between drugs and violence tend to simplify the connection, presenting it in terms of pharmacological determinism (Reinarman and Levine 1997a). In news coverage of the first (and subsequent) methamphetamine scare(s), psychopharmacological explanations of violent behavior committed by users fit with the moral ideologies (e.g., the dope fiend mythology, individualism) of the larger society. Such simplistic constructions of the methamphetamine problem are convenient for journalists and audiences alike. Unambiguous causes (individual/chemical), effects (violence), and solutions (punishment) are easily identified, all while providing sensationalistic "news" and entertainment (see Altheide 1997).

Typifying the Methedrine Problem

One way in which claims makers encourage audiences to ignore the complexity inherent in social life is through the presentation of powerful anecdotes that serve to typify (i.e., characterize) a social problem in a certain way (Best 1990; Loseke 2003). "Atrocity tales" (i.e., extreme and appalling instances of a social problem) are one commonly invoked typification (Best 1990).

Of the three publications shown in Figure 4.1, prior to 1967, attention toward methamphetamine was highest in the *Oakland Tribune*. From 1961 to 1966, the *New York Times* printed only four meth-related articles; *Time* magazine published zero. The striking increase in media coverage by these two major US news sources in 1967 appears to be directly related to the widely publicized rape and murder of eighteen-year-old Linda Fitzpatrick, a "blonde and dreamy-eyed dropout from Maryland's exclusive Oldfields School" and daughter of wealthy Greenwich, Connecticut, parents. Fitzpatrick and James "Groovy" Hutchinson, a "tattooed drifter" and known speed user ("Speed Kills" 1967), were discovered "naked in a grimy tenement basement in Manhattan, their heads beaten by a brick" (Kifner 1967b, 197). A *Time* magazine article suggested the couple may have gone into the cellar to purchase or use drugs or to engage in sex. It also blamed Fitzpatrick's demise on Methedrine: "Since methedrine is a super-pep drug whose 'flash' generates an instant demand for action, it is likely that the onlookers demanded to 'make it' with Linda. Groovy tried to defend the girl and was smashed with one of the boiler-wall bricks, his face crushed. Linda was raped four times and bashed with a brick. Their nude bodies, faces upturned, were found on the dank stone floor" ("Speed Kills" 1967).

News of Fitzpatrick's murder first appeared on the front page of the *New York Times* on October 9, 1967 (Perlmutter 1967). A *Times* article published shortly thereafter discussed the sharp sense of paranoia in New York's East Village, among middle-class hippie émigrés toward "narks" (i.e., narcotics detectives), meth mainliners, and members of local racial and ethnic groups. John Kifner (1967b) suggested that the recent "epidemic of 'burning'—the sale of inferior, highly cut, or false drugs—in the area" (197), including the increasingly popular Methedrine, contributed greatly to intensified fears and anxieties among New York City's hippie community. Fitzpatrick fled to the East Village to join the counterculture ("Speed Kills" 1967), but one of her friends said she ended up becoming "hooked on" Methedrine (Kifner 1967c, 1).

A total of nineteen articles that at least made mention of Linda Fitzpatrick appeared in the *New York Times* during the month of her murder. The last article printed that month, published almost three weeks after her death, suggests the incident (and media coverage of it) stirred up fears among many of the newspaper's subscribers. "An article about Linda Fitzpatrick . . . has brought *The New York Times* many letters and telephone calls from parents concerned about their children and other children in their communities" ("Story of Girl" 1967, 57). Twelve articles containing the word *Methedrine* or *methamphetamine* were published from October to December, including one that appeared on the front page eight days after Fitzpatrick's slaying with the headline, "Methedrine Use Is Growing" (Kifner 1967c, 1). A total of six articles containing the word *methamphetamine* or *Methedrine* appeared in the *New York Times* (any year) prior to Fitzpatrick's death.

The methamphetamine-related murder of Linda Fitzpatrick is a model typifying example that served to frame subsequent media and public discourse about the Methedrine problem in the United States. News coverage of her death struck an emotional chord with the public. By centering on the experiences of specific individuals, atrocity tales allow media consumers to identify with those who are affected by the problem (Best 1990), especially if audiences share certain characteristics (e.g., race, social status, age) with victims (Best 1990; Loseke 2003). The tendency for claims makers to select horror stories to serve as typifying examples of a social problem is referred to by Craig Reinarman and Harry Levine (1997b) as the "routinization of caricature" (24), a core feature of discourse in US drug scares. In the routinization of caricature, "worst cases [are] framed as typical cases . . . [and] the episodic [is] rhetorically recrafted into the epidemic" (24).

Sensationalism and fear sell newspapers. When media consumers draw upon atrocity tales as a referent to understand the methamphetamine problem as a whole, their assessments and reactions are likely to be based on extreme, outlying incidents that do not accurately characterize overall patterns of use and behavior. To be clear, I am not suggesting that the pharmacological effects of methamphetamine have never led users to engage in violence. I am merely emphasizing that the selection of extreme instances of violent and sadistic behavior in framing meth problems distorts reality and ignores the complexity of context.

Conflicting Images of the Methedrine Problem

One of the interesting elements of drug scares is the way in which socially constructed images of drug use and drug users are related to the conventional society. By virtue of their location in middle to upper socioeconomic strata, those non-drug-using members of society who regularly consume mass media and reside in communities that are relatively free from illicit drugs and violent crime have more power and resources to influence public policy. Like any claims-making campaign that attempts to bring some social phenomenon to the forefront of public discourse, in order for claims makers involved in the methamphetamine scare to enlist the support needed for social change, their constructions of meth problems must resonate with members of society who have social power (see Best 1990, 2008; Loseke 2003).

Socially constructed images of drug users may often appear to be paradoxical. On the one hand, drug scares establish an "us versus them" dichotomy between drug users and nonusers. On the other hand, drug scares often frame drug problems as being present among "regular" members of the middle and upper classes. For instance, Methedrine addicts were often depicted by media as members of the lower or working classes. Much like their poor socioeconomic situation, speed freaks were portrayed—implicitly or explicitly—as having acquired their addiction to methamphetamine through an act of free will. At the same time, stories such as the Linda Fitzpatrick murder conveyed the image that methamphetamine was being used by individuals from middle- or upper-class backgrounds. In these portrayals, the message was that dangerous drugs pose a threat to all members of society, regardless of one's social milieu. Superficially, the distinction between the framing of drug scares as "us versus them" and "drugs are being used by everybody, everywhere" appears contradictory. However, these two aspects of the social construction of drug scares actually complement one another.

As a typifying example, Fitzpatrick's slaying was used to orient the larger scope of the Methedrine problem as a threat to all of society, even the "innocent." Other fairly common typifications of the methamphetamine problem during the 1960s described horror stories of its use in prisons or among members of outlaw biker gangs; these characterizations portray methamphetamine use among socially marginalized groups in specific locations. Thus when prisoners and biker gangs were used as common referents, the news-consuming public may not have felt as threatened by Methedrine. Joel Best (1990) notes that typifications may change, sometimes in response to changes in the larger society, other times as a direct result of claims-making efforts.

To borrow a term from David Garland (1996), earlier portrayals of methamphetamine users more often invoked "a criminology of the *alien other* which represents criminals as dangerous members of distinct . . . social groups which bear little resemblance to 'us'" (461; emphasis added). Conversely, news stories that portrayed methamphetamine use as spreading to the more privileged classes, as was typical in the media coverage of the Linda Fitzpatrick tragedy, conveyed the message that drugs can and will ruin the lives of "normal" people. Indeed, in contrast to the typical speed freak, Fitzpatrick was portrayed as a *victim* of meth. Claims makers are more likely to succeed if they typify social problems using victims who are similar to news consumers in terms of race, class, and other meaningful social statuses (Loseke 2003).

Found throughout media coverage of methamphetamine specifically, and other drugs more generally, the contradiction of drug use among alien others and drug use among mainstream society captures audiences because it conveys the threat that the distinction between nonusers and users, between "us" and "them," is eroding. This message resonates with members of the powerful classes who have a stake in maintaining class boundaries. When they hear that Methedrine users are violent, evil beings, and when they also hear that the drug is making its way into the upper strata of society, news consumers will be mobilized to support social policies that, on the surface, appear to prevent the impending epidemic forewarned by claims makers. The ability of claims makers to change typifications is "important because different images emphasize different features of a problem and suggest different solutions" (Best 1990, 4). When images of meth change from use by "them" to use by "them" *and* "us" (or to use by "them" negatively affecting "us"), audiences are more likely to be motivated to back claims makers who promise to do something about the purported problem.

Research by Paul Manning (2006) helps to further illuminate the various "symbolic frameworks"—or, to use a phrase from Loseke (2003), "organizing devices" (16)—through which the news constructs methamphetamine problems. Manning (2006) compares and contrasts British media coverage of volatile substance abuse (e.g., inhalation of chemical solvents) and ecstasy use in England, Scotland, and Wales. Despite the fact that volatile substance abuse was responsible for more than four times as many deaths from 1995 to 1999 as ecstasy, the latter received much more attention in national newspapers. Manning (2006) attributes the discrepancy to "both the *kinds of people* and the *kinds of substance* in question" (51; emphasis in original). Drug use data show that volatile substance abuse is associated with young boys of lower socioeconomic groups, particularly "those who are least visible, most marginalized and most distant from metropolitan political and media elites" (Manning 2006, 55). In contrast, the use of ecstasy is more noticeable and more balanced among both genders and different social classes.

Manning argues that both substances are constructed through separate symbolic frameworks. Almost all of the news coverage of volatile substance abuse utilized a "social pathology framework," where solvent inhalation was portrayed as a disease afflicting members of socially disadvantaged groups. Volatile substances themselves represented grime and filth. By contrast, much of the newspaper coverage of ecstasy fell under the "threat to the innocent" framework. Ecstasy was portrayed as penetrating "the 'safety' of the home with terrible and disruptive consequences for even the most stable, respectable families" (Manning 2006, 60). In other words, ecstasy users, who tended to come from middle- to upper-class strata, were generally depicted as innocent victims of an evil drug pushed upon them from the "outside."

While Manning's research describes social constructions of two separate drugs, his findings help illustrate varying typifications of methamphetamine over time. Americans have illegally (and legally) used methamphetamine for decades, yet media attention has fluctuated substantially. As Methedrine began to be singled out from the other amphetamines around 1960 as the worst form of speed, press coverage over the next six years largely utilized the "social pathology" framework proffered by Manning (2006). Users were shown to be "alien others," segregated by social class and geographic location. Feverish media coverage of Methedrine reached its height shortly after Linda Fitzpatrick was killed. The Fitzpatrick narrative signifies the transition of methamphetamine from a discourse of social pathology to the framework of threatened innocents.

Speed Kills, but How Often?

The impact of Linda Fitzpatrick's tragic murder on the social problems campaign to draw attention to the dangers of Methedrine cannot be overstated. That the phrase "speed kills" first appeared in major US news sources immediately following her death is noteworthy. For example, an article printed in *Time* less than three weeks after Fitzpatrick's passing read, "Speed kills. It really does. Amphetamine, methedrine, etc. can, and will, rot your teeth, freeze your mind and kill your body. The life expectancy of the average speed freak, from the first shot to the morgue, is less than five years. What a drag" ("Unsafe at Any Speed" 1967). Other widely circulated US newsmagazines, including *Newsweek, Reader's Digest, Life,* and *Look,* helped institutionalize the slogan, as the late 1960s witnessed a nationwide "speed kills" crusade that thoroughly demonized the drug (Jenkins 1999). Even elements of the "hip" crowd got involved. In Southern California, an organization called Do It Now formed to convey through music that "speed kills." Grace Slick from Jefferson Airplane and Frank Zappa recorded public service announcements to dissuade radio listeners from using Methedrine and other amphetamines (Rasmussen 2008a).

Public campaigns designed to deter people from using drugs often fail to achieve this goal. The reasons drug-using members of the public do not heed the warnings publicized by politicians and mass media are too numerous to discuss here. However, two explanations that particularly relate to the "speed kills" movement merit mention.

First, highly publicized antidrug campaigns often have the unintended effect of attracting new users. According to Edward Brecher (1972), the considerable amount of media attention dedicated to Methedrine use in the early 1960s may have actually spawned new users by creating general interest in a drug that was "previously known primarily to heroin addicts" (282). Efforts to educate the public about the dangers associated with a drug often include mention of positive user experiences. For example, *Time* magazine reported that the intravenous use of Methedrine led to a "sudden generalized, overwhelming, pleasureful [sic] feeling" and quoted a female user as saying, "It fills you inside, like this churning cloud of light with sparks shooting off, jagged, in all the colors of the rainbow, the universe in the process of creation. And you're a part of it." The article continued, "The overall effect is sexual—in the words of one user, like 'an orgasm all over your body.' It is an aphrodisiac, tending also to prolong the time of sexual activity before climax is achieved" ("Unsafe at Any Speed" 1967).

In a chapter facetiously titled "How to Launch a Nationwide Drug Menace," Brecher (1972) describes how an outburst of press attention toward glue sniffing, a fad isolated among small groups of children in a handful of western US cities, evolved into a self-fulfilling prophecy at the national level. Initial media reports, published in the *Denver Post* in 1959, warned of a glue-sniffing epidemic. Shortly thereafter, kids in other parts of the United States heard about the "feelings of elation" experienced from solvent inhalation. Soon enough, reports of glue sniffing by children in other areas of the country surfaced. In essence, a national campaign warning about the prevalence of glue sniffing "served to popularize rather than to discourage the practice" (Brecher 1972, 332). Scores of stories printed nationally and locally described many of the positive sensations achieved from mainlining Methedrine. Learning of a previously unheard-of drug, media consumers simultaneously discovered that "speed kills" and has orgasmic effects.

A second possible reason for the failure of the "speed kills" movement concedes that the kinds of "facts" conveyed through antidrug campaigns are often exaggerations or outright falsehoods. For example, claims that marijuana is physically addicting, violence producing, or a "gateway" drug are unsubstantiated by virtually everyone who has smoked it. In a similar vein, the claim "speed kills" is not wholly accurate. Medical doses of amphetamines, including methamphetamine, generally range from five to thirty milligrams per day. Heavy users of methamphetamine are known to administer in excess of 1,000 milligrams per binge. In fact, one study reports an individual who injected as much as 15,000 milligrams over a span of twenty-four hours—and lived (Kramer, Fischman, and Littlefield 1967).

"Strictly speaking, speed kills only rarely" (Joseph 2000, 44). According to Harold Kalant and Oriana Kalant (1979), as of 1978, "the world literature include[d] 79 reported cases of death associated in some way with amphetamines" (171), including methamphetamine, over a thirty-five-year period. Roughly twenty-five of these deaths were the result of hyperthermia, cardiac arrest, or cerebrovascular hemorrhage. Furthermore, Kalant and Kalant (1979) do not express absolute certainty that speed was a direct cause of death in some of the seventy-nine cases they examined. For example, several of the persons who died amphetamine-related deaths had also consumed alcohol or other drugs.

Contrary to the popular 1960s and 1970s assertion that "speed kills," the data on amphetamine-related deaths up to 1978 suggest dying from a methamphetamine overdose is difficult. This statement is not meant to imply that speed is not harmful or dangerous to users. Although methamphetamine rarely leads to instantaneous death, prolonged heavy use can cause a variety of ultimately lethal health complications. My point is that the claim that "speed kills" is misleading and erroneous. Though often made with good intentions, deceptive assertions about the purported dangers of drugs sometimes backfire. When people learn through their own experience or the observations of others that their newspapers, televisions, and elected officials have misinformed them, they grow weary of such warnings. Discussing the responses of youth to the misleading anti-marijuana propaganda of the 1960s, Joshua Kaufman, James Allen, and Louis West (1969) suggest that "the horrible reactions to marihuana predicted by various authorities were virtually never seen. [Children who ran away from home to join the drug scene] generally took this to mean that all the widely advertised dangers of drugs were establishment lies. This further alienated them from [society] and made them more willing to experiment with all sorts of chemicals" (719). While one cannot conclusively prove that methamphetamine users ignored "speed kills" warnings because of prior misleading media- and government-facilitated antidrug campaigns, that hysteria-fueled claims often have the tendency to produce effects opposite to their intentions bears noting (Jenkins 1999).

The End of an "Epidemic"

By 1970, "the practice of mainlining speed was depicted as one of the most perilous aspects of the burgeoning drug culture" (Jenkins 1999,

38). Though abuse of this drug was once associated primarily with socially marginalized groups, claims that Methedrine use and its subsequent problems were seeping into mainstream society raised the public's attention to the point of demanding action from government leaders.

We must place the Methedrine panic in the larger political context of the late 1960s and early 1970s. In 1969, illicit drug use was considered the country's gravest social problem (Rasmussen 2008a). Edward Jay Epstein (1990) argues this public focus was precisely what President Richard Nixon wanted. When he entered the Oval Office in 1969, Nixon sought to strengthen the White House's power over domestic and international affairs. In a series of lengthy interviews with previous members of the Nixon administration, Epstein (1990) came to the conclusion that drugs, especially the heroin problem (which was on the decline before Nixon entered office), were a vehicle through which the president attempted to gain wiretapping and other surveillance powers over potential political enemies. An assistant to Egil Krogh Jr., Nixon's liaison to the BNDD, retrospectively observed, "If we hyped the drug problem into a national crisis, we knew that Congress would give us anything we asked for" (Epstein 1990, 140). Moreover, declaring a national emergency over drugs would have the added benefit of potentially distracting citizens' attention away from the uneasy situation that had developed in Vietnam.

One way in which Nixon and his staff sought to hype the drug problem was through the orchestration of a massive media campaign to influence public opinion about the threat of drugs to society. On April 9, 1970, Nixon met with programming vice presidents, production heads, and advertising executives of several major television networks to encourage producers to include antidrug content in their fall programming schedules.[2] The producers responded very favorably to the meeting, and arrangements were made to include antidrug plotlines in fall episodes of popular television shows (e.g., the original *Hawaii Five-O*). A White House communications director assured Nixon's counsel, "At least twenty television programs this fall will have a minimum of one anti-drug theme . . . as a result of our conference" (Epstein 1990, 170). Changes in the content of fall television shows may have succeeded in creating fear among the public, as polls conducted by the Nixon administration in 1971 found that "citizens believed the drug menace to be one of the two main threats to their safety" (Epstein 1990, 172).

To be sure, throughout most of this time period, speed was less a topic of public discussion than marijuana, heroin, and other drugs that were "*not* a source of corporate income" (Graham 1972, 178; emphasis in original). In the legislative hearings held to discuss what ultimately became the Comprehensive Drug Abuse Prevention and Control Act of 1970, street drugs like opiates and cannabis were much more of a focus than pharmaceutical drugs (R. D. Peterson 1985). In its earliest version, Nixon's proposal called for cracking down on illicit drug production but made no mention of controlling domestic manufacturing of amphetamines, barbiturates, or other legally produced drugs (Graham 1972). Nixon's reluctance to take on licit manufacturing could be due to the fact that Attorney General John Mitchell was in close consultation with representatives from major pharmaceutical firms during the bill's drafting phase (Rasmussen 2008a).

The 1970 bill called for a major reorganization of drug regulation in the United States. Up until this point, many drug laws at the national and state levels had been chemical specific. For example, separate federal laws governed possessing, importing, and growing opium poppies (Gahlinger 2004). The Comprehensive Drug Abuse Prevention and Control Act replaced the Harrison Act, "federalized all drug laws, regardless of state laws concerning interstate commerce," and more fully shifted the burden of drug regulation from taxation to direct criminalization (DeGrandpre 2006, 243). Another significant element of this law was Title II, the CSA, which established the drug-scheduling system still in place today.

The CSA lists drugs under one of five "schedules," or categories, according to the federal government's determination of a substance's therapeutic benefits and potential for abuse and dependence. Schedule I drugs, including heroin, LSD, ecstasy, and, yes, marijuana, are deemed to offer no medical value and harbor a high risk of abuse and dependence. Schedule I drugs are completely prohibited, with one exception: scientists may obtain these substances, albeit after navigating a choppy federal bureaucracy, for clinical research purposes only. Schedule II drugs (e.g., cocaine, morphine, OxyContin) are considered to have a high risk of abuse and dependence but are recognized to have valid medicinal uses. Prescriptions for Schedule II drugs are permitted, though refills are not. Federal restrictions and officially recognized levels of potential abuse and addiction decline respectively for those drugs listed in Schedule III (e.g., many anabolic steroids), Schedule IV (e.g., Xanax, Valium, Ambien, Provigil), and Schedule V (e.g., cough medicines with trace amounts of codeine) (DIB 2006; "Controlled Substances" 2013).

In the House and Senate debates over the CSA, legislators did not widely resist plans to include amphetamines in the bill's provisions, largely due to the fact that Nixon's initial draft proposed to list all amphetamines as Schedule III substances, which commanded minimal penalties and controls and exempted them from production quotas. Attorney General Mitchell acknowledged increasing abuse of speed by Americans but argued that since amphetamines had extensive medicinal value, Schedule III was the appropriate classification. Senator Thomas Dodd and several other legislators made multiple attempts to place amphetamines in Schedule II, where they would be subject to tighter restrictions. As expected, these proposals were met with fierce dissention from financially invested drug companies (Graham 1972). Many members of Congress were also against placing amphetamines in Schedule II. Of the bill's many opponents, Representative Robert McClory of Illinois was perhaps most unapologetic: "Frankly . . . there are large pharmaceutical manufacturing interests centered in my congressional district. . . . I am proud to say that the well-known firms of Abbott Laboratories and Baxter Laboratories have large plants in my [district]. It is my expectation that C. D. Searl and Co. may soon establish a large part of its organization [there]" (as quoted in Graham 1972, 196).

Despite the testimony of several physicians, academics, and members of the FDA declaring the negative health consequences of amphetamine use and describing the ongoing diversion of legally produced pills to the black market, efforts to classify all amphetamines in Schedule II were squashed, perhaps due to heavy representation of the pharmaceutical lobby among conferees (Graham 1972). In the end, legislators offered a symbolic gesture to anti-amphetamine crusaders by agreeing to list five of the more than 6,000 products of the amphetamine family in Schedule II (Graham 1972; Rasmussen 2008a). These five products were injectable preparations of liquid methamphetamine, "an insignificant part of the total methamphetamine, not to mention amphetamine, production. . . . It was an easy pill for the [pharmaceutical] industry to swallow" (Graham 1972, 204).

The final bill placed all other forms of amphetamines in Schedule III. This great triumph for the pharmaceutical industry was partly due to its successes in focusing much of the congressional debates about speed on the intravenous use of methamphetamine. This aligned well with speed-related media discourse at the time, the majority of which singled out persons who injected Methedrine, rather than pill poppers, inhaler abusers, or users of other amphetamines. Rather than focus on amphetamine use by much larger segments of (legitimate) society (e.g., athletes, professionals, those who consumed the drug orally without medical supervision), the industry strategically guided the debate onto the small minority of intravenous users. This disproportionate scrutiny is especial-

ly notable considering that by 1970 the majority of injectable methamphetamine was either made illicitly in clandestine laboratories or created
by dissolving Methedrine tablets in water. No evidence existed that
legally produced liquid meth was being diverted in large quantities to
the black market (Graham 1972), as pharmaceutical manufacturers of
injectable meth stopped supplying pharmacies two years before the passage of the CSA (Karch 2001, 2002).

Though drug companies emerged victorious when Congress decided
to place virtually all of the amphetamine preparations in Schedule III,
their success was short lived. Ensuing media coverage of continued
black-market diversion of legally produced speed, combined with a
series of scandals on the overprescribing of amphetamines to hyperac-
tive children and dieting housewives, prompted the BNDD to invoke the
administrative powers it had been granted under the 1970 CSA to reclassify all amphetamines, along with Ritalin, into Schedule II (Rasmussen
2008a). All amphetamine drugs, including methamphetamine, have
remained in this category since 1971.

Judging by the rapid decline in press coverage circa 1971 (as shown
in Figure 4.1), the Methedrine problem appeared to have been "solved"
with the passage of the CSA.[3] Though methamphetamine would enter a
period of cultural dormancy well into the 1980s, the Methedrine panic
forever changed public perceptions of the drug. The decision to place a
few liquid preparations of methamphetamine in the more restrictive
Schedule II legally and socially constructed a boundary between it and
the other amphetamines. From this point forward public discussions of
synthetic stimulants would largely distinguish between the dreadful
"meth" and less scary, though potentially dangerous, other amphetamines. And while Dexedrine, Adderall, and other amphetamines are still
often constructed through a medical framework, the United States' next
two major methamphetamine scares ("ice," in 1989, and "crystal,"
beginning in the late 1990s) were generally void of counterclaims about
meth's potential therapeutic benefits. The fact that meth-related public
discourse post-1971 would rarely invoke the term *Methedrine* supports
the contention that methamphetamine's pop culture transformation from
medicine to drug was complete.

Notes

1. Twiggy was the nickname of Lesley Lawson, a rail-thin British fashion
model, singer, and actress who became internationally famous in the 1960s.

2. Some of the "talking points" for members of Nixon's cabinet to review with network producers were as follows:

"Program content should be carefully designed for the audience that is likely to be tuned in at a given time"; "It would not be accurate to portray the drug problem as a ghetto problem. . . . It is a problem which touches all economic, social and racial strata, of America"; "You will receive a drug information kit. . . . Included in that kit will be a telephone contact list so that you or your script writers can call government officials for clarification and additional information"; "Television subtly and inexorably helps to mold the attitudes, thinking and motivations of a vast number of Americans." (Epstein 1990, 168–169)

3. Many of the methamphetamine-related stories published in the *New York Times* in 1973 discussed meth as one of the amphetamines incurring federally mandated production quotas. Several other articles presented methamphetamine as one of the many illicit substances targeted by New York State's newly implemented drug laws (known as the "Rockefeller drug laws"), promoted by Governor Nelson Rockefeller as "the toughest antidrug program in the nation, with increased penalties for the illicit sale or possession of a wide variety of drugs" (Farber 1973, 16).

5

The Second Scare: Ice

Given the restrictions on the legal supplies and uses of amphetamines, black markets in them grew, and, as so often happens, this change promoted abuse. In the days of legal pills, most users took them by mouth. Today, many people snort powdered amphetamines like cocaine, smoke them, or even inject them. —*Andrew Weil and Winifred Rosen (2004, 55–56)*

The CSA of 1970 functioned to symbolically exorcize the speed demon threat to US society. As exhibited in Figure 5.1, media coverage of methamphetamine dwindled by the mid-1970s, and the drug lay low on the national news radar until 1989. Illicit drugs were a fairly regular staple of the news media across much of this time period, but heroin and, later, cocaine were the specific substances of most concern. Given the historical fluctuations in media attention toward methamphetamine, the casual news viewer may have inferred that meth use was prevalent in the late 1960s and early 1970s and then virtually nonexistent for the next fifteen years. While most researchers did not start gathering nationally representative data on methamphetamine consumption until the 1990s, two sources gauging historical trends are briefly worth mentioning.

Under the direction of the Department of Health and Human Services, the National Survey on Drug Use and Health (NSDUH) is a longitudinal survey of about 70,000 members "of the civilian, noninstitutionalized population, aged 12 years and older in the United States" (SAMHSA 2009b, 229). Researchers selected data from the 2002 NSDUH to construct several retrospective estimates of annual methamphetamine use since the mid-1960s (see Gfroerer and Brodsky 1992; Packer et al. 2002; Gfroerer et al. 2004). Though these data have several

95

Figure 5.1 News Media Coverage of Methamphetamine, 1969–1994

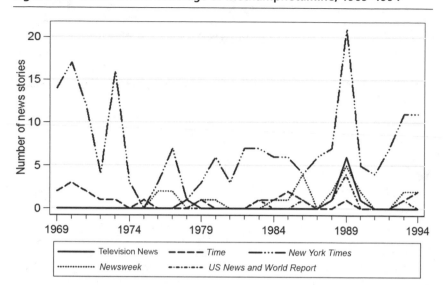

Sources: Vanderbilt Television News Archive, http://tvnews.vanderbilt.edu; *Time* Magazine Archive, www.time.com/time/archive; ProQuest, www.proquest.com; LexisNexis Academic, www.lexisnexis.com/en-us/Home.page.

Note: Television news data represent number of nightly national news segments broadcast by ABC, NBC, and CBS.

methodological limitations and should only be considered rough approximations, the estimates provided are sufficient for talking about broad changes in initiation and use over time (Gfroerer et al. 2004).

Figure 5.2 presents NSDUH retrospective data indicating the number of annual methamphetamine initiates (in thousands) and the rate of initiates per 100,000 population from 1966 to 1994. The lowest number of initiates over this time period was in 1967, when 87,000 US residents were estimated to have used methamphetamine for the first time. This estimate is notable considering 1967 was the first year that *Time* and the *New York Times* devoted any substantial attention to methamphetamine (see Figure 4.1 in previous chapter). Also of note in Figure 5.2, the number and rate of first-time users increased into the 1970s, well after federal restrictions set forth by the CSA.

Figure 5.3 displays NSDUH retrospective estimates of lifetime use of methamphetamine and cocaine for persons age twelve to seventeen and eighteen to twenty-five. In general, the pattern of meth use is similar to what is revealed in Figure 5.2. Usage rates were lowest among

Figure 5.2 Number and Rate of Methamphetamine Initiates, 1966–1994

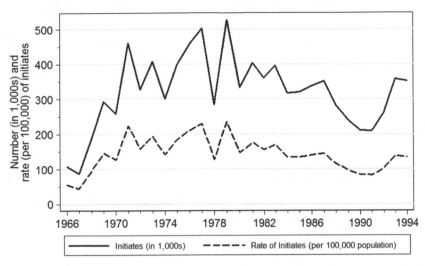

Sources: Data on initiates are from SAMHSA (2003). Population data are extrapolated from decennial figures provided by US Census Bureau (as disseminated by Hobbs and Stoops 2002).

both age cohorts from 1965 to 1970, crested in the late 1970s and early 1980s, and declined thereafter (SAMHSA 2003).

A source of historical data that may help illustrate the extent of early methamphetamine use in the United States is Monitoring the Future (MTF), a survey of thousands of high school students conducted annually since 1975. Figure 5.4 shows changes in the past-year use of several stimulants by US twelfth graders from 1975 to 1994. The overall trend in methamphetamine consumption resembles the NSDUH data presented in Figures 5.2 and 5.3. Specifically, methamphetamine use among high school seniors increased throughout the mid- to late 1970s, peaked in the early 1980s, and steadily decreased into the next decade.

When taken together, longitudinal data on methamphetamine consumption (see Figures 5.2, 5.3, and 5.4) are effectively inversely related to media trends (see Figures 4.1 and 5.1). These patterns raise several questions. Since the strict speed regulations (e.g., production quotas) put into place in the early 1970s essentially eliminated black-market diversion of licitly manufactured methamphetamine, how did so many in the United States illegally obtain and use the drug into the 1970s and beyond? Why was the mass media virtually silent about publicizing the

**Figure 5.3 Lifetime Methamphetamine and Cocaine Use
Among Persons Age 12 to 17 and 18 to 25, 1965–1994**

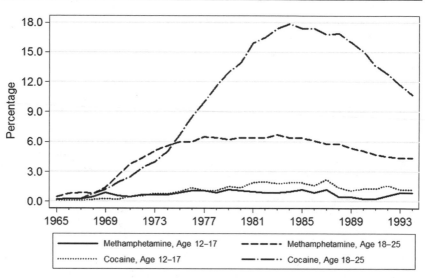

Source: SAMHSA (2003).

Figure 5.4 Past-Year Stimulant Use Among Twelfth Graders, 1975–1994

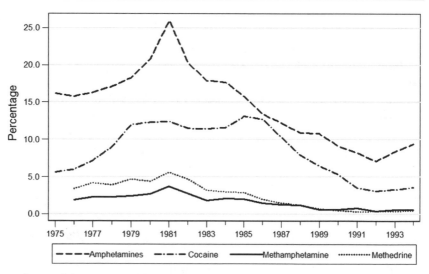

Source: Johnston et al. (2012), Tables 5-2 and E-2.
Notes: Amphetamine and cocaine data are from full sample (weighted annual approximate sample size ranges from 9,400 to 17,800). Methamphetamine and Methedrine data are
from subsample (weighted annual approximate sample size ranges from 2,000 to 3,400).

apparent increase in methamphetamine use over this time period? And why was methamphetamine suddenly revived as a hot topic in national news discourse in 1989, considering survey data indicate consumption substantially declined by this time?

In the remainder of this chapter, I address these questions by first discussing the evolution of the methamphetamine black market during the 1970s and 1980s and then describing the sudden emergence (and retreat) of the ice panic, the United States' second methamphetamine scare. As anti-heroin and anti-cocaine crusaders received the glut of media attention over the fifteen or so years following the CSA, the nature of illicit methamphetamine production and distribution quietly underwent extensive changes. And while on its face, the ice scare of 1989 seemed to arise out of nowhere, its genesis is intimately connected to both the evolution of the black market for meth *and* the late 1980s media frenzy over crack cocaine.

The New Black Market for Methamphetamine

When the illegal diversion of legally manufactured speed diminished around 1972, many illicit stimulant seekers adapted in one of two ways. First, some people, especially those with money, switched to cocaine (Joseph 2000). Increased attention to amphetamine supplies by law enforcement led to an upsurge in cocaine trafficking (Brecher 1972), and cocaine replaced methamphetamine in popularity over the next two decades (Iversen 2006). This market shift was illustrated in Figure 5.3, which showed lifetime cocaine use by teenagers and young adults had become much more prevalent by the late 1970s.

A second way in which persons responded to the lack of lawfully produced amphetamines was by synthesizing their own (Brecher 1972). Clandestine laboratories had existed since 1962, but the CSA of 1970 more fully ceded production to rogue chemists and entrepreneurs operating in various places throughout the country. As the supplier of illegal substances, underground markets determine a drug's production, quality, and price. Since black markets often arise when some good or service is outlawed, it follows that their structure will depend largely on the extent and nature of legal prohibitions. Up until 1962, virtually all illicitly obtained methamphetamine was legally produced by US pharmaceutical companies and diverted to the black market. Generally speaking, prices were relatively low, quality was high, and market control was decentralized. The series of industry and state restrictions implemented over the next nine years (e.g., ending liquid Methedrine sales to pharmacies, the CSA) dramatically altered the black market for methamphetamine by forcing the restructure of production and distribution operations. In turn, these changes facilitated an increase in meth-related harms.

Making Meth

As federal restrictions of legally manufactured amphetamines dried up illicit diversion, outlaw motorcycle gangs and others organized illicit production rings throughout the West Coast and elsewhere to fill the void (Gahlinger 2004; Owen 2007). By the early 1970s, clandestine laboratories (i.e., "meth labs") were the primary source of US methamphetamine. According to Miriam Joseph (2000), the proliferation of meth labs was aided by two factors. First, individuals dedicated to making methamphetamine found that it was not extremely complicated to synthesize. Second, compared to plant-based drugs (e.g., marijuana, cocaine), the illicit production of methamphetamine is more difficult to detect and control. Whereas large-scale cocaine and marijuana operations require many acres of fields for cultivation, meth manufacturing requires relatively little space. Furthermore, trafficking networks involved in the early distribution of methamphetamine covered much less geographic area, as manufacturing occurred relatively close to user populations. In contrast, much of the traffic in other illicit drugs crosses national boundaries, as plants usually originate in faraway lands (e.g., coca in South America, opium poppies in the Middle East) (Joseph 2000).

Meth labs are probably the single most detrimental unintended consequence of legal restrictions on lawfully produced amphetamines. The nature of clandestine manufacturing leads to hazards such as environmental pollution and accidental explosions resulting from improper production methods. In many news stories, claims makers are often quoted saying that "anyone" can make methamphetamine, since most of the required chemicals can be purchased legally at home improvement stores, agricultural business suppliers, and elsewhere. For example, in a 2006 documentary by *National Geographic*, a lieutenant of the Multnomah County Sheriff's Office in Oregon asserted, "If you can make chocolate chip cookies, you can cook methamphetamine" (Crowley 2006). As Joseph (2000) points out, methamphetamine can be created with relative ease. However, the production process is not analogous to baking cookies. Among other requirements, meth makers must possess chemistry equipment, a variety of chemicals, a fairly covert location, and knowledge of the chemistry needed for drug synthesis.

Meth labs vary greatly in size, organization, and output. Though the term *laboratory* connotes images of sterile science classrooms and research facilities, many labs are haphazardly organized. So-called mom-and-pop labs are independently operated by individuals or small groups who produce minor quantities of methamphetamine often just for personal use. Though some mom-and-pop ventures are sophisticated, many are carelessly created in kitchens, hotel rooms, recreational vehicles, tool sheds, garages, basements, and bedrooms (Joseph 2000). In contrast to small-time operations, other clandestine meth labs are very elaborate and well organized. Such large-scale manufacturing outfits (e.g., "superlabs") produce mass quantities for black-market distribution.[1]

Most illegally manufactured methamphetamine is synthesized from other chemicals (called precursors) using one of four methods. The P2P amalgam method uses phenyl-2-propanone (P2P, an organic compound) and methylamine (a derivative of ammonia). The hydriodic acid/red phosphorous reduction and Nazi[2] reduction (also known as Birch) methods utilize ephedrine or pseudoephedrine as precursor chemicals (DIB 2006).[3] In the early 2000s, the "one-pot" or "shake-and-bake" method emerged as a fourth way to cook meth. A variant of the outdated "cold-cook" method, the one-pot procedure yields small amounts of methamphetamine from ephedrine or pseudoephedrine (NDIC 2009; DIB 2012). All four methods require additional chemicals (e.g., hydrochloric acid, aluminum, acetone, lithium) (DIB 2012).

The popularity of each of these synthesis techniques has varied over time, usually in response to legal and interdiction efforts designed to curb illicit manufacturing. From the early 1960s until about 1980, the majority of illegal production operations employed the P2P method (Gahlinger 2004). Referred to on the street as "oil" or "prope," P2P was often used by pest exterminators who acquired it legally in fifty-five-gallon barrels (Jenkins 1999). By 1980, authorities were well aware of P2P's use as a popular precursor chemical and categorized it as a Schedule II substance under the CSA. Some chemists responded by importing P2P from Europe, where it was cheaply and legally available, while others learned how to synthesize P2P from legally obtainable chemicals (Puder, Kagan, and Morgan 1988; Jenkins 1992, 1999).

Nonetheless, increased federal controls of P2P made its acquisition risky and more laborious, and most lab operators eventually switched to synthesis methods that utilized ephedrine or pseudoephedrine precursors (G. Irvine and Chin 1991; Anglin et al. 2000; Joseph 2000; Gahlinger 2004; Franco 2007). Ephedrine—the nature-based stimulant cast from the medical world following the rediscovery of amphetamine in the late

1920s—had a new purpose nearly sixty years later. Frank Owen (2007) suggests a "resourceful chemist" discovered the chemical similarities between ephedrine and methamphetamine when trying to figure out a way to circumvent newly implemented P2P controls (136). Ephedrine was no longer difficult to obtain in bulk, and its more recently synthesized and chemically similar cousin, pseudoephedrine, was in plentiful supply.

In direct response to the DEA's decision to list P2P as a Schedule II drug, ephedrine-based labs first appeared in San Diego, earning the city the nickname the "Bogota of Speed" in the 1980s (Joseph 2000, 57). Throughout the 1980s and into the early 1990s, the use of ephedrine and pseudoephedrine as methamphetamine precursors was prevalent in West Coast labs (G. Irvine and Chin 1991; Owen 2007). From 1978 through the first three-quarters of 1981, over 50 percent of clandestine methamphetamine labs seized by the DEA were determined to have utilized P2P synthesis (Frank 1983). Twelve years later, only 16 percent of seized meth labs were employing P2P, whereas 83 percent were found to be operating with ephedrine (DEA 1994). Virtually all of the 7,622 reported seizures in 2010 were of labs using ephedrine or pseudoephedrine precursors. Only four P2P labs were discovered that year (DIB 2012).

Making Meth More Potent and Harmful

The newly favored synthesis methods, brought about by federal P2P controls, fundamentally and indefinitely altered the nature of the methamphetamine problem (Owen 2007). Ephedrine and pseudoephedrine precursors made illicit manufacture easier and quicker than P2P (Anglin et al. 2000; Scott 2002; Franco 2007). Moreover, the chemical reactions created from ephedrine and pseudoephedrine produce a form of methamphetamine that is molecularly identical to meth made with P2P yet slightly different in structure. Specifically, the outdated P2P technique resulted in dl-methamphetamine (a mixture of dextro- and levo-methamphetamine isomers), whereas ephedrine-based methods yield d-methamphetamine. Dealers and users were more than satisfied with this change in quality, since d-methamphetamine is structurally identical to the pharmaceutical product, and more potent and active than dl-methamphetamine (Derlet 1990; M. A. Miller 1997; Anglin et al. 2000; DIB 2006; Franco 2007; Owen 2007). Also, throughout most of the 1980s, no federal controls restricted production, distribution, and sales of ephedrine and pseudoephedrine. Other chemicals (e.g., ammonia) used in the synthesis process were inexpensive and readily accessible.

When P2P-based dl-methamphetamine dominated the illicit market in the 1970s, "biker meth," often called "crank," was not usually pure enough to be smoked (see Hunt, Kuck, and Truitt 2006, 24).[4] If executed properly, ephedrine reduction techniques can yield very pure methamphetamine powder, which can then be mixed with water or rubbing alcohol and heated. As the liquid solvent evaporates, crystals of purified methamphetamine form (Derlet 1990; DIB 2006). Although *crystal meth* is one of the more popular contemporary slang terms for most forms of methamphetamine, in strict chemical and legal terms, crystallized methamphetamine refers to the volatile (i.e., smokable) and highly pure d-methamphetamine hydrochloride (DIB 2006).[5] Crystallized meth is often referred to as "ice" because the substance looks like ice crystals (Cho and Melega 2002). Typical purity levels of ice range from 93 to 98 percent. According to one source, "the DEA has seized samples [of ice] that have a documented purity of 100%" (DIB 2006, 244).

The increased popularity of smokable methamphetamine afforded by ephedrine and pseudoephedrine synthesis techniques is significant because different routes of drug administration have varying effects on a drug's absorption, the speed with which the user experiences a drug's effects, and the user's health, risk of dependence, and perceptions of risk for dependence (Strang et al. 1998). Of the four main routes of methamphetamine administration, smoking and intravenous injection are the most dangerous, in part because they deliver the drug to the brain almost instantaneously, producing a more intense and immediate "high." Such onset effects tend to "increase the propensity for dependence" (Cunningham, Liu, and Muramoto 2008, 1174). An additional hazard specific to smoking meth is the potential release of toxic compounds (some of which are separate mind-altering drugs) through chemical reactions to heat (Murray 1998; Gahlinger 2004).

The lower-purity, P2P-based dl-methamphetamine prevalent during the 1970s meant that illicit users of this time period were much more likely to swallow or snort speed than they were to inhale it.[6] Oral ingestion (swallowing) is the least dangerous route of administration, partly because a sizable proportion of the drug is absorbed into other parts of the body before ending its relatively long journey (about twenty to thirty minutes) to the brain (Gahlinger 2004; Maisto, Galizio, and Connors 2008). Intranasal administration is the second least dangerous route, in part because snorting or sniffing a drug produces psychoactive effects in three to five minutes (cf. Gahlinger 2004).[7]

Harms from Impurities

When pharmaceutically manufactured meth was being diverted into illicit channels in the 1950s and 1960s, users benefited from the purity and sterility of their drugs (Joseph 2000). Though profit motives likely explain why billions of amphetamine tablets reached the black market, it is also true that pharmaceutical products meet some level of quality control established by industry and legal standards. Illegally produced methamphetamine faces no such standards. When federal policy successfully put an end to most of the illicit diversion of pharmaceutically produced methamphetamine, the black market secured nonsterile drugs, at first from chemical manufacturing plants that shipped in bulk and then increasingly from clandestine laboratories operated by street chemists and biker gangs (Brecher 1972). Since any impurities in legally produced speed are generally inert, fewer risks are involved in using pharmaceutical-grade methamphetamine than in using the illicitly manufactured product.

Impurities found in methamphetamine created in clandestine laboratories may result accidentally (e.g., through poor synthesis methods used by inexperienced chemists) or intentionally (e.g., in the form of adulterants used to "cut" the final product in order to maximize profit) (Burton 1991). Lactose, Epsom salts, monosodium glutamate, baking powder, quinine, photo developer, ether, strychnine, and insecticides are several ingredients that have been used to dilute illegally produced speed (Grinspoon and Hedblom 1975). Chemical analyses of illicit meth seizures have found impurities in the form of methylamine hydrochloride (an ammonia derivative), mannitol (a sugar alcohol), P2P, caffeine, dimethylamphetamine (a less psychoactive amphetamine produced as a "side reaction"), benzyl alcohol (a substance found in perfumes and head lice medications), and the solvent dibenzyl ketone (an acetone-like impurity found in a precursor chemical) (Kram 1977; Puder, Kagan, and J. P. Morgan 1988; Verweij 1989; Inoue, Iwata, and Kuwayama 2008). In the late 1980s, officials in Oregon reported multiple incidents of lead poisoning resulting from the consumption of illicitly manufactured methamphetamine. In one of the cases, a sample of methamphetamine taken from one of twelve users suffering from acute poisoning "contained 60 percent lead" (Norton et al. 1989, as cited in Burton 1991, 55).

As these incidents demonstrate, the destructive consequences of laced methamphetamine may exceed the harmful effects of the drug itself. One does not need a degree in chemistry or physiology to understand that bodily intake of photo developer, lead, or insecticide is unhealthy. Since illicitly produced meth is not subject to production standards, street users are often unaware of the contaminants they may be consuming. Roger Smith (1969b) quotes a street dealer's description of one woman's reaction to adulterated meth: "I had an old lady last year that did about a dime (ten dollar bag) hit cut with rat poison. She turned purple and started gasping for breath and fell on the floor and damn near croaked" (175).

One additional problematic aspect of adulterated methamphetamine is that some "cuts" provide more intense and enjoyable effects than the drug in its pure form. Smith (1969b) notes that street meth containing ether (a substance used in the drying process) provides a greater "flash" feeling when injected. According to Lester Grinspoon and Peter Hedblom (1975), "many speed freaks actually [prefer] certain impurities" because of the greater feelings of pleasure and intensity they provide (26).

Harms from Dosage Irregularities

A problem related to adulterated, impure street drugs concerns dosage. Since purity levels of illicitly manufactured methamphetamine vary, users may not know precisely how much of their product contains the actual drug, and how much contains diluents, both harmful and inert.

For heuristic purposes, imagine a scenario in which every Friday night over the course of a month, a weekend user of powdered methamphetamine purchases one half of one gram (i.e., 500 milligrams, or "a half") from a dealer with whom he shares an apartment complex. Unbeknownst to the user, the meth he has become accustomed to snorting over the past several weekends is 35 percent actual methamphetamine and 65 percent inert adulterants. Further suppose that in response to the arrest and detainment of the dealer next door, the user looks elsewhere to secure his fix for Friday night. Also unbeknownst to the user, the meth scored from his new supplier is 70 percent pure and 30 percent inactive ingredients. A cautious user would first "test" his or her new product by consuming only a small amount and using the subsequent physiological effects to gauge the timing and size of subsequent self-administered doses. Not all users are so cautious. As this hypothetical example illustrates, inconsistent and unknown methamphetamine purity levels can create problems (e.g., overdose) for the user through dosage irregularities endemic to the black market.

Harms from Production

In addition to the bodily harms associated with different routes of administration and inconsistent purity and dosage levels, another series of dangers stemming from the illicit market is more directly related to the proximity of meth production operations. Many of the chemicals utilized in manufacturing can cause physical harm, such as irritation of the eyes, nose, throat, and skin, as well as liver and kidney problems. Some of these chemicals (e.g., ethanol, benzene, petroleum ether) are extremely flammable. Magnesium, potassium metals, and other substances can explode when exposed to water or air (G. Irvine and Chin 1991).

Though the news media tend to routinize the most severe instances of meth cooking gone wrong, accidents do happen. For example, Lynn Willers-Russo (1999) describes a case study of three individuals found dead in a California motel room due to poisoning from phosphine gas, a noxious chemical created by heating red phosphorous. Another study reported that over a sixteen-month period beginning in January 2001, thirteen (9.8 percent) of the 132 patients who received treatment for facial burns across a network of Iowa burn centers were injured "during documented participation in methamphetamine production" (Charukamnoetkanok and Wagoner 2004, 875). Cooks are not the only persons adversely affected by meth production. Neighbors, family members, law enforcement officials, cleanup crews, and even hospital workers are at risk of being harmed. Poorly ventilated and maintained laboratories often contain traces of precursors and chemical by-products long after drug operations have ceased (G. Irvine and Chin 1991; Scott 2002; Sheridan et al. 2006; Melnikova et al. 2011). In recent years, many states have enacted real estate disclosure laws to prevent the purchase and occupation of former meth dens without forewarning.

Another harmful consequence of methamphetamine production is environmental contamination. Optimistically, we might presume that much of the environmental pollution emanating from legitimate industry either meets federal guidelines or results from accidents (e.g., oil spills). The illicit production of methamphetamine is not subject to such protocols. Furthermore, the illegal nature of clandestine laboratories means that cooks will take any necessary steps to avoid detection by authorities, including improperly and haphazardly disposing of chemical waste.

Many of the precursors and chemical by-products associated with methamphetamine production are toxic and corrosive. According to a report by the Department of Justice, "each pound of manufactured methamphetamine produces about 5 to 6 pounds of hazardous waste" (Scott 2002, 4). Although the quantity and quality of waste likely vary according to synthesis method, the expertise of lab operators, and other factors, chemical leftovers are undoubtedly harmful to local ecologies. Residual chemicals, such as phosphorous-based solvents, may be poured into sewers, flushed into septic systems, or dumped onto the ground.

These careless disposal methods contaminate water supplies and agricultural lands and require vast cleanup efforts (G. Irvine and Chin 1991; Scott 2002; Meredith et al. 2005; Sheridan et al. 2006).

The environmental hazards associated with illicit methamphetamine production can also be economically harmful. For example, in 2012, twenty-two separate contractors were licensed in the state of Indiana to decontaminate property polluted by meth labs. "Most companies charge about $2 to $3 per square foot to do a cleanup. Depending on the size . . . the cost can range from $5,000 to $10,000" (Benbow 2012). One comprehensive study estimates that US criminal justice agencies spent a total of $29.2 million cleaning up meth labs in 2005 (Nicosia et al. 2009). Labs are also a detriment to property values. An analysis of one Ohio county found that homes located within an eighth of a mile of recently discovered laboratories sold for 10 to 16 percent less than homes located between one-eighth and one-quarter of a mile away, even after controlling for square footage, age, and other home characteristics (Congdon-Hohman 2013).

Harms from Trafficking

By virtue of their illegality, black markets for illicit drugs are organized and sustained by criminals (Goldstein 1985; Nadelmann 1989; Fish 2006). With no legal supply source, the market for illegal drugs, including methamphetamine, is lucrative. As federal restrictions in the 1960s and early 1970s stymied the diversion of legally produced speed, the early distributors of methamphetamine—physicians, pharmacists, drug wholesalers, and other individuals more closely connected to the white market for drugs—were replaced by organized criminals. According to Edward Brecher (1972), illicit meth manufacturers and traffickers actually favored tighter laws, for they facilitated market monopolies and higher profits. With severely reduced competition due to the decrease in illegally diverted pharmaceutical-grade speed, producers and distributors raised prices, even while often providing a substance of lower purity. Though usually cheaper than cocaine, methamphetamine is costly. Addicts and thrill seekers who cannot afford the drugs they want are likely to engage in other crimes (e.g., prostitution, larceny, burglary) to finance their habits. It is important to point out that illegal drugs are so expensive precisely because they are illegal, not because they are naturally costly to produce and distribute (Nadelmann 1989).

Because they directly or indirectly controlled a sizable proportion of the drug's illicit production, outlaw motorcycle gangs were historically well positioned to become the first organized group heavily involved in methamphetamine trafficking (Jenkins 1992, 1999). During the 1970s, biker groups combined to account for about 50 percent of illicit meth production and a "major part" of its distribution, according to some reports (Jenkins 1999, 51). Many biker gangs established ties to more traditional (i.e., Mafia-like) organized crime networks in some cities, including Philadelphia, where they trafficked in P2P and other precursors (Jenkins 1992, 1999). In fact, most P2P labs in the United States were operated by outlaw motorcycle gangs (Franco 2007).

Between 1960 and 1980, domestic groups distributed virtually all of the illicitly available methamphetamine in the United States. Meth was a quintessentially American drug during this time period, in contrast to cocaine, heroin, and other illicit drugs deriving from foreign nations. As the center of West Coast methamphetamine manufacture shifted from the San Francisco Bay Area to San Diego in the early 1980s, shortly after P2P's classification as a Schedule II drug, Mexican drug-trafficking organizations (DTOs) started to establish a role in illicit meth production and distribution (M. A. Miller 1997; Anglin et al. 2000).

Over the years, the passage of several laws designed to disrupt domestic production activities facilitated greater involvement of Mexican DTOs and other foreign groups in the US trade. For example, when the 1988 Chemical Diversion and Trafficking Act placed controls on bulk imports of ephedrine powder, traffickers secured diversions from legitimate manufacturing plants in India, China, the Czech Republic, and Germany (Suo 2004a). Since many nations have not established importation quotas on ephedrine and pseudoephedrine, DTOs operating in the United States may acquire precursor chemicals elsewhere. Although federal law enforcement agencies attribute much of the methamphetamine trade in the early twenty-first century to Mexican DTOs (e.g., NDIC 2011a; "Drug Fact Sheet" 2012), groups from Vietnam, Korea, Japan, and the Philippines began distributing the drug and its precursors in Hawaii in the 1980s (NDIC 2002). Curiously, this time period was precisely the one during which the news media suddenly experienced a renewed interest in methamphetamine.

From Blip to Panic: The Second Methamphetamine Scare

Following the Methedrine panic of the late 1960s and early 1970s, methamphetamine use in the United States escalated and the black market evolved in ways that created an abundance of new harms. Concurrently, methamphetamine entered the news media doldrums, as evidenced by the dearth of national press coverage from about 1972 until the late 1980s. Methamphetamine *users* were especially absent from news discourse during this time period (Jenkins 1999). The few meth-related stories communicated by major US news sources typically mentioned the involvement of outlaw motorcycle gangs or Mafia groups in crank manufacture and trafficking (e.g., "Nation: Hell's Angels" 1979; "Speed Demons" 1984). In other words, the "threat to the innocent" framework (see Manning 2006) through which Methedrine mania proliferated was replaced by constructions of methamphetamine as a problem of organized crime (Jenkins 1999). The racial/ethnic composition of the criminal groups involved in the US meth trade (e.g., white bikers, Italian American mafiosos) may have been too domestic and familiar to generate much panic. And even though speed's association with patriotism and the medical framework had faded by the 1960s and 1970s, respectively, popular depictions of methamphetamine still occasionally constructed the drug as a workplace performance enhancer, especially among blue-collar whites (Jenkins 1994). Stated differently, during the 1972 to 1987 downturn in national news coverage of methamphetamine, claims makers seeking to publicize the drug were unable or uninterested in constructing meth as a serious threat to deeply held cultural values (e.g., individualism, capitalism).

Methamphetamine's cultural slumber ended in 1989, when media coverage of the drug skyrocketed from blip to sheer panic, seemingly overnight. At this time, politicians and journalists warned that the nation was entering an "ice age" (Jenkins 1994, 1999). However, ice vanished from the mass media almost as abruptly as it appeared. In the remainder of this chapter, I examine news coverage of the mini–ice panic and offer explanations for its quick rise and fall. The United States' second methamphetamine scare was definitely its shortest. Though the ice panic shared some similarities with the Methedrine madness of the 1960s and the crystal meth scare that began in the mid-1990s, the historical and political circumstances surrounding the volatile proliferation and descent of the ice menace are unique and fascinating in their own right. Of particular importance to the birth and initial success of the ice panic was the crack cocaine scare, which had become institutionalized in American culture by the late 1980s.

Piggybacking Crack

Data shown in Figure 5.5 suggest that the crack frenzy peaked in 1989. On September 5 of that year, President George H. W. Bush (1989) delivered a nationally televised speech from the Oval Office outlining his drug control strategy and proposing a $2.2 billion (roughly 35 percent) increase in the federal drug budget. "All of us agree that the gravest domestic threat facing our nation today is drugs," Bush stated. Mentioning heroin and PCP only in passing, the president directed almost all of his attention to cocaine, especially crack. Bush (1989) identified crack users as "the most pressing, immediate drug problem" and repeatedly talked of children threatened by the substance, which he defined as "poison." In dramatic fashion, President Bush (1989) gripped in front of the camera a plastic bag of crack cocaine, telling viewers it had been seized by the DEA "in a park just across the street from the White House." Though it was later revealed that Bush's drug prop had been acquired through an elaborate DEA setup orchestrated by his own administration, the speech seemed to further push crack to the forefront of public discourse (Reinarman and Levine 1997b).[8] By the end of the month, public opinion polls estimated that 64 percent of adult residents believed drugs were "the most important problem facing" the United States, a statistic that was less than 1 percent in 1985 (Reinarman and Levine 1997b, 24).

Figure 5.5　News Media Coverage of Methamphetamine and Crack Cocaine, 1985–1992

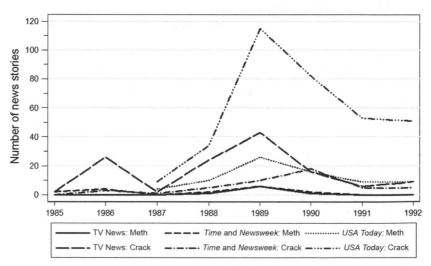

Sources: Vanderbilt Television News Archive, http://tvnews.vanderbilt.edu; *Time* Magazine Archive, www.time.com/time/archive; ProQuest, www.proquest.com; LexisNexis Academic, www.lexisnexis.com/en-us/Home.page.

Note: Television news data represent number of nightly national news segments broadcast by ABC, NBC, and CBS.

To borrow a phrase from Reinarman and Levine (1997b, 18), the "crack attack" of the late 1980s provided a fertile ground from which the second methamphetamine scare sprouted. The timing of the initial media coverage of ice in relation to the escalation of crack hysteria is particularly noteworthy. On September 6, 1989—the day after President Bush's sensationalist crack speech—Dan Rather of *CBS Evening News* introduced a segment about "a new amphetamine in Hawaii known as 'ice'" ("Hawaii / Drugs" 1989). Of all the major national news media sources I examined (see Appendix), this story appears to be the first to refer to methamphetamine as "ice." The following day, ice received its first mention in *USA Today* (MacNamara 1989). *ABC Evening News* followed suit with its own ice feature on September 8 ("War on Drugs" 1989).

By the end of the year, methamphetamine had been mentioned in six nationally televised nightly news broadcasts; from August 5, 1968 (the earliest searchable date in the Vanderbilt Television News Archive), to 1988, ABC, NBC, and CBS presented a total of two stories about meth. *Time* and *Newsweek* presented a combined six stories about methamphetamine in 1989, more than in any other year from 1975 to 1995. Also in 1989, methamphetamine was discussed in twenty-one articles published by the *New York Times* (more than in any year prior) and twenty-six articles by *USA Today* (more than in any year from 1987, the earliest year in which searchable text is available, to 1995). In the midst of a fierce fight against crack cocaine, the United States—especially Hawaii—had fallen victim to a sneak attack from ice. By decade's end, the US drug situation appeared to be spiraling out of control.

One way in which claims makers seek to draw attention to a condition is to connect it with other social problems with which audiences have become familiarized. In some cases, claims makers borrow the rhetoric and imagery of more successful and established social problems (Loseke 2003; Best 2008). In essence, claims makers fueling the propagation of the second methamphetamine scare piggybacked on the achievements of the anti-crack crusade. Crack cocaine was *the* principal drug scare of the late 1900s and, arguably, of US history (see Reinarman and Levine 1997c). The patterns of media coverage presented in Figure 5.5 show that from 1985 until at least 1992, attention to crack cocaine was generally greater than attention to methamphetamine. Figure 5.5 also indicates that coverage of crack on television news broadcasts and in *USA Today* escalated in 1988, at a rate disproportionate to coverage of meth. These trends suggest that in the fall of 1989, when the ice panic began to bloom, US news consumers had been thoroughly exposed to crack cocaine hysteria. Public fears over crack were high, and claims makers interested in adding meth to the mix took advantage of the national drug emergency dominating the social problems marketplace at the time. "In seeking to portray a new problem as serious or dangerous, one well-known rhetorical device is to stigmatize that problem by associating it with another, already familiar issue, thus placing [it] into an existing context" (Jenkins 1994, 16).

The actual content of ice-related news stories provides further evidence of piggybacking. Not only was ice regularly likened to crack, but the former was often depicted as being worse than the latter (Jenkins 1994, 1999). The headline from the *USA Today* article published two days after Bush's televised drug speech read, "More Menacing than Crack, 'Ice' Strikes" (MacNamara 1989, 3A). The director of Hawaii's state mental health department asserted, ice users "go absolutely crazy. . . . They're much more belligerent than those on crack" (Bishop 1989, A1). A journalist from another news source wrote, "As addictive as crack cocaine but far more pernicious, ice . . . is a drug that seems culled from the pages of science fiction" (Lerner 1989, 37). In the *Washington Post*, a National Institute on Drug Abuse (NIDA) adviser suggested, "Ice may pose even more of a social danger than crack." In the same article, a clinical director claimed that ice would not simply replace crack as a drug of choice among crack users. Rather, "it is widening the group of people who are smoking drugs" (L. Thompson 1989, Z11). Another newspaper cited a Hawaiian police officer portending ice "could replace crack on the mainland," and a current user who stated, "It has a lot of side effects, worse than smoking crack. I was getting really violent. I used to hit [my girlfriend] a lot" (Essoyan 1989, 17).

Thus, not only were discussions linking ice with crack commonplace, but whenever differences between the two drugs were offered, they usually regarded the higher destructive potential of ice (Jenkins 1994, 1999). In effect, these reports implied that ice would create exponentially more damage to users and society than the nightmare of crack. Methamphetamine, a drug that had lain dormant, absent from popular culture for so long, would unlikely have received a notable upsurge in press attention under different historical conditions. A public panicked over crack cocaine was well positioned to receive news stories about other threatening drugs, particularly when they were described as worse than crack (Jenkins 1999).

Not coincidentally, methamphetamine earned a boost in news coverage when claims makers altered their constructions of meth as a white, rural, working-class drug to include images of drug-induced harm and violence stereotypical of crack. Although smokable cocaine was usually portrayed as the drug of choice among inner-city blacks, fears of crack cocaine ruining white America permeated media discourse (see Reeves and Campbell 1994; Reinarman and Levine 1997c). One may reasonably suppose that many residents of seemingly crack-free communities perceived the threat posed by methamphetamine, a historically "white" drug, as more credible than the warnings about crack. For many news consumers, crack represented a problem "out there" in black communities. On the other hand, if anti-ice crusaders were to be believed, ice—the "white" version of crack—was likely to be accompanied by similar, if not greater, levels of addiction, violence, and social decay (Jenkins 1994, 1999).

Changing Constructions of Illicit Suppliers

Whereas reports by major national television news programs, newsmagazines, and newspapers portrayed most users of smokable methamphetamine as white Americans (or Native Hawaiians), the rise in ice-related media discourse coincided with the increased involvement of foreign traffickers in the US trade. Asian gangs from Japan, Korea, the Philippines, and Hong Kong were the most frequently cited sources of ice production and distribution (e.g., Bishop 1989; "Hawaii / Drugs" 1989; L. Thompson 1989). By singling out Asian traffickers as ice suppliers, and by identifying them as dangerous foreign "others," the press helped frame the problem as one of national security. Phillip Jenkins (1999) suggests that the image of the criminal Japanese ice trafficker resonated with contemporaneous fears in American society of an economically emerging Japan. Though certainly not the last time domestic methamphetamine problems would be heavily attributed to foreign groups, the short-lived ice panic likely thrived in part because claims makers clearly identified dangerous outsiders as the principal villains. Evil outsiders "are the types of people Americans in general are willing to blame, hate, and punish" (Loseke 2003, 85).

Nationalization and Novelty Claims

Opportune historical conditions and the linking of ice to dangerous foreign groups represent two of the major drug scare ingredients offered by Craig Reinarman (2012). Though connections to crack fostered a rise in media coverage of meth, claims makers vying for the public's attention also sought to distinguish ice from other demonized drugs.

The first *ABC Evening News* story about ice reported a "new illegal drug . . . is sweeping through the state of Hawaii" ("War on Drugs"

1989). In October 1989, the *Los Angeles Times* quoted a US attorney who said, "People in Hawaii are the guinea pigs for the spread of smokable crystal methamphetamine into the U.S. . . . What's happening here is just a sample of what's to come" (Essoyan 1989, 17). In November, *Newsweek* proclaimed that ice, "a devastating drug from Asia has triggered a crisis in Hawaii and now threatens the mainland" (Lerner 1989, 37). That same month, the *Los Angeles Times* reported, "A new concentrated form of methamphetamines known as 'ice' has already overtaken crack on the Hawaiian Islands. . . . While drug experts statewide have yet to encounter that potent form in California, they predict it is only a matter of time" (Fiore 1989, 1). The following month, the *Washington Post* warned that "a hard, smokable form of methamphetamine that causes a half-day high and sometimes bizarre behavior . . . has become popular in Hawaii and spread to parts of California." A Washington, DC, police chief revealed local beat cops were on guard because "ice is coming this way" (Horwitz 1989, A1).

Embedded in these news excerpts are two commonly intertwined themes: novelty and nationalization. Joel Best (1990) refers to novelty claims as "orientation statements" because they help define (or redefine) "a familiar problem in the fresh light of a new perspective" (27). Though some journalists noted ice was one form of methamphetamine, the general tone of press coverage suggested ice was a new drug altogether. Aware that the news media prioritizes original stories, claims makers can strategically invoke the power of novelty when seeking to bring recognition to an allegedly new or previously unacknowledged social problem. "A fresh topic stands a better chance of receiving attention than one that has become all too familiar" (Best 1990, 79). Frequent use of the term *ice*—and not *methamphetamine*, *Methedrine*, or *crank*— aided attempts to construct fear over a "new" and seemingly exotic drug. Ice was not a novel drug, but rather a smokable form of meth made popular by the increased use of ephedrine precursors in illicit production (Cho 1990). For claims makers and audiences alike, understanding ice as a wholly new drug seemed preferable to viewing smokable methamphetamine as a demand-side consequence of failed attempts at supply interdiction and precursor control.

The "nationalization" of ice was conveyed through images of an unknown disease multiplying and spreading geographically (Jenkins 1994, 27). Even though the vast majority of ice use was confined to the Hawaiian Islands, the media often reported the drug was showing up in the contiguous United States. Portraying a local danger as a national menace helps project problems as having a wider significance (Jenkins

1994), while also communicating the fear that the deviant behavior, condition, or group poses an immediate threat to American culture and society (see Loseke 2003). Alarmist in nature, these images serve to demand responses from federal and state governments, often in the form of calls for increased resources to escalate combat operations in the war on drugs.

Political Power and the Rise and Fall of Ice

As indicated in the media coverage cited throughout the second half of this chapter, the ice scare benefited from the actions of claims makers and interest groups situated at the top of the hierarchy of credibility that structures the social production of news (see Molotch and Lester 1974, 1975). Spokespersons representing a variety of government organizations (e.g., police, the courts) dominated media constructions of the ice problem. Of the oft-publicized primary claims makers representing criminal justice or law professions, two in particular help elucidate the role of interest groups and "politico-moral entrepreneurs" (see Reinarman 2012) in constructing and *deconstructing* ice hysteria.

DEA interests. Regularly represented in national media coverage of drugs and drug problems, the DEA's involvement in constructing the United States' second methamphetamine scare might be best described as intermittent. About one year prior to the "ice age," major news outlets began reporting on meth production in clandestine labs located in the continental United States. Federal drug enforcement agents heavily promoted this problem through the mass media. For example, in a November 1988 *New York Times* article, Ron D'Ulisse of the DEA described domestic production as "an astronomical problem. . . . It can't be overstated. There's unanimous agreement out here that, hey, this drug is out of control" (as cited in Gross 1988, A1).[9] In a January 1989 *ABC Evening News* segment on domestically produced and distributed drugs, D'Ulisse defined meth labs on the US mainland as "a problem by Americans, for Americans" ("American Agenda" 1989). In July 1989, several DEA officials warned *USA Today* readers of the increasing popularity of homemade methamphetamine manufactured in labs throughout the western United States (Stewart 1989).

Though a close examination reveals coverage of the DEA in some of the earliest national news stories about ice (e.g., "Hawaii / Drugs" 1989; Lerner 1989), the federal drug agency ultimately adopted a subdued posture on the country's smokable methamphetamine problem

(Jenkins 1994, 1999). In particular, the DEA generally rejected claims of ice spreading from the Hawaiian Islands to the continental United States. An agent from San Diego's DEA office told the *Washington Post* that ice had not yet turned up in any of the newly discovered meth labs in Southern California (L. Thompson 1989). In a House committee hearing, the DEA's assistant administrator for operations, David Westrate, testified, "There still is no evidence to suggest that widespread distribution of ice is occurring on the mainland" (US Congress, House of Representatives 1989, 26). Westrate's testimony indicated his organization was more concerned with crack, heroin, and mainland-located meth labs than it was with Hawaiian ice.[10]

Indeed, much of the *reduction* in public fears about ice can be attributed to the DEA and criminal justice officials who seemed to reverse their positions about ice's national threat (Lauderback and Waldorf 1993; Jenkins 1999). Citing official reports from the DEA and others, a *USA Today* article printed in April 1990 read, "After a year of warnings that 'ice' would become the next major drug epidemic, . . . the threat has not materialized" (Meddis 1990, 3A). Jenkins (1999) suggests the DEA changed its stance because as a result of the crack scare, the agency had already secured many of the resources (or at the very least, formal promises of resources) administrators sought. Figure 5.6 graphs the DEA's annual operating budget from 1972 (when it was still the BNDD) up through 2013. Note the irregularly large budget increase from $654 million in 1990 to $875 million the following year (DEA 2013a, 2013b).[11]

Hawaiian politicking. Jenkins (1994, 1999) attributes much of the explosion and subsequent recession of the ice age to struggles for political power by Hawaiian bureaucrats. When it became increasingly clear that ailing senator Spark Matsunaga was unlikely to survive his term of office, US representatives Daniel Akaka and Patricia Saiki prepared to battle for the soon-to-be-vacated Senate seat. Hyping the ice threat seemed to be a safe political move, and both representatives worked to publicly demonstrate each was tougher than the other on the drugs issue (Jenkins 1999). In a November 1989 *Newsweek* article, Saiki insisted the federal government designate Honolulu as a high-intensity drug-trafficking area, so that the city would be eligible for more federal funding. Representative Saiki demanded that William Bennett, director of the Office of National Drug Control Policy (ONDCP), act immediately "to quell this [ice] plague before it gets to the mainland" (Lerner 1989, 37).

The rivalry turned in Akaka's favor in April 1990, when he was selected as the interim replacement for departed senator Matsunaga

Figure 5.6   Annual Budget of the Drug Enforcement Administration, 1972–2013

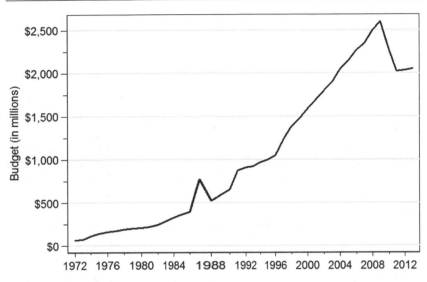

Sources: DEA (2013a, 2013b).

(Jenkins 1999). Two months later, Akaka took part in Senate delibera-
tions that helped shape the Crime Control Act of 1990. Introducing an
amendment that called for increased penalties for ice manufacturers,
traffickers, and dealers, Akaka declared,

> Ice has the potential to become the drug-abuse epidemic of the 1990s.
> We must adopt tougher criminal penalties in order to stop this menace
> in its tracks. Crystal meth is overtaking crack cocaine as the drug of
> choice among America's youth. This insidious drug has already inflict-
> ed such a heavy toll on Hawaii's youth that there is no doubt in my
> mind that strong and immediate action is warranted. (US Congress,
> Senate 1990, S9038)

Akaka's amendment passed with a vote of seventy-nine to twenty (US
Congress, Senate 1990). He went on to retain his Senate seat after
defeating Representative Saiki in the November 1990 election (Jenkins
1999). Although Senator Akaka slipped out of the national media spotlight shortly following the election, his plea to Congress to increase the
severity of punishments associated with smokable methamphetamine
offenses was ultimately codified into the federal law. Nearly fifteen

months after his nationally televised Oval Office speech about the scourge of crack cocaine, President Bush signed the Crime Control Act on November 29, 1990.

Ice Melts

When the media were choosing not to cover the methamphetamine situation throughout the majority of the 1970s and 1980s, the black market was transforming by leaps and bounds in response to the CSA of 1970 and subsequent restrictions on methamphetamine precursors. An important consequence of these regulations was the production of purer, smokable methamphetamine. The fleeting ice scare of late 1989 and early 1990 raised concerns over this newer form, and a popular solution, as communicated via mass media and ensuing policy, was to get tougher on ice suppliers.

By the time the Crime Control Act of 1990 became law, ice was no longer a major topic of media discourse. The 1990 election season had ended, the DEA knew its funding would soon increase, and the press had turned its attention to rapid developments in the Middle East and the First Gulf War that followed (Jenkins 1999). Moreover, exaggerated claims about the prevalence of ice could not be sustained, as evidence of its geographic diffusion never materialized (Lauderback and Waldorf 1993). "Public anxiety quickly evaporated when the ice menace failed to produce the feared 'speed epidemic'" (Morgan and Beck 1997, 138).

Ice had virtually vanished from the national news by 1991. However, in contrast to what happened following the Methedrine scare, methamphetamine's absence from the mass media would not endure another fifteen years. Public attention toward the drug escalated again in 1995, and the third methamphetamine scare that ultimately emerged proved to be the proverbial charm.

Notes

1. A clandestine laboratory is deemed a "superlab" if it can produce at least ten pounds of methamphetamine during a single production cycle (Scott 2002).

2. The origin of the term *Nazi method* is debated. Some claim Germany adopted this procedure toward the end of World War II. Another account posits the name derives from one of the original recipes, which was written on stationery adorned with Nazi symbols (DIB 2006).

3. R. Frank (1983) discusses several variations of these three general methods.

4. Methamphetamine produced using the P2P method was called "crank" because members of outlaw biker gangs who dominated much of the early illicit

production and distribution often stored the drug in the crankcases of their motorcycles (Jenkins 1999). Its original meaning has been lost over the years, as *crank* has become one of the commonly used terms for all forms of street meth.

5. While ice exists in solid rock form, methamphetamine powder may also be smoked, depending on the presence and quality of impurities. When smoking methamphetamine powder, individuals usually place the substance on a piece of aluminum foil and heat the underside with a lighter. The rising vapors are then inhaled using a straw (Derlet 1990; DIB 2006).

6. A NIDA-supported survey of young men living in the United States asked 581 nonmedical users of synthetic stimulants (the majority of whom used amphetamines, including methamphetamine) to self-report their methods of administration. The percentages of respondents who used each route of administration were as follows: oral, 96.7; intranasal, 20.3; intravenous, 8.4; and smoking, 2.2. These percentages sum to more than 100 because some users reported more than one route. Additionally, researchers gathered data through retrospective interviews conducted in the mid-1970s, when respondents were between the age of 19 and 31. Hence, the year of first use for members of the sample varied between 1957 and 1975 (O'Donnell et al. 1976).

7. People may also self-administer drugs sublingually (placing them under the tongue) or transdermally (letting them absorb through the skin) (Maisto, Galizio, and Connors 2008). Even less common routes of administration include rectal, vaginal, and ocular absorption, the latter of which is sometimes accomplished by applying a liquid solution with an eyedropper (Gahlinger 2004).

8. An additional observation of Bush's speech provides insight into how claims makers shape public definitions of drug problems. Bush (1989) said the word *drug* in its various forms (e.g., *drugs*) a total of eighty-two times. He mentioned *cocaine* fourteen times, *crack* nine times, *heroin* twice, and *PCP* once. Bush did not mention any of the following words in his speech: *alcohol, beer, drink, tobacco, nicotine, marijuana, prescription, medicine, pharmaceutical, amphetamine, methamphetamine, speed,* or *ice.*

9. D'Ulisse held a variety of jobs while with the DEA, including divisional security officer, electronic surveillance operations, clandestine laboratory investigations, and media relations. In 2003, he went to work as an executive for Purdue Pharma (D'Ulisse 2013).

10. Members of the Select Committee on Narcotics Abuse and Control seemed more intent than the DEA on hyping the spread of ice. Shortly after Westrate finished stating the DEA had no evidence of ice in the mainland United States, Representative Benjamin Gilman asked, "What has the DEA done to educate our police agencies and the public with regard to the dangers of the methamphetamine—ice—spreading throughout our Nation, just as it has spread in Hawaii?" (US Congress, House of Representatives 1989, 27).

11. The decrease in the DEA's 2010 budget (and data for subsequent years) may not be as abrupt as indicated in Figure 5.6. Budget information published by the DEA (2013a, 2013b) contradicts figures provided in ONDCP's Fiscal Year Budget and Performance Summary. For example, the DEA's website reports its 2011 budget as $2.02 billion (DEA 2013a), whereas ONDCP (2012) lists the DEA's fiscal year 2011 budget as $2.31 billion.

6

The Third Scare: Crystal Meth

We are in the midst of one of the worst drug epidemics in world history.
—*Alex Stalcup, as quoted in Chris Cuomo and Jon Scott (1998)*

Any historical analysis of methamphetamine in American culture must emphasize that the United States' first two episodes of meth mania were largely overshadowed by other substances of concern. During the 1960s and early 1970s, Methedrine had to contend with heroin, LSD, and marijuana for the media spotlight. In the late 1980s, ice played a rather peripheral role in a drug problems marketplace dominated by crack cocaine. Unlike the two previous panics, the third methamphetamine scare did not face a great deal of competition from claims makers touting the evils of other drugs.

Perhaps this lack of competition helps partly explain why the amount of hysteria generated during the "crystal meth epidemic" easily exceeded the combined amounts accorded to Methedrine and ice. Virtually all the US news sources included in Figures 6.1 and 6.2 show revived attention to methamphetamine in 1995. In general, coverage of meth by major news outlets grew gradually over the next ten years. Though each of the sources examined displays unique year-to-year fluctuations, as a whole, the media trend data indicate that national discourse over methamphetamine crested in 2005. Declaring meth "America's New Drug Crisis," the August 8, 2005, cover of *Newsweek* symbolized a decade-long consummation of growing hostility and dread toward the drug. Only two years later, national coverage of methamphetamine began a steady decline such that by 2012, meth was no longer a provocative national issue.

121

Figure 6.1   National Newsmagazine and Television News Coverage of Methamphetamine, 1987–2012

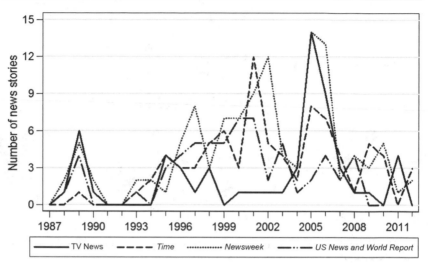

Sources: Vanderbilt Television News Archive, http://tvnews.vanderbilt.edu; *Time* Magazine Archive, www.time.com/time/archive; LexisNexis Academic, www.lexisnexis .com/en-us/Home.page.

Note: Television news data represent number of nightly national news segments broadcast by ABC, NBC, and CBS.

Figure 6.2   Major Newspaper Coverage of Methamphetamine, 1987–2012

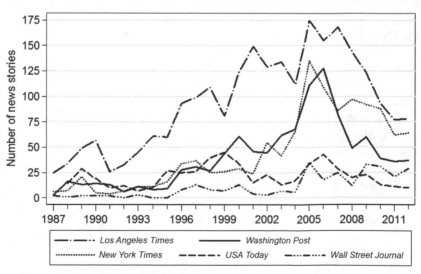

Source: ProQuest, www.proquest.com.

In this chapter, I examine the social construction of the third methamphetamine scare in the United States and detail how crystal meth surpassed crack cocaine to become *the* demon drug of the early twenty-first century. Although it shared several themes with the short-lived ice age of 1989 (e.g., appeals to novelty), the crystal meth scare ultimately carved out a unique cultural identity for methamphetamine, in part due to the discovery of a new set of folk devils: "tweakers," gay men, and Mexicans. In an analysis of the various claims makers involved in drawing attention to this third meth problem, I find that initial portrayals of methamphetamine under a "social pathology" framework were largely replaced by discourse of meth as a "threat to the innocent" (see Manning 2006). Specifically, early media descriptions suggested that crystal meth problems were local and regional, whereas later constructions painted methamphetamine as a Mexican-perpetuated menace victimizing the nation. These later portrayals profoundly inflamed public concerns over the drug and ultimately spurred governmental intervention.

Clichéd Claims

When methamphetamine returned to the national news in the mid-1990s, many of the initial claims were unoriginally reminiscent of times past. In particular, claims makers touted novelty and epidemic themes and made frequent comparisons to crack cocaine. Though somewhat clichéd, these claims were important to rejuvenating methamphetamine as a national topic of discussion.

Another "New" Drug

Novelty claims help establish a social problem's domain and attract the public's attention (Best 1990). Though methamphetamine has existed since 1893, much like some of the news stories published during the ice scare, the tone of several press reports circulated in the late 1990s suggested meth was a new drug. For instance, a *Washington Post* article cited a claim by the ONDCP that methamphetamine represented a "new and dangerous trend in US drug use" (Farah 1997, A01). The headline of one *US News and World Report* article declared, "A New Drug Gallops Through the West" (Witkin 1995). While the author later pointed out that methamphetamine was used during World War II, the headline illustrates the tendency for the news industry to frame an issue as novel in order to generate (or regenerate) consumer interest and establish the grounds for renewed public discourse.

New incidents of "old news" have to be recrafted as novel and original in order to maximize audience appeal (Best 1990). Most media
accounts embodying the novelty theme reconstructed older meth problems by presenting new forms, sources, or threats. While the term had
been employed sparingly since at least the late 1980s, *crystal meth* (or
crystal) became the popular name for methamphetamine during the third
scare. To some extent, utilization of this new name helped distinguish it
from the methamphetamine of past drug scares (i.e., Methedrine and
ice). Also, as some of the illicit production operations moved outside of
the United States, media claimed that the "new" methamphetamine
being produced in foreign lands was more dangerous and potent. In
addition, as law enforcement accounts of previously unknown or unre-
ported methamphetamine problems in various locales surfaced, the press
employed the newness theme by discussing novel threats to specific
towns and cities.

Constructing novelty to regenerate public interest in a decades-old
problem was not just limited to media accounts of the late 1990s. In
2006, *FOX Evening News* aired a brief segment on a "new, more powerful form of methamphetamine, meth ice," which was reported to be popular in California ("Drugs / Meth Ice" 2006). The next year, *NBC
Nightly News* featured a story about a "new, more dangerous form of
methamphetamine called ice" ("In Depth" 2007). Apparently, news
directors at FOX and NBC had not seen the reports about ice broadcast
by ABC and CBS back in 1989.

The Meth "Epidemic"

Another early theme in the third methamphetamine scare that would
persist for its duration was the use of the "epidemic" metaphor to
describe the magnitude of the problem. Shortly after signing the
Comprehensive Methamphetamine Control Act of 1996 into law,
President Bill Clinton delivered a speech about the drug's harms.
Identifying the bill as a preventive measure, Clinton (1996) said, "I am
particularly pleased that we are acting before this epidemic spreads"
(1746). According to several national media sources, it was too late.
Earlier that year, John Coonce, head of the DEA's meth lab task force,
told *Time* magazine that the drug was "absolutely epidemic" (Toufexis
1996). A year prior, he was quoted in *USA Today* describing meth as "an
epidemic that's getting worse" (Davis 1995, 7A). That same year, a *New
York Times* headline announced, "Mexican Drug Dealer Pushes Speed,
Helping Set Off an Epidemic in US" (Dillon 1995a, A7).

Despite Clinton's hopes, the plague continued to worsen over the next decade, according to his own appointees, the press, and other claims makers.[1] In 1997, Clinton's ONDCP director, colloquially referred to as the nation's "drug czar," General Barry McCaffrey, described the geographic spread of methamphetamine to a *Washington Post* reporter by saying, "The analogy to cancer may be a very helpful one. . . . It pops up in very unpredictable manners" (Suro 1997, A01). Law enforcement was reported to be "facing an epidemic" of meth labs in 2001, according to an *NBC Nightly News* segment ("Focus: Methamphetamines" 2001). Describing his community, a sheriff from Snohomish County, Washington, told the *New York Times,* "We've got a meth plague" (Egan 2002, A14). During the 2004 presidential campaign, Senator John Edwards called meth a "cancer" and promised a group of midwestern reporters that if he and running mate Senator John Kerry were elected president, they would allocate $30 million to fight the drug (Archibold 2004, A22). The editor of *Newsweek* wrote, "The nation's latest drug epidemic first hit with a vengeance in California" (Whitaker 2005, 4). A district attorney from Portland, Oregon, proclaimed meth "an epidemic and a crisis unprecedented" (Jefferson et al. 2005a, 41). In 2006, *Newsweek* reported, "The methamphetamine epidemic continues to ravage the country" (Skipp and Campo-Flores 2006, 9).

As these excerpts demonstrate, highly alarmist images of methamphetamine as an epidemic construct a reality of uncontrollable, indiscriminate death and disease. Methamphetamine was and remains a problem in cities and towns throughout the United States. However, to gain perspective, we must contemplate the meaning of the word *epidemic* by placing it in context. As Clayton Mosher and Scott Akins (2007) point out, Europe's Bubonic Plague of the 1300s killed one-third of the population, or 25 million people. One-eighth of Ireland's population perished during the Potato Famine of the mid-1800s. Conversely, a liberal estimate of the total number of US deaths directly—and indirectly—attributable to methamphetamine use is probably several thousand.[2] Also, according to the annually implemented NSDUH, 0.1 to 0.3 percent of US residents age twelve and older (which translates into roughly 314,000 to 731,000 people per year) were "regular" meth users (defined as having used methamphetamine at least once in the past thirty days) from 2002 to 2011 (SAMHSA 2012b). Like previous meth scares, the crystal meth panic contained a "kernel of truth" (see Reinarman 2012); people in the United States used methamphetamine, and some did very horrible things to both themselves and others as a result. Yet defining the problem as an "epidemic" is a bit careless when the term is considered in its historical context.[3] Indeed, the word *epidemic* is so often used in constructions of drugs and other social problems (e.g., gambling, text messaging) that it seems to have lost its original meaning.

Put simply, disease metaphors are so often invoked because they are effective. Referring to a chemical substance as a plague is common to virtually all drug scares. Images of systematic death and decay invoke fears among the public. When people are afraid they are quick to support groups and policies that promise protection. Hence, the social construction of fear is advantageous to claims makers who offer solutions to stop the spread of disease.

Crack of the 1990s

Given the frequent use of the word *epidemic* to describe the crack cocaine problem of the late 1980s and early 1990s, perhaps it is not surprising that claims makers involved in promoting the crystal meth problem chose similar terminology. Much like media coverage of the ice panic, the third scare continued to invoke comparisons with crack, the quintessential US drug scare of the late twentieth century. A *New York Times* article discussing the popularity of methamphetamine in urban areas of the West and Southwest ran the headline "Speed Catches Up with Crack" (Dillon 1995b, D2). Another *New York Times* article reported, "Locally made methamphetamine . . . has become the small-town Midwest's drug of choice, authorities here say, the kind of scourge that crack cocaine has long been to the inner city" (Wren 1997, A8). In 1996, drug czar McCaffrey warned that meth could become "the crack of the 1990s" (Bai 1997, 66). McCaffrey's quotation, along with similar statements from President Clinton, Attorney General Janet Reno, and other high-ranking officials, was publicized repeatedly by many news sources. Still on the crack theme in 1999, McCaffrey warned methamphetamine "could be the crack cocaine of the next century if we don't get ahead of the problem" (McGraw et al. 1999, 12).

Like many media reports of ice circa 1989, crystal meth was often portrayed as being worse than crack. While one reporter wrote that meth "is considered just as addictive as crack cocaine" (Owen 2004, I1), another cited "many experts [who] say it is more addictive and toxic than . . . crack" (Jacobs 2002, B1). The following is a sample of quotations from various claims makers comparing the two drugs:

- New York State police officer: "Meth makes crack look like child's play, both in terms of what it does to the body and how hard it is to get off" (Butterfield 2004a, A1).

- Iowa medical doctor: "Crack, wicked as it is, cannot compare to the destructive power of methamphetamine" (D. Johnson 1996, A1).
- UCLA researcher: "The appeal of meth is even greater than crack. . . . [It] is just as cheap but packs a more potent and prolonged high" (Jacobs 2006, B1).
- Healthcare professional in Spokane, Washington: "Eight years ago I thought injectable cocaine was the worst drug in the world. . . . Six years ago I thought crack was the worst and now I think it's crank" (Goldberg 1997, D16).

The crack craze of the 1980s and early 1990s was still fresh in collective memory when the crystal meth panic gathered steam in the late 1990s. In drawing analogies to crack, claims makers involved in the social construction of the meth problem borrowed much of the frightening imagery associated with crack. Indeed, media portrayals of the "tweaker"—a central folk devil of the United States' third methamphetamine scare—shared several similarities with the cocaine-smoking "crack head" of the previous decade, particularly with respect to images of desperation and propensity for violence.

Tweakers: Constructions of Crystal Meth Users

Beginning in the mid-1990s and continuing throughout the duration of the crystal meth scare, the "tweaker" arose as the reincarnation of the Methedrine-mainlining "speed freak" of the 1960s and early 1970s. Ostensibly, the term originates from automobile mechanic lingo that "speak[s] of 'tweaking' an engine to make it perform better" (Will 1996, A31). Some chronic methamphetamine users are known to tweak, or tinker with appliances and other mechanical gadgets. Miriam Joseph (2000) calls this phenomenon the "MacGyver Effect," named after the 1980s American television show protagonist who consistently escaped danger by assembling elaborate tools and contraptions out of paper clips, rubber bands, and other miscellaneous common materials. However, the term *tweaker*, when invoked to refer to a methamphetamine user, has evolved to describe someone who is deranged, deformed, or strung out from the drug.

A *US News and World Report* article explained tweakers as users who "load up on . . . homemade speed and stay up for three days grinding their teeth and taking apart carburetors for fun" (McGraw and Witkin 1998, 33). In another passage, the authors describe a former tweaker named John:

> After a divorce several years ago, John, 26, moved in with some
> friends and began snorting meth. Early on he found that the rush
> helped him work harder on his construction job and took the edge off
> the tedium. Soon he began staying up for three days at a time, drinking
> beer with buddies and staring at the TV for hours. But meth is a pro-
> gressive drug, and the more John used, the worse the high became. He
> became paranoid and started stealing tools from work to support his
> habit. He got into pointless fights in bars. . . . He thought he saw peo-
> ple outside his house looking for him; they turned out to be shrubs.
> (McGraw and Witkin 1998, 33)

Other media reports depicted meth tweakers as "bedraggled [and] rail-
thin, with greasy hair and open sores" (D. Johnson 2004, 41), "antisocial
zombies . . . [who are] hostile and delusional" (Owen 2004, I1), and
"cadaverous, pallid creatures with bad skin and phosphorescent eyes who
chatter as if possessed" (Holden 2007, E10). A DEA agent described the
typical tweaker as follows: "The user is mowing his lawn at 3 a.m. Or the
user unintentionally kills his or her baby by shaking it too hard. It gets
users so wired they can stay awake for three or four days. Which makes
them crazy, and dangerous" (Will 1996, A31). One article even acknowledged "tinkle tweakers"—users who are so desperate for the drug that
they "store their urine in bottles so they can reprocess it to extract
methamphetamine" (A. Johnson 2003, B4).

Meth Mouth

As these quotations indicate, many discussions related the effects of
methamphetamine on users' physical health or appearance, a theme that
was especially prominent during the height of the crystal meth scare
(circa 2004–2006). One of the commonly mentioned physiological consequences of taking the drug was "meth mouth," a condition referring to
the poor oral health (e.g., tooth decay, gum disease) of some chronic
users. A *New York Times* piece adequately summarizes media depictions
of meth mouth: "In short stretches of time, sometimes just months, a
perfectly healthy set of teeth can turn a grayish-brown, twist and begin
to fall out, and take on a peculiar texture less like that of hard enamel
and more like that of a piece of ripened fruit" (Davey 2005, A1).
Ghastly photos of meth users' mouths have appeared in many newspapers and magazines and on numerous television news programs.

   The majority of "meth mouth" mentions portray the phenomenon as
a direct and sole consequence of methamphetamine use. While the clinical research literature documents oral health problems among metham-

phetamine users (e.g., Klasser and Epstein 2005; Shetty et al. 2010), medical researchers and news reporters rarely consider the potential role of mediating factors that may contribute to meth mouth. Though they did not investigate illicit drug use specifically, Kenneth Hudson, Jean Stockard, and Zach Ramberg (2007) found that income, education, and regular (at least annual) visits to a dentist were negatively associated with tooth decay and tooth loss, even after controlling for alcohol and tobacco use. Consumption of sugary sodas, poor dental hygiene habits, and lower levels of income, education, and dental insurance among some methamphetamine users are likely to at least partly contribute to their development of meth mouth (Mosher and Akins 2007).

Faces of Meth

A second noteworthy portrayal of the tweaker's decrepit physical appearance is in media coverage of "faces of meth." What began as a newspaper article in a December 2004 issue of Portland's *Oregonian* eventually received national attention from a variety of other news sources and anti-meth crusaders. "The Faces of Meth," by Joseph Rose (2004), presented before-and-after photographs of methamphetamine users arrested for various crimes in Portland, Oregon. Put bluntly, many of the "after" photographs are revolting and sickening to the typical viewer. Meth users are shown to be weary, wrinkly, and wired. Several photos show users with open sores and bandages on their faces, a result of compulsively scratching away imaginary "meth bugs."[4]

In 2005, the year in which methamphetamine received the highest level of national media attention, *CBS Evening News* ran a "faces of meth" story during the final day of a three-part special series examining meth use in the United States ("Meth Crisis" 2005). Four months later, *NBC Evening News* featured the "faces of meth" during its four-day special series on the drug ("The Meth Crisis: Danger at Home (Part IV)" 2005). The photographs became very popular, making their way into other news outlets, law enforcement websites, and advertising campaigns. An August 2013 Internet search of "faces of meth" on Google returned 2.55 million results.

Montana Meth Project

Gruesome portrayals of tweakers were also central in media created by the Montana Meth Project (MMP) organization. In 2005, the MMP introduced a major methamphetamine prevention program, largely through the release of a series of television advertisements depicting the ills associated with use of the drug (Erceg-Hurn 2008). The majority of the ads feature children or teenagers who have turned into "tweaked-out" monsters bent on crime and destruction. In one advertisement, a teenager violently punches and kicks the door to his parents' house, commanding, "Let me in! I'm gonna kill you!" In another, a ghostlike teenage boy ferociously runs into a public self-service laundry facility, steals customers' money, and screams in the faces of terrified women and babies. In a third MMP ad, two young, emaciated teenage girls casually offer up their bodies to male strangers in order to acquire "meth money." After accepting the proposition, the commercial ends with the girls entering a grimy bathroom and the men removing their coats. Virtually all of the advertisements are punctuated with shrieks and music reminiscent of a horror film. The tweakers resemble zombies, as evidenced by their pale skin, blackened eyes, open sores, cracked lips, rotten teeth, and overall disheveled appearance. The majority of scenes in which meth use takes place are cold, dank, and dirty ("View Ads" 2013).

Beginning in Montana, the MMP "rolled out across the nation . . . [and received] considerable public funding" after the campaign was her-alded as a massive success in reducing use and increasing anti-meth atti-tudes (Erceg-Hurn 2008, 256). In 2006, *NBC Evening News* featured an MMP segment, airing several of the advertisements and interviewing Tom Seibel, the program's founder ("Drugs / The Meth Crisis" 2006). The next year, *ABC Evening News* aired two separate stories on the MMP, citing its effectiveness in reducing meth use in Montana ("A Closer Look" 2007; "Key to Success" 2007).

In a critical analysis of a series of state and national surveys, David Erceg-Hurn (2008) finds that contrary to media, political, and organiza-tional claims, the MMP has not significantly reduced use or pro-methamphetamine attitudes. For example, the percentage of Montana teenagers who "strongly disapproved" of methamphetamine use decreased steadily, from 98 percent in 2005 to 91 percent in 2008. The percentage of Montana teens who reported lifetime use of methampheta-mine was 2 percent in 2005, reached 6 percent in 2006, and dropped to 3 percent in 2008. Erceg-Hurn (2008) attributes some of the MMP's apparent lack of effectiveness to exaggerated portrayals of methamphet-amine hazards, as reported by about one-half of those surveyed. A sub-sequent study employed a more robust statistical analysis of the MMP's utility and similarly concluded the prevention program had "no effect on meth use" (Anderson 2010, 741). Additional opportunities for research on the prevention outcomes of MMP abound: since 2008, the organization has launched similar meth projects in Colorado, Georgia, Hawaii, Idaho, and Wyoming ("The Meth Project" 2013).

Meth mouth, "faces of meth," the MMP's morbid images of tweakers, and other horrific depictions of meth users' physical appearance have a "shock and awe" appeal. Although monster-like constructions of addicts may not actually deter meth use, they have great potential to instill a sense of alarm among news consumers, especially those who know little to nothing about the drug. Additionally, such representations function to stigmatize meth users as deformed "others" through a perpetuation of the dope fiend mythology.

From Serial Killing to Necrophilia: Portrayals of Violence

Beyond their depictions as zombie MacGyvers, tweakers were also often shown as impulsively and overpoweringly violent. Behaviors characterized by aggression and psychosis were two of the most common media-cited effects of meth use. For example, one reporter described the methamphetamine high as "an intense 'rush' followed by a state of high agitation that can lead to volatile behavior" (Howlett 1997, 1A). Another article told the story of a man who, after using meth, "fled his workplace to get a gun, terrified that helicopters were coming after him." The same article also asserted that tweakers "greeted . . . police with psychotic tirades" during standard traffic stops (Kirk Johnson 1996, 1A). In *Time* magazine, a hospital doctor recounted the following interaction with a meth user: "One night a boy came in so out of control he thought I was the police and the police were trying to kill or kidnap him. He was incredibly violent—biting, slapping, grabbing doctors' private parts. We got hold of his folks and found out he's usually a good student. Even if he does this only once every two years, given his psychotic reaction to the drug, he could end up killing someone" (Kirn 1998). In another news story, a UCLA pharmacologist brushed off a reporter's inquiry about a beheading committed by an Arizona meth user, stating, "That is really pretty mild compared to the kind of cases we're seeing. . . . We're seeing everything from serial killing to necrophilia" (Davis 1995, 7A).

Another set of news reports was devoted to rich descriptions of specific murders and other heinous, hideous acts committed by methamphetamine users (e.g., Howlett 1998). The decapitation mentioned above and briefly in Chapter 1 was repeatedly referenced in gory detail by multiple news sources. For example, Debbie Howlett (1997) cited a

Minnesota state trooper who referred to the murder "as an example of how dangerous the drug is. In that case, Eric Smith—high on meth for 24 hours—stabbed his 14-year-old son 29 times and then cut off the child's head. He told police he thought the boy was possessed" (1A).

Reporters at the *Los Angeles Times* wrote about the mayhem created by Shawn Nelson, a methamphetamine user and former army tank crewman who broke into a San Diego armory, stole a military tank, and went on a "destructive urban rampage" in May 1995. "[Nelson] wreaked about 22 minutes and six miles of havoc: He rammed at least 40 vehicles, slightly injuring a mother and child by smashing into their van, attempted to hit pursuing police cars and plowed into bridges, utility poles, fire hydrants, signal lights, a bus bench and finally a concrete freeway divider, where the tank became stuck in a cloud of dust" (Rotella and Kraul 1995, A1). According to the *Vancouver Sun,* witnesses claimed, "Nelson, whose head was sticking out through the hatch, was smiling and laughing as the tank rumbled along" ("Man Shot" 1996, A15). Nelson was eventually shot to death by police. Footage of his infamous tank offensive was broadcast by news organizations throughout the country and even appeared on an episode of the reality-genre television show *World's Wildest Police Videos.*

Although a few of the original news stories about Nelson's tank joyride mentioned he had ongoing struggles with alcohol and methamphetamine, neither drug was cited as the sole cause of his erratic behavior. Rather, the initial press coverage described a man who had recently experienced a string of grave misfortunes, including loss of employment, financial problems, and failed relationships. Almost two months after the incident, the *San Diego Tribune* reported that the toxicology analysis found Nelson "had a blood-alcohol level of .24 percent and a trace amount of methamphetamine in his system" (J. Hughes 1995, B1). This news article appears to be one of the only ones discussing the official postmortem toxicology results.

Original depictions of the complex cascade of bad breaks Nelson experienced prior to the tank rampage that ultimately resulted in his death were soon replaced with a simplistic, one-dimensional explanation. Pop culture references to Shawn Nelson make little mention of his heavy level of alcohol intoxication (three times the legal limit in many states) or series of late-life troubles.[5] Rather, his behavior is generally attributed to methamphetamine, a trace amount of which was found in his body. For example, eight months after the incident, a *New York Times* article about San Diego's many methamphetamine problems made specific mention of Nelson in passing. "A San Diego man . . .

stole a tank from a National Guard armory last year and took it for a joy ride on a freeway before being shot to death by the police. Friends said he had abused [meth] for years" ("In San Diego" 1996, A19). Nelson's demolition also appeared in the opening scene of an hourlong A&E documentary about the growing methamphetamine problem in the United States, narrated with, "A man wired on crank gets behind the wheel of an M-60 tank. For 30 minutes, he provides the nation with a window into his twisted and violent world" (Kurtis 1997). In 1998, a cable news program special feature titled "Meth Madness" showed video of the event, explaining that Nelson procured the tank during "a meth stupor" (Cuomo and Scott 1998).

Shocking narratives of decapitations and stolen tank rampages function as typifying examples of the crystal meth problem. Atrocity tales are often used to typify social phenomena; they serve as a point of reference from which the overall problem is publicly defined (Best 1990). This approach is evident in the aforementioned article by Howlett (1997), in which the state trooper uses the beheading to characterize the general scope of the methamphetamine problem. It is also evident in the A&E documentary's opening scene, in which the narrator warns, "Those who know crank say an M-60 tank is just the beginning" (Kurtis 1997), or in the cable news program's lead-in to Shawn Nelson's tank joyride: "San Diego County is an example of what happens when methamphetamine reaches [an] urban environment. It's not a pretty picture" (Cuomo and Scott 1998).

Atrocity tales embody the routinization of caricature, a rhetorical technique in which claims makers construct extreme instances as normative (Reinarman and Levine 1997b). From 2002 to 2011, an annual average of roughly 1.1 million US residents age twelve and older used methamphetamine at least once (SAMHSA 2013a). Presenting worst cases as typical serves to shape public perceptions of the behavior of all users. These criticisms are especially important regarding news presentations of methamphetamine, a drug that—unlike alcohol, marijuana, or even cocaine—has been relatively uncommon in the United States and strongly patterned by class and region. Drug users who "exist beyond the realms of our daily intercourse are the subject of immense misperceptions," and the mass media play a major role in the construction of such distorted images (Young 1971, 105–106). Atrocity tales likely provide much of the epistemological basis of methamphetamine and its users, particularly for news consumers with no prior experience with the drug, including the large segment of society geographically separated from the traditional meth "hubs" located throughout the western and midwestern United States.

Changing Frames of Crystal Meth

As shown earlier in Figures 6.1 and 6.2, methamphetamine reentered the national news around 1995, but the crystal meth scare did not begin to truly blossom until the turn of the century. At about this time, claims makers began to more fully distinguish methamphetamine from other demonized drugs. Though comparisons to crack persisted throughout the duration of the third methamphetamine panic, social constructions of the drug evolved such that by 2005 meth was no longer just the "poor white man's cocaine." In this section, I examine several transformations in the frames through which crystal meth was defined by primary claims makers (e.g., law enforcement) and the national news media. The upsurge in methamphetamine-related public discourse during the early 2000s occurred concomitantly with increased claims of geographic and socioeconomic diffusion, meth use among gay men, meth's many innocent victims, and the involvement of foreigners in the illicit trade.

From Local to National, from Poor to Affluent

During the first few years of the crystal meth scare, users tended to be portrayed as socially marginalized "others" who were poor, rural, uneducated, white, and mostly confined to western pockets of the United States. Media depictions of the physical environments in which methamphetamine was used were often illustrated with scenes of trailer parks, rusty pickup trucks, and farms. In 1996, a journalist at the *New York Times* wrote that meth was mostly preferred "by blue-collar white males, sometimes in rural areas" (Wren 1996, A16). One university researcher described users as "moms trying to juggle jobs and three kids and day care, and women working as waitresses on their feet for 12 hours a day. And it's truck drivers, carpet layers, people who work long hours doing tedious, repetitive tasks" (Goldberg 1997, E16). An article published on the front page of *USA Today* described typical meth users as "white, working-class men in their 20s or 30s" (Howlett 1997, 1A). Politico-moral entrepreneurs helped shaped this image. For example, ONDCP director Barry McCaffrey remarked, "It's possible we're seeing methamphetamine, the poor man's cocaine, replacing, to some extent, crack cocaine" (Suro 1997, A01).[6] McCaffrey also appeared in an *NBC Nightly News* story about escalating meth use in rural areas of the US West and South (James 1998).

At the same time that claims makers acknowledged regional and socioeconomic patterns of meth use, they also warned that the drug was moving eastward and away from the margins of society. Such claims represented the "nationalization" theme (see Jenkins 1999) and were often made in the context of the epidemic metaphor of methamphetamine spreading like an uncontainable disease. Attorney General Reno remarked, "When I first took office, people talked about [methamphetamine] being a problem in the West. . . . Let us disabuse ourselves of that notion and recognize that it is spreading across this country" (Wren 1996, A16). One *New York Times* reporter noted that historically, meth was a problem in the southwestern United States, but that "the drug is now making its way across America, ruining lives and families along the way and raising the concern of policy makers in Washington" (D. Johnson 1996, A1).

The unprecedented level of media attention devoted to crystal meth in the early 2000s was likely at least partly due to the increasing tendency of news outlets to portray the drug as a threat to "regular" citizens in all geographic corners of mainstream America. For example,

- "[I]t's not just six figures and stock options that keep Tim going. When his workload gets overwhelming, Tim cranks up on methamphetamine, sometimes for weeks at a stretch" (Beiser 2002, 34).
- "The methamphetamine epidemic has often been associated with drug labs hidden away in the countryside, but today's users frequently defy that image, whether they are urban professionals or suburban homemakers" (M. Irvine 2005, A5).

The 2005 *Newsweek* cover story perhaps best captures the nationalization and professionalization themes embedded in many of the later media depictions:

Once derided as "poor man's cocaine," popular mainly in rural areas and on the West Coast, meth has seeped into the mainstream in its steady march across the United States. Relatively cheap compared with other hard drugs, the highly addictive stimulant is hooking more and more people across the socioeconomic spectrum: soccer moms in Illinois, computer geeks in Silicon Valley, factory workers in Georgia, gay professionals in New York. The drug is making its way into suburbs from San Francisco to Chicago to Philadelphia. In upscale Bucks County, Pa., the Drug Enforcement Administration last month busted four men for allegedly running a meth ring, smuggling the drug from California inside stereo equipment and flat-screen TVs. Even Mormon Utah has a meth problem, with nearly half the women in Salt Lake City's jail testing positive for the drug in one study. (Jefferson et al. 2005a, 42)

From Capitalistic to Sinful

Donileen Loseke's (2003) insights into the ways in which successful claims makers frame social problems suggest that audience members, politicians, business leaders, and others would be less anxious about the methamphetamine problem if speed were often constructed as compatible with capitalistic values. Indeed, its traditional association with the Protestant work ethic is one of the primary reasons meth has historically received a relatively low amount of media and political attention, when compared with other drugs (e.g., marijuana, crack). Evident in some of the quotations in the previous section, the workplace performance enhancement theme remained popular during the crystal meth scare. However, in the early 2000s, pro-capitalist constructions of methamphetamine began to be contested by newer images of addicts motivated by more hedonistic desires. Specifically, depictions of meth as a "party" drug, especially among gay men, became quite common. Gay-themed media coverage was particularly popular in news stories about meth use in the northeastern United States, an area with comparatively low overall usage rates.

News reports of crystal meth use among gay populations often described the drug's role in dangerous sexual practices. A *Newsweek* exposé described in detail the "ugly underground of meth-fueled sex" among gay men in New York City. The opening paragraph is worth quoting in its entirety:

> It's Saturday evening in Manhattan, and three dozen men are crammed into a one-bedroom suite in an upscale hotel across from Ground Zero. After shelling out $20 apiece to the man who organized tonight's event over the Internet, the guests place their clothes in Hefty bags for safe-keeping and get down to business and pleasure. A muscular man in his mid-30s sits naked on the sofa and inhales a "bump" of crystal methamphetamine. Within minutes, he's lying on the floor having unprotected sex with the host of tonight's sex party, whose sunken cheeks, swollen neck glands and distended belly betray the HIV infection he's been battling for years. In the bedroom, a dozen men, several of them sweaty, dehydrated and wired on meth, are having sex on the king-size bed. There's not a condom in sight. "It's completely suicidal, the crystal and the 'barebacking' [unprotected anal sex]," says one of two attendees who described the scene. "But there's something liberating and hot about it, too." (Jefferson et al. 2005b, 38)

Many of the news stories about gay users communicated concerns about methamphetamine's potential to foster the spread of the human immunodeficiency virus (HIV) and with it acquired immune deficiency syndrome (AIDS). An *ABC Evening News* segment told of the "growing use of meth by a number of gay men in big cities, which correlates to risky behavior and a spike in AIDS" ("Drugs/Meth Wars" 2005). According to the *Washington Post*, "AIDS experts were uniformly worried . . . about . . . a strain of highly virulent and drug-resistant HIV [that] had been found in a gay man in New York." New York City's health commissioner said that "the man had 'many' episodes of anal intercourse with men met through the Internet. Many of the encounters . . . occurred under the influence of crystal methamphetamine" (Brown 2005, A16).

Some of the media reports of meth use within gay subcultures had empathetic themes, but most causal explanations were located at the individual level. Depictions of gay methamphetamine users as uncontrollable, irresponsible, sickly, and self-loathing fit with the dope fiend mythology's image of the drug addict as a moral degenerate who uses drugs because of abnormal or inferior personality traits (see Lindesmith 1940a, 1940b; Reasons 1976). And while the crystal meth panic certainly was not the first time users were constructed as moral degenerates, the increased news coverage of meth-driven gay sex challenged the well-established workplace performance-enhancer theme that had once dominated popular explanations of user motivations. At last, many of the moral entrepreneurs involved in the third US methamphetamine scare had accomplished what claims makers from the previous two could not: firing up public indignation toward meth by portraying the drug as a hedonistic, sinful threat to heteronormative, capitalistic society, and to widely cherished values of self-control, utilitarianism, and hard work. As folk devils, gay methamphetamine users represented an exceptionally deviant kind of tweaker.

Crystal Meth's Many Victims

In addition to promoting moral outrage over methamphetamine's use in the gay club scene, and intensifying fears of a geographically and socioeconomically spreading epidemic, news coverage of the crystal meth scare dedicated a great deal of attention to the many innocent nonusers victimized by the drug. Blameless victims, especially those who are "weak, [and] engaged in a respectable activity," are rhetorically advantageous to social problems campaigns (Best 1990, 34). In the crystal meth panic, children, quaint communities, Mother Nature, and law enforcement officials emerged as oft-cited victims.

Children. As in many other drug panics, media coverage of the third meth scare was rife with stories of harmed children. Accounts of children neglect-

ed by meth-using parents, "meth babies," and kids harmed in clandestine
meth lab accidents were popular topics.[7] For example, one *ABC Nightly
News* broadcast included a story of three children who died in a suspected
meth lab explosion in California ("California / Methamphetamines" 1995).
An *NBC Nightly News* report featured "meth orphans" abandoned by their
addicted parents, and a discussion by one user who spoke of meth use by
kids in local schools ("Drug Abuse" 2004). *Newsweek* claimed that "a new
generation of 'meth babies' is choking the foster-care system in many
states" (Jefferson et al. 2005a, 41).

Many news sources quoted alarming statistics about the impact of
methamphetamine on children and child welfare programs. For instance,
one newspaper article reported that seventeen children were taken away
from their homes in Boone, North Carolina, in 2003 after their parents
were discovered operating meth labs. Nationally, "the young 'meth
orphans'—3,300 of whom were removed from homes with meth labs
nationwide last year—have become a particularly acute health concern"
(Hickman 2004, A14). Another newspaper stated that from 2004 to
2005, the number of foster children rose 16 percent in Oklahoma and 12
percent in Kentucky, yet it did not indicate specifically what proportion
of the increase was attributable to methamphetamine. In addition, the
author cited Oregon officials who insisted the child welfare "caseload
would be half what it is now if the methamphetamine problem suddenly
went away" (Zernike 2005a, 1). The article also conveyed DEA statistics on the national scope of child endangerment: "Over the last five
years 15,000 children were found at laboratories where methamphetamine was made. But that number vastly understates the problem . . .
because it does not include children whose parents use methamphetamine but do not make it and because it relies on state reporting, which
can be spotty" (Zernike 2005a, 1). Similar statistics provided by the
DEA appeared on an *NBC Nightly News* segment, which also included a
comment by drug czar John Walters on the damage of methamphetamine to children in the United States ("The Meth Crisis: Danger at
Home [Part II]" 2005).

Ascertaining the validity of the many statistics quantifying methamphetamine's role in displacing children and overburdening social service
agencies is difficult. However, in the social problems marketplace, one
threatened or harmed child is one too many (Best 1990). This discussion
is not intended to undercut the plight of the countless kids and families
harmed by methamphetamine. At the same time, we must acknowledge
the fact that much of the child endangerment problem is a historical consequence of the black market's response to supply-side measures taken

in the 1960s. Prior to these restrictions, zero children were placed in foster care as a result of parental methamphetamine production. Stimulant-seeking parents did not operate meth labs at that time because speed was attainable through less hazardous channels. Virtually all media presentations of methamphetamine's effect on children and society neglected this fact, along with many of the other historical antecedents that helped shape the contemporary problem. Instead, children were portrayed solely as helpless, innocent victims of their parents' methamphetamine addictions (cf. Linnemann 2010).

In addition to news coverage of "meth babies," "meth orphans," and child lab victims, one perhaps more idiosyncratic threat to children warrants mention. A handful of news reports surfacing around 2007 warned about "strawberry quick," a pink-colored, strawberry-flavored form of methamphetamine. A headline in *USA Today* read, "DEA Sees Flavored Meth Use; Trend May Be Effort to Lure Young Market." The article opened, "Reports of candy-flavored methamphetamine are emerging around the nation, stirring concern among police and abuse-prevention experts that drug dealers are marketing the drug to younger people" (Leinwand 2007, 3A). According to one DEA agent, "drug traffickers are trying to lure in new customers, no matter what their age, by making the meth seem less dangerous." After a bag of pink meth was found in Missouri, a local police officer referenced a recently issued police bulletin about strawberry quick in Nevada, saying, "It seems to have progressed very quickly from west to east." The bulletin read, "Teenagers who have been taught meth is bad may see this flavored version as less harmful. 'Strawberry Quick' is designed for the younger crowd" (Leinwand 2007, 3A). Scott Burns of the ONDCP commented, "The traffickers know the word is out about what a horrible drug this is. . . . They are having a tough time selling this product, especially to young people . . . [so] they have to come up with some sort of gimmick" (Leinwand 2007, 3A). Reports of strawberry quick appeared in several other newspapers, including the *Seattle Times* (Gambrell 2007), and were also circulated via e-mail (Mikkelson 2012).

Claims that dealers were creating strawberry-flavored meth to intentionally entice children into using the drug are characteristic of urban legends and suspect for several reasons:

1. Children are lousy customers because they usually do not have a great deal of money to spend on drugs.
2. Although people have likely combined methamphetamine with sugar or candy in order to achieve a smoother or more enjoyable

administration of the drug, such methods are doubtfully often used in a concerted attempt to get kids hooked (see point 1).

3. The *USA Today* article reported the police officer did not actually taste the confiscated meth. Rather, he stated the drug "had a slight strawberry smell to it" (Leinwand 2007, 3A).

4. Different chemicals used in the production process can result in different colors of methamphetamine (Gahlinger 2004).

This fourth point is particularly significant since some legal distributors of anhydrous ammonia, a chemical used to dissolve ephedrine and pseudoephedrine, add a pink dye to their product in an attempt to deter thefts committed by methamphetamine cooks. "The dye produces a pink meth" (DIB 2006, 242). As early as 2004, a DEA publication acknowledged that fertilizer manufacturer Royster-Clark began adding a substance called GloTell to their anhydrous ammonia products. The company declared that clandestine manufacturers who used GloTell-laced agricultural chemicals as precursors would end up with methamphetamine of "an unbleachable pink color" ("Company Announces" 2004, 183).

The Partnership at Drugfree.org (formerly known as the Partnership for a Drug-Free America) responded to media-reported law enforcement alerts about strawberry (and cola and chocolate) meth, saying, "Flavored meth is somewhat akin to the Loch Ness Monster: everyone has heard of it, but firsthand sightings are hard to track down and verify" (Join Together Staff 2007). The organization also warned that the wide publicity of candy-like meth may have the unintended consequence of attracting more young users, creating "a trend where none exists." When contacted, one of the original sources of claims about strawberry quick could not determine whether the methamphetamine seizure was actually flavored or merely dyed pink (Join Together Staff 2007).

Urban legends, a feature of contemporary folklore, convey the risks of the modern world (Fine 1985; Best 1990). Though specific in content, urban legends embody greater, more unmanageable fears felt by members of society (Best 1990). In a noteworthy turn of events, a revised version of the strawberry quick story was circulated via e-mail in October 2007. The new tale was titled "Halloween Warning for Parents" and was purportedly issued by a special agent of the US Department of Homeland Security (Mikkelson 2012).[8] Joel Best (1990) discusses the popular urban legend of Halloween sadism, illustrated by claims that seem to surface every October warning about the dangers of trick-or-treating (e.g., razor blades in candy). After investigating seventy-eight incidents of Halloween sadism printed in major US newspapers between 1958 and 1989, Best (1990) found that the overwhelming majority of reported cases were either greatly exaggerated or outright falsehoods. Urban legends "reflect the conditions of modernity and raise the concerns of the age. They represent attempts by the public to deal with the massive social dislocations affecting them" (Fine 1985, 63–64). Fears about strawberry quick help to demonize meth dealers, but they also symbolize a more general fear about the overall safety of children in rapidly changing times.

Communities. Another innocent victim depicted in media coverage of crystal meth was Anytown, USA. Communities described as inhabited by good, honest, faithful, and hardworking people were shown to be under siege by methamphetamine. A *Time* magazine article about a Pennsylvania Amish settlement offers a prototypical example of the destruction of Anytown. The author describes Abner Stoltzfus, an Amish teenager who, as a result of meeting a member of a motorcycle gang, began selling cocaine and methamphetamine at town dances to finance his addictions. "It's a familiar story, barely noteworthy, except for one detail: Abner Stoltzfus is Amish." The article concludes by warning about the potential damage drugs can cause to the stability of the Amish community (Labi 1998).

Another news story, published in *Newsweek,* further illustrates crystal meth's role in the obliteration of quaint American towns:

> As spring settles in, the Red River is certain to swell, threatening the tidy homes and industrial shops that line its banks. But folks here will tell you that Fargo's streets are already flooded—with the drug methamphetamine—and more than a few lives have been washed away. Just last month, a meth addict who burned his house down while hallucinating, killing his own mother, pleaded guilty to manslaughter. . . . Residents have been locking their doors since an elderly woman was shot to death by four teens on meth last year. Life on the prairie may never be the same. (Bai 1997, 66)

The general lesson to be learned from these and other accounts of simple, old-fashioned communities being victimized by meth is that if methamphetamine can ruin Amish Country or Fargo, North Dakota, it can devastate any place at any moment.

Other news reports examined small cities and towns affected by meth-related property crimes. For example, an article about the destruction wrought by methamphetamine on Laramie, Wyoming, read, "Like many towns in the West and Midwest, [Laramie] has been unnerved by the scourge of methamphetamines, and by the resulting property crimes and social decay that accompany drug addiction" (Kirk Johnson 2006, A19). Fox Butterfield (2004b) wrote that in the small town of Lovell, Wyoming, because of methamphetamine, "property crime has skyrocketed, as addicts commit burglaries or break into cars" (A10). The *New York Times* cited a statistic claiming that 85 percent of Oregon's property crimes were "committed by [meth] addicts, many of whom steal ID's, passports and tax information" (Heffernan 2006, E8). According to Mosher and Akins (2007), this "85 percent" statistic appeared in at least fourteen articles published in the *Oregonian* from 2002 to 2006.

Very few press reports explained the relationship between drug use and property crime as a consequence of the black market. Illegal substances tend to cost a great deal more than they would in a free market, particularly when illicit supplies face interdiction threats (Nadelmann 1989). While law enforcement agencies often proclaim victory upon learning illicit drug prices have risen (under the assumption that high prices will deter use), hard-core addicts often resort to criminal activities to support their increasingly costly habits. Furthermore, if statistics purporting that the great majority of property crime rates are attributable to methamphetamine were true, longitudinal variations should strongly correlate with usage data. Perhaps this lack of relationship is why Mosher and Akins (2007) ask, "If methamphetamine (or any other illegal drug, for that matter) were eliminated, would all property crime also be eliminated?" (31). Referring to one analysis, Mosher and Akins (2007) point out that Oregon's property crime rate was greater in the "pre–meth epidemic" years than in the early 2000s (31).

Mother Nature. The natural environment was a third frequently cited victim of crystal meth. As I discussed in Chapter 5, clandestine methamphetamine labs generate hazardous waste, and lab operators often dispose of chemical by-products carelessly. Media gave a great deal of attention to the ecological damage done by domestic illicit methamphetamine production. The *New York Times* described Mother Nature's victimization as follows:

> At the abandoned laboratories, often a trailer, a vacant house, a campground or the back of a car, officials find acid, flammable solvents, sodium hydroxide, lithium and ammonia, often accompanied by pressurized cylinders like fire extinguishers or scuba tanks. "We see it everywhere," said Paul O'Brien, the leader of a spill response team for

the Department of Ecology. "Sometimes they'll just dump it by the side of the road. It gets washed down into streams and kills salmon or poisons other forms of life." (Egan 2002, A14)

A *USA Today* headline read, "Drug Labs Poisoning Forests." The article's author wrote that "several national forests have become chemical dumping grounds for illegal drugmakers" (Kevin Johnson 2001, 3A). Another news source cited "toxic chemical waste dumped in water or spilled on soil during or after the often-crude manufacture of" methamphetamine (Sanchez 2001, A03). In a story about meth lab dump sites found in hunting grounds across the upper Midwest, Mark Johnson, the director of the Minnesota Deer Hunters Association, asked, "How can people abuse our natural resources like this?" (Keen 2006, 3A).

As these media reports demonstrate, methamphetamine cooks were constructed as the principal victimizers of the environment. Though perhaps less tangible for audiences than children or Anytown, USA, Mother Nature's portrayal as another blameless victim of crystal meth indirectly serves to construct and reinforce the victimization of all humans, who suffer health consequences from lab-polluted water, land, and air.

Law enforcement. Members of law enforcement organizations were a fourth commonly represented victim of the US meth problem.

> After seven years of chasing drug traffickers, Richard Fass was no novice when it came to dangerous undercover work. His easy charm and fluent Spanish made him one of the Drug Enforcement Administration's most effective agents. From his Phoenix base, Fass saw methamphetamine, a synthetic drug cooked in rural Mexican and American labs, pouring into the city. Meth was becoming the new scourge of the '90s, and Phoenix one of the top three markets for the white crystals. On June 30, 1994, Fass was on his last day at work undercover. He was being transferred to a desk job in Mexico, and his wife and four children were waiting for him to go shopping for the move to Monterrey. But Fass had one more drug gang to bust, a job that turned out to be his last. (Robinson 1998, 35)

This *US News and World Report* article subsequently described the tragic and appalling details of the federal agent's murder, mentioned the dangers faced by drug enforcement officers, and attributed partial blame to a corrupt Mexican government. Reported in numerous national news publications over the next several years, the Fass tragedy symbolized the death of drug war soldiers fighting the good fight, but losing to the forces of evil.

Beyond being discussed as physical casualties of the illicit trade, law enforcement officials were also regularly portrayed as underfunded, understaffed, and overwhelmed in their fight against meth. For example, one police officer said that citizens in his community were justified in complaining that law enforcement was not doing enough to stop the local methamphetamine problem. One hundred meth labs were busted in the officer's county in 2003. "With more resources . . . it could have doubled or tripled that number. The unit is spending nearly as much time and money on meth as it spends on every other drug combined" (D. Johnson 2004, 41). One news story described the budget of the Jefferson County Sheriff's Office in Missouri as so "meager" that it could not even purchase a "fingerprint kit, a camera to photograph suspects, or . . . bulletproof vests," let alone deal with its burgeoning meth problem (Butterfield 2002, A1). Another press report stated that methamphetamine "is particularly prevalent in poorer and rural communities with few resources to combat it . . . [and] poses a significant safety threat to law enforcement officials" (Eggen 2005, A2).

Numerous media outlets quoted a statistic showing that 58 percent of county law enforcement agencies cited methamphetamine as their most urgent drug problem (e.g., "Drugs / Meth Wars" 2005; Goddard 2005; Jones 2005; Leinwand 2005; Zernike 2005b). *Newsweek* announced, "In a survey of 500 law-enforcement agencies in 45 states released last month by the National Association of Counties, 58 percent said meth is their biggest drug problem, compared with only 19 percent for cocaine, 17 percent for pot and 3 percent for heroin" (Jefferson et al. 2005a, 42). It is instructive to point out how the manner in which *Newsweek* presented these data aids in the social construction of the "58 percent" statistic.

- Five hundred law enforcement agencies were surveyed, a relatively large (and thus, significant) number.
- Only five states were excluded from the study, indicating its wide scope.
- The survey was conducted by the National Association of Counties (NACo), a rather official- and objective-sounding organization.[9]
- Fifty-eight is a much larger number than 19, 17, and 3, the statistics associated with three other detested drugs. These numerical differences imply that threats posed by cocaine, marijuana, and heroin pale in comparison to the nation's methamphetamine problem.

As a more general note, "58 percent" conveys a much greater level of severity than, say, a statistic indicating that 0.2 percent of US residents age twelve and up were "current" methamphetamine users in 2005 (according to SAMHSA 2009a).

Media reports of the "58 percent" statistic failed to provide any discussion of the methodological procedures employed by NACo survey administrators. As several critics have noted (Gillespie 2005; Mosher and Akins 2007), the actual survey from which this statistic derived is flawed from the use of leading statements and questions. Implemented as a telephone survey, the interview for "The Criminal Effect of Meth on Communities' Law Enforcement" study began as follows:

> As you may know, methamphetamine use has risen dramatically in counties across the nation. Formerly a rural problem, it is slowly moving into a more urban setting. At the same time, it has not yet arrived on the national radar screen. The National Association of Counties is conducting a telephone survey of public safety officials in counties to determine the impact of meth use on public safety activities. Can you take a few minutes to answer a few questions that will provide information for a national report that will be released in July? (Kyle and Hansell 2005, 9)

Ten of the survey's eleven questions dealt specifically with methamphetamine. Though it omits a number of important methodological details (e.g., response rates, as suggested by Gillespie [2005]), the original NACo report indicates that zero of the twenty-seven counties in Connecticut, Massachusetts, and Rhode Island—three states with very low rates of methamphetamine use—were included. Additionally, seven of the 500 responding counties had a population of 500,000 or more, while 312 had populations of less than 25,000 (Kyle and Hansell 2005). These details are important because they suggest that methamphetamine affects a lower proportion of the populace than is indicated by the statistic of 58 percent. None of the aforementioned national news sources included a discussion of this information.

Jonathan Simon (2007) argues that victims, especially law enforcement victims, are central "to the meaning of crime and to the force of law" (131). In public opinion and policymaking discourse, law enforcement officials serve "as a prime example of the victims of crime, injured both by criminals and by the lax handling of criminals by courts and corrections" (Simon 2007, 98). Police officers exist to protect the rights and freedoms of citizens. When law enforcement is portrayed as victims of a methamphetamine pandemic, subject to the harms of deficient policies that do not protect or provide them with enough resources, the logically implied solution is to grant them more funding and control. This line of discussion is not meant to deny the fact that the many honorable men and women employed as narcotics officers or in other areas of law enforcement do not face real dangers on the job. Rather, I seek to point out that in an arena where agencies compete for public monies, claims about the extent of illegal drug problems affect reallocation of resources. With money at stake, constructing law enforcement officials as victims functions to increase their power not only in fighting drugs but in shaping popular understandings of how drug problems *should* be fought (see Altheide and Michalowski 1999). The close and regular proximity of police organizations to mass media (see Chermak 1994) assured law enforcement of a central role in defining the parameters of the crystal meth problem.

From Domestic to Foreign, from White to Brown

A final major transformation in social constructions of crystal meth concerns depictions of race and nationality. Whereas methamphetamine has historically been associated with white Americans, media coverage of the country's third scare grew saturated with claims condemning foreigners for their involvement in the illicit trade. Several news stories invoked North Korea (e.g., J. Brooke 2003) and Middle Eastern terrorist groups (e.g., "US Drug Ring" 2002) as methamphetamine producers and traffickers, but these reports were usually presented in the context of larger international issues (e.g., fears about North Korea's nuclear weapons program, post-9/11 terrorism hysteria) and only mentioned meth as an ancillary concern.

Although domestic labs received much media attention during the third methamphetamine scare, Mexican producers and traffickers emerged as a primary threat to innocent children, communities, and law enforcement. As ephedrine and pseudoephedrine became more difficult to obtain legally, a sizable proportion of the production operations shifted to outside the United States. Consequently, many of the trafficking networks evolved to include persons from Mexico, Asia, and elsewhere.

The *New York Times* headline mentioned previously merits repeating: "Mexican Drug Dealer Pushes Speed, Helping Set Off an Epidemic in US" (Dillon 1995a, A7). Though merely one of hundreds published during the crystal meth scare, the article captured a theme present in many news stories on the subject. After avoiding a federal indictment for cocaine trafficking, Jesus Amezcua of Mexico "retreat[ed] to safety south of the border, [and] shifted from cocaine to a drug then surging in popularity across the American West, and now sweeping east: methamphetamine, or speed" (Dillon 1995a, A7). Sam Dillon (1995a) casually noted that Amezcua owned a $50,000 BMW. The journalistic practice of describing the lavish lifestyles of drug dealers and traffickers was common in press reports.[10] Such depictions likely instilled a sense of envy or injustice in the typical, legitimately employed news consumer. Dillon (1995a) continued, "Elbowing aside the American motorcycle gangs who once dominated production and trafficking, the Mexican drug mafias have in recent years flooded the Western United States with methamphetamine" (A7). The image of Mexican gangsters "flooding" the country with drugs completely neglects the demand side of the US methamphetamine problem. Like many US drug policies and policy-makers, news reporters tended to single out illicit suppliers as the root cause of society's troubles with meth.

Dillon was certainly not alone in assigning responsibility to Mexico. A *US News and World Report* article claimed, "Powerful Mexican drug cartels have hit rural America," and stated that most of the meth in one rural Iowa county "is not the home-grown variety. Newly powerful Mexican drug lords have muscled in on virtually every aspect of the illegal drug business to such a degree that there is a direct pipeline of methamphetamine from Mexico to Marshalltown" (McGraw and Witkin 1998, 33). A map displaying various locations and "hubs" for methamphetamine trafficking was accompanied by the claim that in Iowa, "an established market of users and an influx of cash-strapped illegal immigrants have enabled the meth trade to flourish" (McGraw and Witkin 1998, 33). A *Time* article described Mexican drug traffickers as "border monsters" who "pay off . . . or kill off . . . anyone who stands in [their] way." Two Mexican brothers were said to have smuggled "hundreds of tons" of drugs, including methamphetamine, into the United States each year (Padgett and Shannon 2001). In 2006, *CBS Evening News* showcased a two-part series on the Mexican drug trade. The second part reported that despite a decline in domestic meth labs, the United States was witnessing an "explosion of meth use," purportedly because of Mexican trafficking syndicates ("The War Next Door" 2006).

Several news stories explicitly mentioning that most methamphetamine users were white leaned toward explaining white, US-born addicts as victims of foreign suppliers. An article about methamphetamine use in rural Georgia, published in the *New York Times,* illustrates this tendency. After describing a history of drug problems among local white (and black) residents, the author wrote, "But where local methamphetamine cooks might turn out a couple of pounds of the drug at a time, Mexican traffickers offer much larger quantities and lower prices, . . .

attracting dealers from nearby areas of Tennessee and North Carolina"
(Golden 2002, A1). Another article stated that the "vast majority of meth
users are white," but most distributors are Mexican: "Although methamphetamine isn't completely new to the area, the business was once dominated by motorcycle gangs and truckers. Then it exploded in the
Shenandoah Valley within the past decade, as the Latino population rose
by more than 400 percent" (Boorstein 2004, C08). Like the previous
article, this account attributes the main cause of the United States'
methamphetamine problem to Mexicans and other Hispanic groups.

Echoing this theme, a third news story described Candy, a white
woman, mother, and former defense attorney who "was a pit bull when
it came to protecting kids" but later lost everything through her addiction to meth. After acknowledging that the preponderance of methamphetamine users in the United States were white and briefly discussing
the early illicit domestic trade, the author noted that by the 1980s,
"Mexican cartels . . . discovered a lucrative market in cooking up the
drug and exporting it north. Over the next 15 years, meth's use exploded
in Southern California and spread from there. By the mid-'90s, Eugene,
Ore.—where Candy had hung out her shingle as a juvenile-defense
attorney—was flooded with the stuff" (Singer 2006, W22). The implica-
tion is clear: Candy became addicted to Mexican-produced methamphetamine because Mexican distribution networks had successfully inundat-
ed her town.

Inferred from these news reports is the general sentiment that before
Mexicans became involved in the trade, the US methamphetamine problem was minor, almost tolerable; but since white motorcycle gangs and
other domestic groups had ceded control to brown foreigners, action
was needed to stifle what had become a deplorable scourge. The periodic portrayal of white American crystal meth addicts as victims of sneaky,
greedy, and ruthless Mexican trafficking syndicates is remarkably different from previous depictions of Methedrine, ice, and many other
drugs that have faced public scorn. In my admittedly incomplete reading
of media coverage of the crack cocaine scare, I do not recall any news
stories describing black crack addicts as victims of Colombian cocaine
kingpins. This interpretation is consistent with research by Jennifer
Cobbina (2008), who found that US newspaper accounts were more
likely to portray white methamphetamine users as victims of methamphetamine than they were to present black users as victims of crack
cocaine.

Even though Asian suppliers were cited as a foreign menace in news
coverage of the ice age, their connections to Hawaii—and not the US

mainland—meant that they were too distant to endure as a serious threat. Thus, the racial component of the crystal meth scare makes it notably distinct from the first two methamphetamine panics. Considering that the most successful US drug scares have linked drugs to racial/ethnic minorities (Reinarman 2012), the ability of claims makers to regularly identify Mexicans as a dangerous group responsible for the problem must at least partly explain why the crystal meth scare prospered in ways the Methedrine and ice scares did not. Levels of meth hysteria fully proliferated only after constructions of methamphetamine producers shifted from white and domestic to brown and foreign.

Ancient civilizations practiced live sacrifice in order to ward off or bring an end to plagues and other outside threats (Szasz 1974). In spite of the fact that white Americans continued to be portrayed as the typical user group, foreign suppliers—particularly Mexicans—served as a common scapegoat for the rising crystal meth "epidemic" and the focus for combating it. Rather than defining the methamphetamine problem in terms of a US demand for stimulants, a media largely focused on Mexican folk devils helped minimize the extent to which the domestic roots of the problem (i.e., America's apparent need for speed) were entertained in public discourse.

* * *

Over the course of approximately ten years, methamphetamine culturally evolved from a localized nuisance into a national catastrophe. Perhaps with the exception of 1989's ice panic, from the early 1970s to the mid-1990s the minimal media attention accorded to methamphetamine tended to construct the drug from a social pathology framework (see Manning 2006). Meth was perceived to be made by Americans, used to enhance the job performance of blue-collar laborers, and confined to "poor white trash" in rural enclaves of the western United States. By 2005, instrumental motivations had been somewhat supplanted by images of a gay party drug, and crystal meth had become understood as a countrywide problem affecting persons from all socioeconomic backgrounds.

Through the use of evocative case studies and often questionable statistics, the news media painted a horrible picture of victimization. Claims makers construct victims to evoke sympathy from audiences. Implicit in constructions of innocent victims are motivational frames (i.e., appeals to news consumers to take an interest in the problem and call for change). "Why should audience members care? They should care because good people are unjustly harmed" (Loseke 2003, 79). The most persuasive strategies tend to portray victims as pure, "anyone," middle class, hard-working, and suffering greatly (Loseke 2003). These characteristics were heavily apparent in depictions of methamphetamine corrupting innocent youth, ruining charming, tight-knit US towns, raping Mother Nature, besieging police departments, and imprisoning white addicts. In marked contrast to popular images of meth over most of the previous three decades, the voluminous media coverage of the wide variety of blameless victims indicates that the crystal meth scare—especially in its later stages—framed methamphetamine as a threat to innocence (see Manning 2006). Accompanied by constructions of tweakers and Mexicans as new folk devils to rally around, the transition from definitions of methamphetamine use as pathological to a framework of innocent victims coincided with crystal meth's high point in public discourse.

Solutions to the Crystal Meth Problem

According to Loseke (2003), claims makers involved in the social construction of social problems strive to diagnose the problem, motivate people to care about the problem, and offer ideas on how to solve the problem. Up to this point, I have outlined the diagnostic and motivational frames inherent in the crystal meth scare. Methamphetamine came to be defined as a national disaster caused by careless clandestine meth cooks and evil foreign traffickers. The social construction of meth's many victims provided audiences with ample reason to be concerned about crystal methamphetamine and demand action.

The extent to which the dope fiend mythology was a guiding ideology in the crystal meth scare perpetuated calls for individual-level and supply-side solutions. Despite their periodic victim status, meth users were largely viewed as weak minded, violent, and morally corrupt tweakers whose addictions were the result of inferior personalities and bad personal choices. Domestic meth makers were depicted as neglectful of their children and environmentally irresponsible. Traffickers were portrayed as materialistic Mexican drug lords or illegal immigrants who sought to hook as many US citizens as possible on meth. The overall methamphetamine problem was discussed as a problem of supply rather than demand (or rather than a problem of both supply *and* demand). As is typical in media constructions of social problems (see Altheide 1997), the complex social, historical, and legal forces involved in shaping contemporary meth problems were generally ignored in favor of a discourse of fear in which personal troubles and convenient moral truths prevailed. This collective understanding of the United States' crystal meth problem (i.e., the ways in which it was socially constructed) logically implied the need for increases in resources for social control agents, harsher punishments for users and suppliers, and stricter laws limiting the availability of precursors. I have already discussed more resources for law enforcement agencies as one media-conveyed solution to the meth problem. Hence, in the remainder of this chapter, I focus on other commonly proffered strategies to ending the epidemic.

Punish Users

Calls for punitive sanctions on methamphetamine users, as a solution, can be summarized with a quote from the feature in *Newsweek* that deemed meth "America's Most Dangerous Drug." Published at the height of the crystal meth panic, one of the article's concluding statements read, "The sobering fact is that, like addiction itself, this epidemic can only be arrested, not cured" (Jefferson et al. 2005a, 48). Certainly, some news reports featured claims makers calling for more drug treatment programs or included former users who had successfully recovered from their addictions. However, punishment was more often invoked as a favorable solution to treatment, partly due to the widespread belief that methamphetamine is a uniquely addictive drug. A medical director of a city hospital said, "I don't have any great treatment options right now. This drug really terrifies me, and I think what we're seeing is the tip of the iceberg" (Jacobs 2004, B1). One journalist wrote, "Most specialists believe . . . [methamphetamine addiction] is one of the hardest to treat, requiring that a patient stay in treatment for up to two years" (Butterfield 2004a, A1). Echoing this sentiment, another reporter wrote, "Health experts say . . . [methamphetamine] addiction is particularly hard to treat" (Paley 2006a, C1).

Many years ago, one scholar wrote, "Some of the most persistent misbeliefs [among the public] are that a single dose of a drug can cause addiction, and that an individual once addicted is beyond all hope of rehabilitation" (Hein 1968, 99). If, as many have asserted, this claim were true for methamphetamine, approximately 9.8 million US residents would be addicted to meth, the estimated number of persons in the United States who have used the drug at least once in their lifetimes (SAMHSA 2012a).

Contrary to many of the media reports, methamphetamine addiction is treatable. For example, Amy Copeland and James Sorensen (2001) found no difference in treatment success among methamphetamine and cocaine users, suggesting "that highly specialized substance abuse treatments for methamphetamine patients may not be needed" (91). In one study of a midwestern drug treatment court program, researchers discovered that treatment lowered recidivism rates for persons arrested for methamphetamine offenses, but not for those arrested for driving while intoxicated (Bouffard and Richardson 2007). Ryan King (2006) summarizes results from studies in fifteen states showing that treatment programs help many methamphetamine users successfully recover from their addictions.[11]

Claims of instant and permanent addiction embody the ideology of pharmacological determinism and conflict with reality. The framing of drugs in this manner necessarily implies criminal justice approaches as the only viable solution and spreads misinformation and fear among media consumers. When members of the public later learn such claims are grossly exaggerated, they become more likely to respond cynically when presented with truthful information about other social problems.

Punish Producers and Distributors

Increased penalties for methamphetamine manufacturers and traffickers were offered as a third solution to the methamphetamine problem. For example a *New York Times* article explained, "One problem [a] sheriff [from North Carolina] faces is that [the state's] current penalties for manufacturing methamphetamine are light, the same as for growing one marijuana plant. A first-time offender faces a maximum sentence of six to eight months in jail and can get out on bond for as little as $1,000. 'So they can be back cooking before we finish the paperwork' [the sheriff said]" (Butterfield 2004a, A1). Even legislators from Connecticut, the state with one of the historically lowest levels of methamphetamine use, vowed to get tough on suppliers. After introducing a bill that would give stiffer penalties to methamphetamine dealers and manufacturers, Connecticut governor Jodi Rell proclaimed, "The changes I am proposing will move us forward in the fight against meth" (Holtz 2006, 14CN2). No evidence exists to suggest Connecticut had any serious methamphetamine problem to fight at that time. The state ranked dead last in the percentage of residents age twelve and older who used the drug at least once annually from 2002 to 2005 ("State Estimates" 2006). Also, from 2004 to 2006, a total of seven meth lab incidents were recorded in Connecticut, compared to 6,543 in Missouri over the same time period (DEA 2013c).

Several news reports discussed the implementation of a "meth registry" as another practical solution to the methamphetamine problem. Like the sex offender registry, meth registry laws require that persons convicted of making or dealing methamphetamine disclose their names and addresses in a publicly available database. Justifying his state's adoption of a meth registry law, a spokesperson for Minnesota governor Tim Pawlenty explained, "We want to arm citizens with information, so they can protect themselves and their communities" (Leinwand 2006a, 1A). Another article cited legislators who called the public database a "safety measure" that "will allow landlords, real estate agents and neighborhood residents to check for meth offenders" (Leinwand 2006b, 3A). Little consideration was given to the possibility that the degree of public shaming created by meth registry laws could effectively prevent the reintegration of offenders into society and instead push them back into meth making or other deviant activities.[12]

Restrict and Interdict Supplies

A fourth solution claims makers proposed was stricter controls on the availability of ephedrine and pseudoephedrine. Citing an "epidemic-like" spread, environmental pollution, and child endangerment, lawmakers from around the country voiced support for precursor restrictions. Nebraska governor Dave Heineman espoused a bill that would require pseudoephedrine products to be stored in locked containers behind store counters, saying through a spokesperson, "Anything we can do to take that drug from the shelves and make it harder to obtain is a help" (L. Copeland 2005, 5A). A member of the legislative counsel for the International Association of Chiefs of Police declared, "The chain [of methamphetamine supply] is only as strong as the weakest link. . . . States that have less-strict laws are going to become the stopping point for people looking to pick up pseudoephedrine" (Paley 2006b, B5). In a letter to the editor of the *New York Times,* Arizona attorney general Terry Goddard wrote, "Meth has a devastating impact on users, their families and communities. We need more tools to combat it. Passing . . . [a] federal bill to impose tighter controls on the sale of pseudoephedrine would be an effective start" (Goddard 2005, A22).

A series of national and state precursor laws were enacted from 1988 to 2006 to combat clandestine methamphetamine manufacture. As I will discuss in the next chapter, producers and traffickers adapted to each new law and continued supplying illicit meth to those who demanded it. Occasionally, national news presentations of meth precursor regulations referenced the historical cat-and-mouse game between illicit producers and law enforcement (e.g., Witkin 1995). However, the general solution emanating from these reports was more supply-side efforts. The message was that if legislators were just a little tougher—if they enacted just one more interdiction-based policy, if they allocated just a few more resources to law enforcement organizations—they would ultimately outsmart and overpower meth makers, thereby finally solving the methamphetamine problem in the United States.

Notes

1. In 1998, President Bill Clinton wrote, "The methamphetamine and crack cocaine epidemics, which in recent years were sweeping the Nation, have begun to recede" (as cited in McCaffrey 1998, iii). The mass media did not appear to regard his proclamation very seriously.

2. This liberal estimate is based on three factors. First, up until 1978 the total number of worldwide deaths linked to methamphetamine was seventy-nine (Kalant and Kalant 1979). Second, the total number of methamphetamine-involved deaths in the United States in 2005 was estimated to be 895. However, this figure does not disentangle the proportion of these deaths that occurred in combination with alcohol use (Nicosia et al. 2009). Third, the Drug Abuse Warning Network (DAWN), which records annual drug-related visits to US hospital emergency departments, offers no data on deaths from methamphetamine use because yearly counts are too low to provide reliable estimates.

3. This is precisely why I have placed quotes around the term *epidemic* periodically throughout this manuscript.

4. Some chronic methamphetamine users experience formication, the sensation that many bugs are on or beneath the surface of the skin. This condition encourages constant scratching and picking of the skin, which often results in sores and scabs.

5. An exception is the 2002 documentary *Cul de Sac: A Suburban War Story*, produced by Icarus Films. Directed by Garrett Scott, the film offers a sociologically rich analysis of Shawn Nelson by situating his life story in the context of the declining US working class.

6. As Jenkins (1999) points out, the description of meth as the "poor man's cocaine" would be repeated "hundreds of times" by news organizations (21).

7. Use of the term *meth babies* (i.e., children born to mothers who used methamphetamine while pregnant) is one additional example of how claims makers involved in the meth scare borrowed rhetoric (i.e., "crack babies") from the institutionalized crack scare (Jenkins 1999).

8. According to Barbara Mikkelson (2012), calls to the phone number listed in the Halloween e-mail were greeted with this recorded message from Special Agent Todd Coleman of the US Department of Homeland Security: "If you're calling regarding crystal meth information, that information is false and inaccurate."

9. According to its website, NACo (2012) "is the only national organization that represents county governments in the United States." As a lobbying interest group, NACo strives to provide "essential services" to county governments in the United States, including funding for county law enforcement agencies.

10. For example, a *Washington Post* article described the residence of a suspected Mexican meth trafficker as a "Mediterranean-style mansion in Mexico City's posh Las Lomas de Chapultepec neighborhood" (Duggan and Londo 2007, A01).

11. See Weisheit and White (2009, 209–214) for additional discussion of the challenges and successes of methamphetamine treatment.

12. During the height of 9/11 hysteria, in 2003, a Boone, North Carolina, prosecutor charged a methamphetamine lab operator under a North Carolina "weapons of mass destruction" law, enacted in November 2001. The prosecutor argued that the law was applicable because of the toxic and combustible chemicals used in illicit production: "The law reads, in part, that the term *nuclear, biological or chemical weapon of mass destruction* applies to 'any substance that is designed or has the capability to cause death or serious injury and . . . is or contains toxic or poisonous chemicals or their immediate precursors'" ("Prosecutor Fighting" 2003, emphasis added).

7

Context
and Consequences

As you know, we always ask for more resources in the budget process.
—*David Westrate, DEA (US Congress, House of Representatives 1989, 30)*

My social constructionist approach to the methamphetamine problem in
the United States posits that longitudinal patterns in media coverage are
based more on the successes and failures of claims makers than on temporal trends in rates of drug use and drug-related harms. Parts of
Chapters 4 and 5 demonstrated that from the mid-1960s to the early
1990s, national news attention toward methamphetamine essentially
shared an inverse relationship with levels of meth consumption, as estimated by the few available historical sources. Fortunately, over the past
couple of decades, a variety of data measuring multiple angles of
methamphetamine incidence have emerged. These data provide an
excellent opportunity to examine the crystal meth scare in its epidemiological context.

In the first part of this chapter, I briefly explore the extent to which
several contemporary methamphetamine prevalence indicators parallel
changes in both the quantity and content of media coverage. After
observing that the relationship between news attention and epidemiological data is not as straightforward as the generally negative association
observed during (and between) the nation's first two methamphetamine
scares, I discuss the larger sociohistorical context surrounding the climax
of the crystal meth panic. Specifically, I argue that the United States'
third meth scare fully flourished when claims makers directly or indirectly connected methamphetamine to other (i.e., nondrug) social problems
campaigns prominent during the early 2000s. Through a brief analysis of

news coverage trends of the two most demonized drugs over the last thirty years, I also argue that methamphetamine reached "epidemic" levels
of media attention during the early 2000s in part due to the efforts of
criminal justice organizations seeking to supplant faded crack cocaine
hysteria with a new drug crisis. Finally, though one of my main arguments throughout has been that social problems—as constructed by interest groups, moral entrepreneurs, and news organizations—are not always
correlated with objective social conditions, I must reiterate that drug
scares have real, lasting effects on society (Renairman and Levine 1997d;
Adler and Adler 2012). In this spirit, in the third part of this chapter I
investigate how some of the more contemporary drug policies instituted
as solutions to the methamphetamine problem have influenced changes
in the black market.

Epidemiology of Methamphetamine, ca. 1995–2012

In this section, I draw on several data sources in order to understand the
epidemiology of methamphetamine during the crystal meth scare. In
addition to examining national prevalence patterns, I discuss several
demographic correlates of methamphetamine (e.g., regionality, race).
Each data source varies in its longitudinal scope, though when it is
available, I include information from 1995 to 2012.

   Figure 7.1 presents annual rates of methamphetamine and cocaine
use among high school seniors and US residents age twelve and older
with data from MTF and the NSDUH, respectively. Past-year "crystal
methamphetamine (ice)" use by twelfth graders hovered between 2 percent and 3 percent from 1995 to 2005 and declined thereafter. In 1999,
MTF introduced a separate survey question asking high school seniors
about their past-year consumption of "methamphetamine." That year,
4.7 percent reported using methamphetamine, a statistic that steadily
declined to 1 percent by 2010 (Johnston et al. 2012). NSDUH data indicate a slow decline in methamphetamine use among the general population of US residents age twelve and up, from a high of 0.7 percent in
2002 to a low of 0.3 percent in 2011, the years for which comparable
data are available. One half of 1 percent of this population was estimated to have used methamphetamine in 2005. Both surveys indicate that
past-year use of cocaine was much more common than that of methamphetamine over the time periods covered (SAMHSA 2006a–2006c,
2009a, 2009c–2009e, 2011, 2012a, 2012c; Johnston et al. 2012).

**Figure 7.1 Past-Year Stimulant Use Among Twelfth Graders
and Persons Age 12 and Older, 1995–2011**

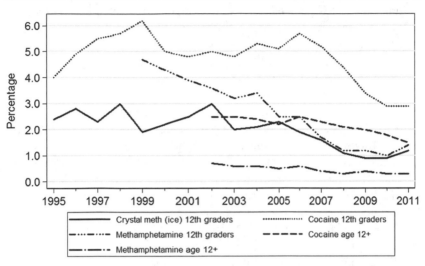

Legend:
— Crystal meth (ice) 12th graders   ········· Cocaine 12th graders
—····—···· Methamphetamine 12th graders   — — — Cocaine age 12+
—·—··· Methamphetamine age 12+

Sources: SAMHSA (2006a–2006c, 2009a, 2009c–2009e, 2011, 2012a, 2012c; Johnston et al. (2012).

Due to confidentiality concerns, geographic data on methamphetamine users are not publicly accessible in the annual results published by the NSDUH. Thus, to streamline my discussion of demographic correlates, I examine the NSDUH's Restricted-Use Data Analysis System (R-DAS), which provides information combined from the 2002 to 2009 surveys. Over this time period, 0.6 percent of males and 0.4 percent of females above the age of eleven were estimated to have used meth at least once annually. An annual average of 949,000 non-Hispanic whites (0.6 percent of all non-Hispanic whites age twelve and up) reported past-year use between 2002 and 2009. Rates for other races/ethnicities were as follows: black (0.1 percent), Native American (1.1 percent), Native Hawaiian (1.6 percent), Asian (0.2 percent), multiracial (1.3 percent), and Hispanic (0.5 percent) (SAMHSA 2013b).

R-DAS data show a negative relationship between methamphetamine use and education. Excluding respondents under the age of eighteen, 0.9 percent of persons without a high school degree were annual meth users from 2002 to 2009, compared with 0.7 percent of high school graduates, 0.6 percent of those with some college education, and 0.2 percent of college graduates. Of the nine urban/rural classification codes defined by the US Department of Agriculture, past-year methamphetamine use was most common in small cities not adjacent to metropolitan areas (1.0 percent), less common in rural areas (0.6 percent to 0.7 percent, depending on population size and proximity to metro areas), and least common in metro areas with populations of over 1 million inhabitants (0.4 percent) (SAMHSA 2013b).

R-DAS data collected from 2002 to 2009 also indicate substantial regional variation in methamphetamine consumption. On average, 1 percent of persons living in the western United States were estimated to have used meth at least once in the past year, compared with 0.4 percent in the Midwest and South, and 0.1 percent in the Northeast. Data at the state level show that methamphetamine use was most common in Nevada (1.6 percent), Arkansas (1.4 percent), Wyoming (1.2 percent), and Idaho, Nebraska, and Oregon (1.1 percent), and least common in Connecticut (less than 1.0 percent, or an average of about 1,000–2,000 residents annually) and Massachusetts, New Hampshire, New Jersey, New York, and Vermont (0.1 percent) (SAMHSA 2013b).

Data from a much more limited population—adult males arrested in various counties throughout the United States—also show substantial regional variation in methamphetamine use. Implemented quarterly from 1998 to 2003, and again beginning in 2007, the Arrestee Drug Abuse Monitoring Program (ADAM) has asked probability-based samples of men arrested for various crimes to provide urine specimens to test for the presence of different drugs.[1] Table 7.1 lists the percentage of adult male arrestees who tested positive for methamphetamine at different ADAM study sites from 2000 to 2003. Honolulu, Hawaii, had the highest percentage of positive tests, ranging from 35.9 percent in 2000 to 44.8 percent in 2002. Other western counties, including Multnomah County, Oregon; Maricopa County, Arizona; and Sacramento County, California, had relatively high rates of adult male arrestee methamphetamine use. Less than 1 percent of arrestees tested positive in New York City, Philadelphia, Detroit, and Washington, DC. For example, from 2000 to 2003, a total of 3,352 adult male arrestees in the New York City sample provided a urine specimen. Six tested positive for methamphetamine (ADAM 2000, 2001, 2002, 2003).[2]

ADAM data also show that arrestees prefer cocaine over methamphetamine by a ratio of more than two to one. For those ADAM sites in which data were collected every year from 2000 to 2003, 28.4 percent of arrested men tested positive for cocaine, 12.8 percent for methamphetamine (ADAM 2000, 2001, 2002, 2003).

Table 7.1 Adult Male Arrestees Testing Positive for Methamphetamine in Various US Counties (percentages), 2000–2003

	2000	2001	2002	2003
Honolulu	35.9	37.4	44.8	40.3
Sacramento	29.3	29.4	33.5	37.6
San Diego	26.3	27.9	31.7	36.2
San Jose	21.5	30.2	29.9	36.9
Portland, OR	21.4	20.4	21.9	25.3
Spokane	20.4	19.5	22.3	32.1
Phoenix	19.1	25.4	30.9	38.3
Des Moines	18.6	22.0	20.2	27.9
Las Vegas	17.8	20.6	22.9	28.6
Salt Lake City	17.1	17.2	22.8	25.6
Oklahoma City	11.3	10.9	14.3	12.3
Omaha	11.0	15.6	21.0	21.4
Seattle	9.2	11.1	10.9	12.1
Tucson	6.9	5.4	9.2	16.0
Albuquerque	4.7	9.5	6.7	10.1
Denver	2.6	3.4	3.8	4.7
Dallas	2.1	1.7	3.1	5.8
Minneapolis	1.6	2.4	3.9	3.3
Charlotte	1.4	0.5	0.2	0.6
Indianapolis	0.7	0.6	1.5	1.9
San Antonio	0.2	2.6	2.3	3.5
Anchorage	0.2	0.8	1.5	0.7
Birmingham	0.2	0.1	0.6	1.2
New Orleans	0.2	0.0	1.3	2.6
Cleveland	0.1	0.1	1.5	0.3
Chicago	0.0	0.2	0.3	1.4
New York City	0.0	0.1	0.5	0.0
Philadelphia	0.0	0.0	0.0	0.6
Capital Area (Albany, NY)	0.0	0.0	0.0	0.0
Atlanta	0.5	—	2.3	2.0
Laredo	0.0	0.0	0.0	—
Detroit	0.0	0.0	—	—
Fort Lauderdale	0.0	—	—	—
Miami	0.0	—	—	0.4
Kansas City (Jackson County)	—	1.0	—	—
Woodbury County (IA)	—	—	15.3	14.3
Los Angeles	—	—	14.8	28.7
Tulsa	—	—	14.4	17.5
Washington, DC	—	—	0.0	0.7
Tampa	—	—	—	1.6

Sources: ADAM (2000, 2001, 2002, 2003).
Notes: Dashes indicate no data were gathered that year. Data are weighted.

Another source of nationally gathered methamphetamine data is the El Paso Intelligence Center (EPIC). Figure 7.2 shows the annual number of clandestine meth production operations uncovered in the United States by law enforcement officials.[3] EPIC distinguishes between lab *seizures* and lab *incidents*. Since the latter are defined as the discovery of meth labs, dump sites, chemicals, or glassware, the annual number of lab incidents is larger than the number of actual labs seized. Law enforcement seizures of meth labs peaked in 2003 at 10,094, or an average of 27.7 per day. The number of meth lab incidents was highest in 2004, when 23,829 were reported. These numbers declined over the next three years and then increased from 2008 to 2010. Data from 2011 and 2012 indicate a slight decrease in domestic meth manufacture from 2010 (DEA 2013c).

A study by Ralph Weisheit and Edward Wells (2010) found substantial variation in methamphetamine lab discoveries across the country. Analyzing data from 2004 to July 2008, they determined that almost half of US counties (46.3 percent) experienced zero meth lab seizures. Over this time period, only 5.3 percent of counties reported twenty or more lab busts (Weisheit and Wells 2010). An examination of state-level

Figure 7.2   Methamphetamine Lab Seizures and Incidents, 1995–2012

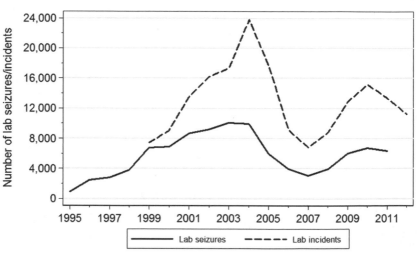

Sources: Carnevale (2005); NDIC (2005, 2007a, 2011a); DEA (2008, 2013c). Data for 2011 lab seizures approximated from Kerlikowske (2012).
Note: "Incidents" include labs, dump sites, or chemical and glassware seizures.

EPIC data indicates that domestic clandestine meth production has been most common in the West and Midwest. California, Washington, Texas, Oklahoma, Iowa, and Missouri are several states with consistently high numbers of meth lab incidents, while the opposite is true for many eastern states. For example, from 2004 to 2012, a total of thirteen lab incidents were reported in Vermont, compared with 4,863 in Iowa over the same time span. Interestingly, some of the western states witnessed a marked decrease in discoveries of clandestine meth production a few years into the new century, while some southern states have experienced a substantial increase. For example, EPIC registered 632 lab incidents in Oregon in 2004, but only nine in 2012. Conversely, from 2004 to 2006 Kentucky averaged 516 annual meth lab incidents; from 2010 to 2012 it averaged 1,342 (DEA 2013c).[4]

While these data are certainly valuable, lab discoveries are not necessarily indicative of actual methamphetamine use. For instance, from 2004 to July 2008, lab seizure rates in the Midwest and South were about double the rate in the West. Yet over this time period, rates of self-reported methamphetamine use were roughly 50 percent greater in the West than in the Midwest and South (Weisheit and Wells 2010).

Two additional sources of nationally gathered methamphetamine data—the Drug Abuse Warning Network (DAWN) and Treatment Episode Data Set (TEDS)—warrant brief mention. DAWN provides annual estimates of drug-related visits to emergency departments (EDs) through a stratified random sample of nonfederal hospitals. An ED visit is classified as "drug related" if a person's recent drug use—intentional, accidental, illicit, or licit—is a direct or indirect reason for needing to visit a hospital's emergency room (DAWN 2011). From 2004 to 2010, the time span for which comparable data are available, the rate of methamphetamine-related ED visits was highest in 2004, at 45.3 visits per 100,000 population. This number corresponds to roughly 133,000 nationwide ED visits that year. The rate of meth-related visits reached a low of 20.9 per 100,000 in 2009 and rose to 30.7 the following year. Over the same seven-year time span, the annual rate of cocaine-related ED visits was at least 3.6 times greater than that of visits due to methamphetamine. Also, meth accounted for an annual average of 4.8 percent of the roughly 1.6 million to 2.3 million yearly drug-related visits from 2004 to 2010. During this time, cocaine accounted for an annual average of 26.6 percent of all drug-related ED visits (DAWN 2012).[5]

Finally, TEDS contains information on the annual number of admissions to many drug treatment facilities in the United States. From 1995 to 2010, TEDS recorded an average of 95,223 and 240,312 annual drug treatment admissions in which methamphetamine and cocaine, respectively, were cited as the primary drugs of abuse. The percentage of treatment admissions listing meth as the primary substance of abuse increased almost every year from 1996 (2.5 percent) to 2005 (8.2 percent). By 2010, the gap between meth and cocaine as primary drugs of choice among treatment seekers reached its narrowest point (5.7 percent and 8.2 percent, respectively) (TEDS 2012).[6]

The Relationship Between Methamphetamine Data and Media Trends

Whereas the nation's first two methamphetamine scares did not appear to coincide with increases in US meth consumption (as estimated by the few available historical data sources), the picture is a little less clear for the crystal meth panic. Data from two of the most systematic and controlled longitudinal surveys of drug use in the United States do not generally follow national media trends. MTF shows a general decrease in methamphetamine consumption by high school seniors from 1995 to 2011, and the NSDUH indicates that annual use among those age twelve and older followed a similar decline from 2002 to 2011. ADAM data show that meth use among male arrestees was geographically regionalized and moderately increased from 2000 to 2003; however, due to the program's postponement, no data from this specialized population of users exist during the years in which the meth panic reached its peak in national news discourse. Data on hospital admissions provided by DAWN reveal a moderate decrease in methamphetamine-related ED visits from 2004 to 2010.

Of all the sources examined, drug treatment admissions (TEDS) and data on meth lab discoveries (EPIC) most closely fit the temporal patterns of national media attention shown in Chapter 6. Of all the annual drug treatment admissions from 1995 to 2010, the largest percentage involving methamphetamine as the primary drug of abuse occurred in 2005. Laboratory seizures and incidents reached their highest levels in 2003 and 2004, respectively, but the overall trajectory of meth lab busts from the mid-1990s up through most of the first decade of the twenty-first century parallels national media trends fairly closely.

Data from DAWN and EPIC (and to a lesser extent, ADAM and TEDS) show a slight to moderate increase in respective national indicators of methamphetamine use and problems in 2010. However, national media coverage of meth was lower in 2010 than in most of the previous fifteen years (see Figures 6.1 and 6.2 in previous chapter). *US News and World Report,* as well as prime-time television news programs broadcast by ABC, NBC, and CBS, presented zero stories about methamphetamine in 2010. In addition, the *New York Times, Washington Post, Los Angeles Times, Wall Street Journal, USA Today,* and *Time* magazine all saw decreases in meth-related news articles from 2009 to 2010. The lack of media coverage of methamphetamine in 2010 is noteworthy considering that meth-related hospital ED visits that year were at their highest levels since 2005 (DAWN 2012), and methamphetamine lab and incident seizures were at their highest levels since 2004 (DEA 2013c).

In regard to media depictions of user characteristics, the epidemiological data appear more consistent with news coverage during the late 1990s. Meth is less prevalent in major cities and more popular among persons with low levels of education. African Americans are the racial group least likely to use methamphetamine. Although Native Americans and Native Hawaiians have the highest rates of past-year use, population dynamics reveal that the majority of methamphetamine users are white. Contrary to claims of an exploding meth "epidemic," the percentage of the general population who have used methamphetamine remained relatively low and stable throughout the third scare, though ADAM data show meth use among arrested males increased markedly in several urban areas (e.g., Phoenix, Tucson, Omaha) from 2000 to 2003. And while EPIC data indicate an uptick in clandestine meth labs in some southern states during the later years of the crystal meth panic, the regional variation patterns exhibited by ADAM and the NSDUH challenge blanket assertions that methamphetamine had "swept the nation."

Why the Methamphetamine Scare Peaked in 2005: Context

Given the indistinct relationship between epidemiological indicators and media coverage, a more complete account of the temporal variation in national news attention could be supplemented by attention to heretofore underdeveloped social constructionist explanations. In Chapter 6, I argued that the crystal meth scare reached extraordinary levels of national media attention in the early 2000s largely because primary and secondary claims makers changed the framework through which they defined and communicated the United States' methamphetamine problem.

Depictions of economically marginalized and geographically segregated users gave way to images of Mexican-manufactured meth victimizing members of all socioeconomic classes across the nation. Although many of the drug scare "ingredients" (e.g., media magnification, politico-moral entrepreneurs) developed by Craig Reinarman (2012) were invoked in Chapter 6, other social problems prominent around the time crystal meth reached its pinnacle of notoriety were overlooked. Drug panics have a greater chance to prosper if historical "conflicts—economic, political, cultural, class, racial, or a combination—[provide] a context in which claims-makers" can convincingly portray drugs as a threat to society (Reinarman 2012, 164–165). In this section, I present two separate but related conflict-based historical conditions that help more fully explain the timing of the third methamphetamine scare's high point in public discourse.

Three Prominent Social Problems

During the first few years of the twenty-first century, gay rights, illegal immigration, and environmental devastation emerged in the social problems marketplace as three frequently communicated and contested issues. That these issues came to the forefront is significant, considering that gay men, Mexican traffickers, and the ecological pollution caused by clandestine meth labs were three popular themes in media coverage of crystal meth.

Figure 7.3 graphs the number of nationally televised nightly news segments dedicated to gay marriage, global warming, and illegal immigration from 1995 to 2007. I chose to only examine these subjects up to 2007 since most national media outlets significantly reduced their attention to methamphetamine by this year.

Gay marriage received more media attention in 2003 than in the combined years since 1995. In 2004, a presidential election year, gay marriage was mentioned a great deal in the national news. In 2005, the number of televised news stories about gay marriage dropped but remained at a higher level than in 2003. Media discussions about the use of methamphetamine by gay men were much more frequent in the early 2000s than in the late 1990s. For instance, a LexisNexis Academic search of *USA Today,* the *Washington Post,* and the *New York Times* found a total of seventy-three articles about methamphetamine and gay men published from 1995 to 2007.[7] Of these articles, sixty-four (88 percent) appeared from 2002 to 2007, including fifteen in 2004 and twenty-five in 2005.

Figure 7.3 National Television News Coverage of Gay Marriage, Global Warming, and Illegal Immigration, 1995–2007

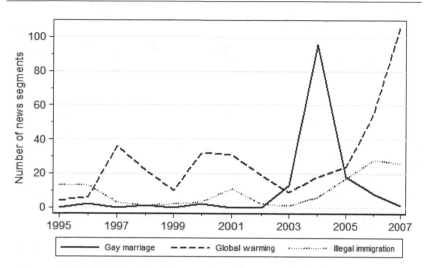

Source: Vanderbilt Television News Archive, http://tvnews.vanderbilt.edu.
Note: Data represent number of nightly national news segments broadcast by ABC, NBC, and CBS.

With gay marriage a popular subject of news discourse in the early 2000s, that methamphetamine was more often linked to gay men during this time period is noteworthy. Claims about methamphetamine and gay men possibly resonated with the public more during the 2000s because of increased attention to gay rights at the time, as evidenced with the heightened news coverage of gay marriage shown in Figure 7.3. It should also be noted that methamphetamine use within lesbian, gay, bisexual, and transgender populations was a popular area of scholarly inquiry in the early 2000s, particularly in those cities characterized by relatively low overall rates of consumption (Weisheit and White 2009). In fact, medical researchers and other academics often appeared as claims makers in news reports on the subject.

Illegal immigration was a more popular subject of discussion in nightly televised news stories in 2005 than in any year since 1995. In 1996, a total of thirty-eight newspaper articles in the *New York Times,* the *Washington Post,* and *USA Today* associated methamphetamine with Mexico or illegal immigration.[8] From 1997 to 2004, that number fluctuated annually from fifteen to twenty. In 2005, discussions of meth and illegal immigration or Mexico were presented in thirty articles, followed by thirty-four in 2006, and forty-three in 2007. That claims linking methamphetamine problems to Mexico were more likely to be taken seriously during this time seems a reasonable conclusion, as media coverage of illegal immigration (much of which discussed Mexican immigrants specifically) began escalating in 2004 and continued to grow over the next few years.

Global warming was a third frequently discussed social problem concomitant with the crystal meth scare. Though prime-time television news coverage of global warming was more consistent year to year than illegal immigration and gay marriage, the topic received more media attention in 2005 than it had since 2001, and much more exposure in 2006 (the year Al Gore's documentary *An Inconvenient Truth* was released) and 2007. Clandestine production of methamphetamine has little effect on global warming. In fact, none of the major US news sources I consulted explicitly linked these two topics. I use global warming only as a proxy indicator of media attention and public concern about the environment.

According to LexisNexis Academic, a total of 202 articles printed in *USA Today,* the *New York Times,* and the *Washington Post* from 1995 to 2007 discussed clandestine methamphetamine labs.[9] Of these, forty-nine appeared from 1995 to 2001. A total of forty-two articles were published in 2005 alone, more than in any other year over the time period examined. Thirty-eight articles about methamphetamine labs appeared in 2006, and twenty-eight in 2007. Much of the increased news attention to meth labs, especially in 2006, reported on new federal legislation restricting cold and allergy medications containing pseudoephedrine. However, if media coverage of global warming is an indicator of overall heightened concerns with environmental health, the escalation of the crystal meth scare during the early 2000s is likely partly related to the growth in environmental consciousness among the US media and public.

In contrast to many previous drug scares in the United States, environmental organizations had great incentive to join or support the anti-methamphetamine crusade, since most other illegal drugs do not involve domestic production operations that are as harmful to the environment as those resulting from meth manufacture. Thus, the crystal meth scare likely benefited from the backing of environmental activists as an additional interest group specifically concerned about the ecological harms stemming from the proliferation of domestic labs. Worth highlighting is that much of the production and use of methamphetamine in the United States has taken place on the West Coast, an area with particularly high levels of environmental awareness and local news attention toward methamphetamine.

Social problems do not exist in clearly marked boundaries, separate from one another (Best 1990). Therefore, one could reasonably suppose that individuals involved in public discourse over gay marriage, illegal immigration, or the environment at times tailored their claims to focus on threats posed by methamphetamine. For example, an opponent of immigration may point to the involvement of undocumented aliens in the production and trafficking of meth, in order to bolster support for immigration reform from anti-meth crusaders. Conversely, persons campaigning against meth may emphasize the role played by Mexican DTOs in order to attract allies from the anti-immigration social problems marketplace. Moral entrepreneurs seek strength through the formation of alliances and coalitions with claims makers involved in a variety of social problems movements (Adler and Adler 2012). US media coverage of methamphetamine likely peaked in 2005 in part because claims makers enlisted support from persons concerned with other social problems (i.e., gay marriage, illegal immigration, environmental destruction) prevalent at the time.

Criminal Justice System Demands

Much like drugs themselves, drug scares are subject to forces of supply and demand. In a general sense, much of the populace seems to demand sensationalist news stories. Indeed, the public's fascination with the spectacle of the staged trial and punishment of norm violators is a cultural tradition in the United States and elsewhere. Whereas in times past social deviants were "parad[ed] . . . in the town square or expose[d] . . . to the carnival atmosphere of" public hangings, contemporary demands for fantastic forms of entertainment are met largely through media consumption (Erikson [1966] 2012, 19).

But heightened attention to methamphetamine circa 2005 cannot be explained by a general public need for sensationalism. Such demands could easily be met with an array of subject matter on crime, deviance, and scandal. More to the point, criminal justice agencies, largely through the mass media, help supply the nation with drug scares. In serving as source organizations for news outlets (see Chermak 1994), law enforcement demands for more power and resources are subtly and not so subtly conveyed to audiences. As Clayton Mosher and Scott Akins (2007) argue, "criminal justice system officials need psychoactive substances in order to justify increases in . . . resources devoted to their organizations" (2). To illustrate this point to its logical extreme, if crime and drug use ceased to exist, many people (including me, perhaps) currently employed in legitimate occupations would lose their jobs.

Claims makers often face the problem of audience saturation, which occurs "when audience members become bored with repeatedly hearing the same claims" (Loseke 2003, 62). In the mid-1980s and early 1990s, crack cocaine hysteria ensured a steady supply of taxpayer assistance for the DEA (an organization that actively fueled the crack scare), sectors of the Federal Bureau of Investigation and Central Intelligence Agency, and other law enforcement organizations at both national and local levels. When the crack cocaine scare became institutionalized following the enactment of several federal laws, by the turn of the century, the drug had become a very passé subject in public discourse. In order to sustain or increase government funding, the DEA and other criminal justice agencies needed new drug threats. While heroin and ecstasy served some of that purpose into the late 1990s, the emergence of the crystal methamphetamine scare, especially over the first few years of the twenty-first century, was crucial to criminal justice organizations. Additionally, a new drug scare may have been of particular importance following September 11, 2001, as many drug enforcement agencies faced budget cut threats due to reallocation of government monies to fight terrorism.

Figure 7.4 displays coverage of methamphetamine and crack cocaine by nationally televised nightly news programs and the newsmagazines *Time* and *Newsweek* from 1993 to 2007. In a comparison of drug coverage within sources, crack generally received more attention than meth during the mid-1990s. However, from 1999 to 2006, one prime-time television news segment about crack was broadcast, compared with twenty-nine for methamphetamine over the same time period. Also, a total of twenty meth-related articles appeared in *Time* and *Newsweek* in 2005 alone. From 2003 to 2007, these publications discussed crack in a combined seventeen articles. Clearly, methamphetamine took over the national news drug spotlight in 2001, a position it held until about 2007.

Philip Jenkins (1999) speculates that the DEA's commitment, in 1989 and 1990, to remaining cautious about "the highly speculative ice issue enhanced [their] credibility about other claims" (114–115). Perhaps the DEA's historical decision to jump off the nationalization-of-ice bandwagon paid off when it came time to promote the methamphetamine "epidemic." As demonstrated in Chapter 6, the DEA and other agents of the modern drug war were among the most commonly cited

Figure 7.4 National Newsmagazine and Television News Coverage of Methamphetamine and Crack Cocaine, 1993–2007

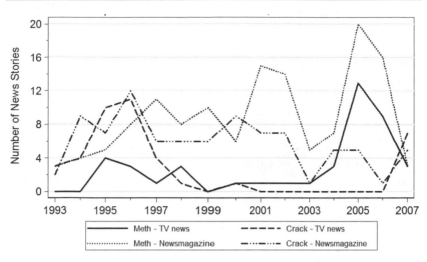

Sources: Vanderbilt Television News Archive, http://tvnews.vanderbilt.edu; *Time* Magazine Archive, www.time.com/time/archive; LexisNexis Academic, www.lexisnexis.com/en-us/Home.page.

Notes: Television news data represent number of nightly national news segments broadcast by ABC, NBC, and CBS. Newsmagazine data represent number of articles in *Time* and *Newsweek*.

claims makers in mass media coverage of the crystal meth scare. News stories of law enforcement officials victimized by haphazard meth cooks were regularly accompanied by pleas for more resources and alarming statistics about the proliferation of domestic meth labs. Although such statistics are useful for many reasons, they can be significantly limited by the nature in which clandestine labs are discovered.

To illustrate this limitation using a nondrug example, suppose an animal abuse task force receives a multimillion-dollar grant to study the magnitude of dogfighting operations and puppy mills in a particular area. Such an increase in monetary resources would allow this task force to hire more personnel and purchase new technologies conducive to detecting various forms of animal abuse. Very likely, the increase in resources—in terms of both manpower and cutting-edge equipment—would lead to the discovery of dogfighting operations and puppy mills that would have remained undetected (and absent from official statistics) if the task force never received the grant in the first place.

Uncovering and cleaning up meth labs cost money. In order to acquire financial or logistical governmental assistance to combat methamphetamine problems, federal, state, and local law enforcement agencies must demonstrate they are under the utmost levels of distress. As agencies receive more resources to dedicate to drug interdiction efforts, they are bound to discover more drug trafficking and production operations. What results is a feedback loop, whereby more resources lead to the detection of additional meth labs, which in turn leads to more claims of a meth lab problem, and pleas for more resources. Hence, areas with more officially recorded meth labs may be policed by agencies expending more energies looking for labs. Data on lab seizures in areas where law enforcement officers are exerting little effort detecting clandestine production operations may underestimate the presence of local methamphetamine manufacture.

Ryan King (2006) points out that the large increase in methamphetamine lab seizures from 1998 to 2004 coincided with the creation of the "Meth/Drug Hot Spots" program, which allocated $385 million in federal aid to state and local law enforcement organizations "for the detection and eradication of clandestine labs. . . . In all likelihood, this increase in lab seizures was the product of expanded law enforcement efforts targeting methamphetamine production facilities in response to financial incentives" (15).

A more contextualized example of the relationship between resources and seizure data was detailed in a 2012 article in the *Washington Times* (as well as several other news sources, such as CBS, FOX, and NPR). In February 2011, states that relied on federal money to help cover the costs of cleaning up toxic meth lab sites suddenly fell victim to budget cuts on Capitol Hill. Consequently, many local law enforcement agencies abruptly stopped looking for labs, and a national decrease in lab seizures and incidents shortly ensued (see Figure 7.2). The director of Tennessee's Meth Task Force stated that lab seizures in his state dropped 75 percent after the federal funding cuts, remained low for four months, and then increased 73 percent following a state-funded cleanup program (Salter 2012). EPIC data report 1,748 lab incidents in Tennessee in 2011 (DEA 2013c). The director anticipated his Meth Task Force would have managed over "2,300 seizures" that year if Tennessee had not lost federal funding (Salter 2012).[10]

As alarm bells from the previous century's crack scare grew silent, methamphetamine surfaced as the "new" drug on which many criminal justice agencies came to depend for justifying increased budgets. Although analysis of news media finds law enforcement made minimal claims linking methamphetamine to gay men, frequently expressed concerns over the ecological hazards associated with domestic labs and, to a lesser extent, Mexican suppliers fit nicely within the larger social problems marketplace of the mid-2000s that had come to construct environmental pollution and illegal immigration as significant social issues. Fearing reduced economic and political clout, and facing new forms of competition, the DEA, state and local drug enforcement organizations, and other pro-interdiction interest groups (e.g., NACo) succeeded in constructing meth as the new crack. And like the dominant, law enforcement–shaped public definitions of the crack crisis, framing methamphetamine primarily as a criminal justice problem ensured steady legislative and financial support for supply interdiction solutions.

Cat and Mouse Redux:
Contemporary Meth Acts and Consequences

Throughout the commotion and hysterics surrounding the crystal meth scare, claims makers rarely considered the contributions of previous policy decisions to ever-evolving methamphetamine problems. In the final section of this chapter, I discuss several laws and drug interdiction strategies implemented from the late 1980s up to the early 2010s designed to stamp out methamphetamine production and trafficking.

As detailed in Chapter 6, precursor regulation was one of the resounding media-conveyed solutions to the crystal meth problem. However, precursor controls were favored solutions well before the nation's third methamphetamine scare. In 1988, Congress passed the Chemical Diversion and Trafficking Act, which attempted to control the international cocaine trade. However, the 1988 act also amended the CSA by placing federal controls on twenty chemicals used in the manufacturing of illicit drugs (Abood 2005). Ephedrine and pseudoephedrine made the list of restricted chemicals. Partly due to pressures from pharmaceutical industry lobbyists, the amendment only regulated ephedrine and pseudoephedrine in powder (bulk) form, not pills or capsules (Suo 2004b; Franco 2007).

With tighter controls on powder supplies, many domestic illicit methamphetamine manufacturers simply obtained ephedrine and pseudoephedrine in tablet form (Suo 2004b). In response, the Domestic Chemical Diversion Control Act, passed by Congress in 1993, increased restrictions on ephedrine—but not on pseudoephedrine (Franco 2007). Black-market manufacturers adapted by relying on pseudoephedrine tablets more than before. Legal imports of pseudoephedrine increased

41 percent from 1994 to 1996, and the precursor began showing up in a higher proportion of lab seizures (Suo 2004b).

Congress responded with the passage of the Comprehensive Methamphetamine Control Act of 1996, which expanded restrictions on ephedrine and pseudoephedrine to include tighter regulations on tablets sold as OTC cold medications (Franco 2007). Specifically, retail distributors were required to keep records of transactions involving products with any amount of ephedrine or more than twenty-four grams of pseudoephedrine (approximately ten boxes, or 500 pills, depending on dosage). However, "blister packs"—packages containing pills individually wrapped in foil—were exempted from this twenty-four-gram threshold (Kurtis 1997; Konnor 2006). Lawmakers knew that lab operators preferred bottles of pills over blister packs, since tablets in the former could be accessed for processing much more quickly (Suo 2004b).

Meth cooks were not deterred. According to Steve Suo (2004b), law enforcement discovered blister packs at 47 percent of labs seized in 1999 and 2000. The Methamphetamine Anti-Proliferation Act of 2000 lowered the record-keeping threshold from twenty-four to nine grams, but blister packs were still exempt (Franco 2007). The annual number of meth lab seizures and incidents increased, reaching their highest levels from 2000 to 2004. In 2004, Oklahoma became the first state to declare all tablet forms of pseudoephedrine as controlled dangerous substances under state statutes. Whereas the new federal act specified that individuals could purchase no more than nine grams of pseudoephedrine products per day, the Oklahoma law prohibits persons without a prescription from buying that amount over a thirty-day period (DEA 2004). In 2005, Oregon required that all pseudoephedrine products, regardless of dosage, be available only by prescription. By early 2006, a total of forty states had implemented varying controls on pseudoephedrine pills (Mosher and Akins 2007).

In early 2006, the year in which most of the national news sources I examined began to decrease their coverage of methamphetamine (see Figures 6.1 and 6.2 in the previous chapter), President George W. Bush signed into law the latest in the series of federal legislative acts that seek to control precursors, the Combat Methamphetamine Epidemic Act (CMEA) of 2005 (Title VII of the USA PATRIOT Improvement and Reauthorization Act). Among its many provisions, the CMEA further reduces record-keeping exemptions, limits monthly purchases by individuals to 7.5 grams, and requires customers to show identification and sign a logbook when buying any products containing more than sixty milligrams of pseudoephedrine (Franco 2007). Since low doses of Sudafed, one of the leading product brands, contain thirty milligrams of pseudoephedrine per tablet, virtually all purchases are subject to this control.

Supply-Side Successes

The logic behind precursor regulations and other supply interdiction attempts is that if pseudoephedrine and other meth precursors are difficult to obtain, prices will increase. An increase in price should foster a decrease in demand (Nonnemaker, Engelen, and Shive 2011). Put simply, people will stop using drugs if they become too expensive.

Several studies have found support for this reasoning. Carlos Dobkin and Nancy Nicosia (2009) studied trends in methamphetamine-related hospital admissions in California from 1994 to 1997. In May 1995, the DEA executed two major raids of US-based ephedrine and pseudoephedrine distributors after determining the companies were principal suppliers of the black market for illicit meth manufacture. Analyzing data from the DEA's System to Retrieve Information from Drug Evidence (STRIDE), Dobkin and Nicosia (2009) observed an abrupt increase in the street price of illicit meth immediately following the raids and a consequent decrease in meth-related hospital visits. Another study attributed the rise in the average per-gram price of methamphetamine sold in the United States—from $101 in April 2005 to $284 in October 2007—to precursor restrictions enacted by the US and Mexican governments (Gizzi 2011). Analysis of criminal justice data specific to Mesa County, Colorado, found that the number of felony arrests for methamphetamine possession and trafficking decreased significantly from 2007 to 2009. Treating arrest patterns as proxy measures of methamphetamine use and availability, Michael Gizzi (2011) credited much of the decline to DEA reports that area meth prices more than tripled between 2006 and 2008.

Another series of studies has investigated the effects of various supply restrictions on clandestine meth lab seizures. Analyzing data from California, James Nonnemaker, Mark Engelen, and Daniel Shive (2011) determined that while the Methamphetamine Anti-Proliferation Act of 2000 had no impact on lab seizure rates, a 2000 state law restricting blister pack sales likely contributed to the subsequent decline in statewide lab discoveries. Duane McBride and colleagues (2011) found states that enacted precursor and sales restrictions from 2004 to 2006 were more likely to report significant decreases in small toxic lab seizures than states without such policies. However, their analysis is limited by the omission of seizure data from eighteen states, including some that have been known to have relatively high rates of methamphetamine use and production (e.g., New Mexico, Texas, Tennessee).

Other literature more casually examines before-and-after counts of meth labs in states that have enacted their own precursor controls. An article published in the *Harvard Law Review* reported Oklahoma saw a 50 percent decrease in lab seizures following the passage of its 2005 precursor restriction law ("Cooking Up Solutions" 2006). Oregon's 2005 decision to mandate pseudoephedrine sales as prescription only is one potential explanation for the state's marked decrease in meth lab discoveries in subsequent years, though critics point out lab seizures were on the decline several years prior, and seizure rates similarly declined in neighboring states (i.e., Washington and California) without prescription requirements (Stomberg and Sharma 2012). As of early 2013, Mississippi was the only other state to have passed a law requiring a prescription for products containing any amount of pseudoephedrine (NDIC 2011a; Cha 2013). In 2010, the year in which Mississippi instituted its prescription-only law, 912 lab incidents were recorded. Over the next two years, the state registered 321 and 5 incidents, respectively (DEA 2013c).

A number of researchers point to the longitudinal nationwide trend in annual lab seizures and incidents to illustrate the successes of contemporary supply-side policies. By the end of 2005, a total of thirty-eight states had enacted precursor restrictions ("Cooking Up Solutions" 2006). As shown earlier in Figure 7.2, the number of lab discoveries began falling around this time and continued to fall after the 2006 implementation of the federal CMEA. Many scholars agree that this federal law played a major role in the national decrease in lab seizures that followed (e.g., Weisheit and Wells 2010; Maxwell and Brecht 2011).

As these studies and others indicate, contemporary methamphetamine laws and drug interdiction efforts have had positive outcomes. Whether or not they are directly or indirectly related to supply-side policies and procedures, decreases in hospital admissions, meth-related arrests, and lab seizure rates are certainly welcomed by politicians, law enforcement, and the public at large. Many of these policy successes, however, have been offset by a slew of new harms.

Supply-Side Failures

One of the most consistent findings from longitudinal studies of the effectiveness of various supply interdiction policies is that observed successes are usually short lived. For example, Dobkin and Nicosia (2009) found that both the price of methamphetamine and the number of meth-related admissions to California hospitals were back to their "normal" levels only several months after the May 1995 DEA raids on two large precursor distributors. Dobkin and Nicosia (2009) also found that in the months immediately following the rise in price, arrests for robberies increased, suggesting that "methamphetamine users who rely on crime to support their consumption responded to the higher price by committing more crimes" (341). STRIDE data indicate that after nearly tripling between 2005 and 2007 (Gizzi 2011), the average price per pure gram of methamphetamine was back down to pre-2005 levels by 2010 (Maxwell and Brecht 2011). And though the number of lab seizures decreased substantially in the years immediately following the United States' strictest state and federal meth precursor laws, clandestine meth operations detected by law enforcement increased consistently from 2008 to 2010. EPIC data from 2011 and 2012 indicate no substantial decline even in the face of cuts to task-force budgets.

P2P II: Trafficking evolves. Contemporary methamphetamine regulations have facilitated significant changes in trafficking networks. One of the most noteworthy black-market adaptations has been the shifting of production and supply to countries with less government resources to deal with drug problems. If reports published by the US Department of Justice are an appropriate gauge (e.g., NDIC 2005, 2007a), claims about the role of Mexico as a major source of methamphetamine in the United States were among the more accurate media portrayals of the crystal meth scare. When P2P restrictions put many of the motorcycle gangs out of business in the 1980s, Mexican DTOs, in recognition of an opening in the market, stepped up to meet demand by obtaining precursors in bulk and manufacturing meth in superlabs for export to the United States (Reding 2009; NDIC 2011a). More recently, the Department of Justice has named Mexican DTOs as *the* primary production source of illicit methamphetamine consumed in the United States (e.g., NDIC 2010a, 2011a).

Upon securing much of the market, many Mexican DTOs mastered chemical synthesis techniques to the extent that they learned how to mass-produce highly pure methamphetamine in smokable (i.e., ice) form (NDIC 2006, 2007b, 2008). This black-market adaptation is crucial when we remember that inhalation (i.e., smoking) of methamphetamine produces greater health and dependence problems than oral ingestion or intranasal use (i.e., snorting) (Cunningham, Liu, and Muramoto

2008). Multiple studies indicate this change in product quality has facilitated more harms in user populations.

Examining data on admissions to California-based drug treatment programs from 1992 to 2004, James Cunningham, Lon-Mu Liu, and Myra Muramoto (2008) found that the number of treatment seekers who smoked methamphetamine increased steadily beginning in 1997, the year pseudoephedrine regulations from the Comprehensive Methamphetamine Control Act went into effect. Because treatment admissions for persons using other routes of administration did not rise over this time period, the researchers indicated an upsurge in Mexican-manufactured ice—afforded by the newly implemented domestic restrictions on pseudoephedrine—likely explained the increased popularity of smoking (Cunningham, Liu, and Muramoto 2008). In an analysis of national data from TEDS, Jane Carlisle Maxwell and Mary-Lynn Brecht (2011) learned that starting in 1998, smoking became the primary method of administration among clients seeking help for methamphetamine abuse. Smokers made up 12 percent of meth-related treatment admissions in 1992, but 68 percent by 2008. Nonnemaker, Engelen, and Shive (2011) found that after the enactment of the Methamphetamine Anti-Proliferation Act of 2000, street prices actually decreased, while purity levels and meth-related treatment admissions grew. The researchers note that one of this law's unintended consequences was a potential increase in methamphetamine supplies from international traffickers. In a review of ten studies, the influx of methamphetamine and its precursors from neighboring nations is cited as a principal factor undercutting much of the long-term effectiveness of US precursor regulations (McKetin et al. 2011).[11]

In 2006, Mexico began implementation of a series of precursor controls when it severely lowered its importation of pseudoephedrine. In 2007, Mexico passed a law mandating that persons obtain a prescription in order to purchase pseudoephedrine products. That same year, the Mexican government shut down a major "rogue" chemical company that had been illegally dealing in precursors. In 2008, Mexico enacted a complete ban on pseudoephedrine, which puts the popular meth precursor legally on par with heroin and other Schedule I drugs in the United States.[12] Research by Cunningham and colleagues (2010) demonstrates that some of these supply interferences, particularly the closing of the rogue chemical company, led to a significant reduction in voluntary admissions to Mexican and Texan facilities for methamphetamine treatment.

Subsequent literature shows that Mexican DTOs have responded in at least three ways to their government's supply-side successes in limiting pseudoephedrine availability. First, some Mexican DTOs have actually chosen to relocate their production operations to the United States (mainly to California), evidently because pseudoephedrine and other precursors are more easily obtainable there (NDIC 2008; UNODC 2011). Second, Mexican manufacturers and traffickers have increasingly come to rely upon South Africa, China, India, and countries in Central and South America with little to no precursor restrictions as source nations (Maxwell and Brecht 2011; Kerlikowske 2012). A third way in which Mexican DTOs have adapted to their government's disruption of pseudoephedrine supplies is by adopting P2P precursor methods.

Considering that the outdated synthesis technique once championed by domestic biker gangs of the 1960s and 1970s resulted in the less centrally active, usually unsmokable, dl-methamphetamine, the reversion to P2P by Mexican manufacturers should facilitate a reduction in physiological harms and dependence. To the contrary, Mexican lab chemists have improved upon old formulas such that they are now able to produce the purer, more potent, smokable d-methamphetamine from P2P (Maxwell and Brecht 2011; UNODC 2011; Kerlikowske 2012). Since the government of Mexico maintains tight restrictions on P2P, some DTOs have gone as far as synthesizing P2P from other chemicals (referred to as "pre-precursors"), such as phenylacetic acid and phenylacetyl amide (Maxwell and Brecht 2011; UNODC 2011).

"Smurf's Up": Domestic adaptations. At the same time that Mexican methamphetamine manufacturers have adapted to contemporary international control efforts, US meth cooks have also modified their operations to find ways around newly implemented federal and state precursor restrictions. Many domestic lab operators have resorted to a technique dubbed "smurfing"[13] to overcome the monthly pseudoephedrine purchase limit of 7.5 grams (NDIC 2010a; McBride et al. 2011). Andrew Goetz (2007) distinguishes between two smurfing strategies. The "multiple-purchases" technique occurs when multiple partners in crime enter a store (while pretending not to know one another) and buy the maximum amount of pseudoephedrine allowable by law. In the "multiple-stores strategy," individuals will hop from store to store until they have acquired a desired amount of pseudoephedrine. Of course, these strategies are not mutually exclusive.

Though the federal law requires virtually all purchasers of pseudoephedrine to sign their names in logbooks, no comprehensive national tracking system exists to help catch persons utilizing the multiple-stores strategy. Recognizing the increasing trend in smurfing, some states have implemented electronic databases that are capable of sharing real-time pseudoephedrine purchase data with law enforcement. Ostensibly, persons seeking to buy pseudoephedrine for the purpose of making methamphetamine would rely more heavily on the multiple-purchases strategy to better avoid detection in states with tracking systems. And while many smurfing operations are small scale, law enforcement agencies have discovered rather sophisticated pseudoephedrine purchasing networks in some places. Some ventures have been known to involve up to "100 individuals . . . [who] travel throughout their regions using false identifications to obtain pseudoephedrine. . . . The groups then sell the pseudoephedrine to brokers, who in turn sell the pseudoephedrine to methamphetamine producers" (NDIC 2011a, 35). In other words, federal law has inadvertently created a black market for OTC cold and allergy medications. The Department of Justice reports that the increase in domestic methamphetamine lab incidents and seizures since 2008 is due in large part to the emergence of smurfing operations (NDIC 2010a).

Domestic meth manufacturers have also adapted to recent precursor restrictions by relying more heavily on the "shake-and-bake" or "one-pot" method of production (McBride et al. 2011). EPIC data suggest the rise in popularity of the shake-and-bake process is a direct consequence of the CMEA of 2005. Ten one-pot labs were seized from 2000 to 2006 (the year in which the CMEA was signed into law), whereas 10,205 were discovered from 2007 to 2011 (DIB 2012). Although the shake-and-bake technique yields small amounts of meth, usually only enough for personal use, the compact nature of the operation and the rapid time in which it allows for methamphetamine synthesis appeal to cooks worried about drawing the attention of authorities ("Meth Labs" 2010; NIDA 2010). Chemists can make high-purity d-methamphetamine in as little as forty to sixty minutes via shake-and-bake, compared with several hours or days using more traditional production methods (Hamilton 2010; DIB 2012). At least one state law enforcement agency has claimed that the incognito compatibility afforded by shake-and-bake has encouraged the movement of meth labs into urban areas ("Meth Labs" 2010).

Beyond fostering more harmful routes of administration, meth of higher purity, Mexican drug cartels, smurfing activities, and urban meth labs, a final unintended consequence of contemporary supply interdiction policies is the propensity for some users to replace their demand for stimulation with cocaine. As noted in Chapter 5, federal methamphetamine regulations enacted in the early 1970s helped bring about a boom in the cocaine trade (Brecher 1972). According to Rebecca McKetin (2007), "in the real world, drug users have a habit of shifting from one drug to another depending on availability and cost" (522). Though some reports find no evidence of a rise in cocaine use following policies that reduce methamphetamine supplies (e.g., Cunningham et al. 2010; McKetin et al. 2011), other research provides support for the so-called water balloon theory. One longitudinal study of rural stimulant users discovered that while the number of months exposed to state precursor regulations was unrelated to methamphetamine use, precursor laws were associated with a significant rise in powder cocaine use (Borders et al. 2008). The researchers suggest that "methamphetamine legislation reduced the supply of methamphetamine and, in turn, contributed to increased demand for cocaine" (806). Gizzi's (2011) study in Mesa County, Colorado, found that when arrests for methamphetamine decreased as the drug became more expensive and less available, cocaine arrests increased. "The high cost of methamphetamine forced the drug's users to find alternative drugs, and for a short time, cocaine use in Mesa County increased, in an ironic situation where powder cocaine was considerably less expensive than methamphetamine" (120).

A brief examination of ADAM data provides further support for the contention that in drug markets where one stimulant is scarce, the user population's demand for stimulation is satisfied by another, psychopharmacologically similar substance. Figure 7.5 shows the percentage of adult male arrestees testing positive for stimulants in select US counties, from 2000 to 2003. Excluding Des Moines, Iowa, variation in positive tests is quite low across locales. While cocaine use is exceptionally more common among arrestees in Chicago and New York, methamphetamine is the illicit stimulant of choice among males arrested in San Diego and Honolulu (ADAM 2000, 2001, 2002, 2003). ADAM sites are more easily differentiated by the *type* of stimulant consumed, rather than by differences in their overall rates of stimulant consumption.

* * *

From the moral panic perspective, the enactment of major federal legislation in 2006 (i.e., the CMEA) signified an end to the threat. Crystal meth mania reached its media saturation point, and despite mild increas-

**Figure 7.5   Percentage of Adult Male Arrestees Testing Positive for
Methamphetamine and Cocaine, by Select ADAM Site,
2000–2003**

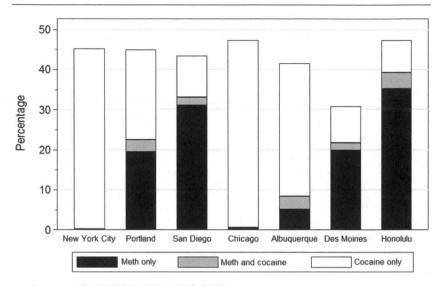

Sources: ADAM (2000, 2001, 2002, 2003).

es in several indicators of methamphetamine incidence at the end of the
decade, the topic was no longer sensationalist enough to command
national headlines.[14] To borrow a term from Craig Reinarman (2012),
the crystal meth panic had a larger "kernel of truth" when compared
with the two previous meth scares. Methamphetamine, especially the
smokable version popularized in the late 1990s, has the potential to create a great number of harms in users. But in another similarity to moral
panics over other drugs, the dominant rhetoric of the crystal meth scare
was too emotional and superficial to search beyond molecular and individual-level causes. And although methamphetamine had become old
news by 2010, another drug panic was on the horizon.

Notes

1. Of course, not all arrestees consent to an interview or agree to provide a
urine specimen. In 2003, for example, 56.7 percent of eligible male arrestees

agreed to be interviewed by ADAM researchers; 91.4 percent of those interviewed provided a urine sample (ADAM 2003). Also, I excluded data collected in 1998 and 1999 because subsequent methodological changes in the ADAM program do not permit comparisons with later years.

2. After being postponed in 2004, ADAM resumed data collection in 2007, but with some modifications (e.g., only ten counties now participate). More recently collected ADAM data still indicate regional variation in meth use by male arrestees. For example, Portland, Oregon, and Sacramento consistently exhibit the highest rates of positive tests. From 2007 to 2011, less than 1 percent of male arrestees in New York City, Atlanta, Charlotte, and Chicago tested positive for methamphetamine. Washington, DC, was the only ADAM location that bucked the trend, when it saw a rise in meth-positive tests in 2007, but a return to low levels in the following years (ADAM II 2011, 2012).

3. Since EPIC does not systematically and publicly disseminate national lab seizure and incident data, I had to rely on several secondary sources to compile the information presented in Figure 7.2. The specific sources are as follows: incident data from 1999–2003 (DEA 2008), incident data from 2004–2012 (DEA 2013c), seizure data from 1995–1998 (Carnevale 2005), seizure data from 1999–2001 (NDIC 2005), seizure data from 2002–2004 (NDIC 2007a), and seizure data from 2005–2010 (NDIC 2011a). The statistic of 6,400 lab seizures in 2011 is an estimate from Kerlikowske (2012), who testified to Congress in July 2012 that "US methamphetamine lab seizures have increased . . . to nearly 6,400 in 2011" (5). This statement contradicts numerous press reports circulated in February 2012 (e.g., Salter 2012), which stated 2011 lab seizures increased at least 8.3 percent from 2010. Since NDIC (2011a) reported 6,768 seizures in 2010, an 8.3 percent increase suggests a total of 7,330 labs were seized in 2011. All of the statistics in Figure 7.2 purport to originate from EPIC's National Seizure System database. At the time of this writing, I was unable to locate data on the number of 2012 lab seizures.

4. For several reasons, a healthy degree of caution is urged when interpreting EPIC data. First, a single "incident" could include anything from the discovery of a few empty boxes of Sudafed littered in the forest to a highly sophisticated superlab churning out fifty pounds of crystal per production cycle. Of the 17,356 incidents recorded in 2003, 143 (0.8 percent) were deemed superlabs (NDIC 2004). Of the 6,768 lab seizures in 2010, nearly 85 percent were determined to be capable of producing only two ounces of meth or less (NDIC 2011a). A second limitation concerns the fact that EPIC mostly relies on voluntary reports of lab seizures and incidents. Only three states (Missouri, California, and Oklahoma) are mandated by law to submit data to EPIC (Franco 2007).

5. DAWN data are limited in that they do not disentangle methamphetamine (or cocaine) from other drugs in ED visits by poly-drug users. Also, DAWN includes ED visits for drugs in combination with alcohol but does not provide data on alcohol-only ED visits. See Mosher and Akins (2007) for a detailed discussion of DAWN limitations.

6. One limitation of TEDS is that data are compiled from state administrative systems. States vary in the extent to which they report hospital, prison, and

private provider treatment admissions. States also vary in the amount of public funding available for treatment facilities and the extent to which coercion plays a role in treatment referrals (TEDS 2010).

7. The specific search command used was as follows: (methamphetamine OR "crystal meth") AND ("gay men" OR "gay sex" OR "sex with men" OR "gay man" OR "homosexual man" OR "gay club").

8. The specific search command used was as follows: (methamphetamine OR "crystal meth") AND (Mexic* OR "illegal immigra*").

9. The specific search command used was as follows: (methamphetamine OR "crystal meth") AND ("clandestine production" OR "meth lab*" OR "methamphetamine lab*")

10. Unclear is whether Tennessee's Meth Task Force director anticipated 2,300 lab *seizures* or *incidents*. State-level data on lab seizures are not available at the time of this writing. Since EPIC reported 1,748 lab incidents for Tennessee in 2011 (DEA 2013c), one can assume fewer lab seizures took place that year.

11. In 2007, the United States and Mexico reached an agreement for the United States to appropriate $1.3 billion in anticrime and counterdrug assistance (e.g., helicopters, corrections, military training) to Mexico, Central America, and several Caribbean nations. Though the Mérida Initiative was originally due to expire in fiscal year 2010, the "partnership" was expanded into at least 2012. At that time, appropriations had totaled $1.6 billion since the program's inception (Vaughne 2010; "The Merida Initative" 2012).

12. Mexico decriminalized simple possession of marijuana, cocaine, and heroin the year after it enacted its complete prohibition of pseudoephedrine.

13. The origin of the term *smurfing* is somewhat debated. According to one source, *smurfing* derives from the fact that many pseudoephedrine tablets are blue, the same color of the Smurfs (characters in a popular children's cartoon and movie by the same name) (Pretti 2011). A more sensible explanation traces the term's origin to the banking industry, where *smurfing* refers to a money-laundering technique in which individuals split up large cash deposits into smaller ones so as to avoid coming under government scrutiny (C. Adams 2009).

14. Many of the methamphetamine mentions by news organizations following the decline of the crystal meth scare have discussed the drug in relation to celebrities (e.g., Andre Agassi admitting to using the drug during parts of his professional tennis career), Mexican drug wars, and the critically acclaimed meth-themed television show *Breaking Bad*.

8

New Panics,
New Approaches

It was a scene as creepy as a Hannibal Lecter movie. One man was shot to death by Miami police, and another man is fighting for his life after he was attacked, and his face allegedly half eaten, by a naked man on the MacArthur Causeway off ramp Saturday. . . . The horror began about 2 p.m. . . . According to police sources, a road ranger saw a naked man chewing on another man's face. . . . [A police] officer . . . approached and, seeing what was happening, . . . ordered the naked man to back away. When he continued the assault, the officer shot him. . . . The attacker failed to stop after being shot, forcing the officer to continue firing. —*Daniela Guzman and Julie Brown (2012)*

Presumably due to its uniquely bewildering and shocking details, this May 2012 incident originally reported by the *Miami Herald* quickly gained national and international attention. Surveillance camera videos of the cannibalistic attack and photographs of the victim's bloodied, mangled face were posted online, soliciting gasps of horror from anyone brave enough to look. Before the autopsy was completed, innumerable news sources proclaimed the attacker was high on "bath salts," a colloquial term for a class of stimulants known as synthetic cathinones.

As might be expected, a variety of claims makers, including persons in the medical field, members of law enforcement, and politicians, competed for ownership of the bath salts problem by communicating their perspectives through the mass media. As the story of the so-called Miami cannibal broke, the president of the city's Fraternal Order of Police told one news outlet he suspected the attacker had been under the influence of bath salts, which "cause [users] to go completely insane and become very violent" (Lendon 2012). Five days after the incident, a Florida-area nurse wrote to the *Miami Herald* warning that bath salts represented a "new and dangerous street drug that has created a crisis across the United States" (Barden 2012). According to an *ABC News* report, the following Monday, Senator Chris Coons from Delaware delivered a statement saying, "Dangerous drugs like bath salts are terrorizing our communities and destroying lives. . . . Stricter measures must be taken to stem the growing prevalence of bath salts and other new designer drugs" (Dolak 2012).

The widely reported attack resonated with American pop culture's peculiar fascination with zombies (see Platts 2013) and seemed to fit with a handful of other gruesome cannibalism-themed news stories publicized around this time. Perhaps these factors led one journalist to half-jokingly speculate that the United States might be experiencing the dawn of a "Zombie Apocalypse" (Trapasso 2012, 20). Apparently, the brief wave of human-eating-human occurrences raised enough of a legitimate concern that a spokesperson from the Centers for Disease Control felt compelled to issue a formal statement, saying, "CDC does not know of a virus or condition that would reanimate the dead (or one that would present zombielike symptoms)" (Trapasso 2012, 20).

By the time the media frenzy began to subside, several new details over the Miami cannibalism incident emerged. Although he survived, victim Ronald Poppo suffered permanent blindness and scars from the attack (Robles 2012). Also, the autopsy results revealed that the attacker did not actually swallow any of Poppo's flesh ("Causeway Cannibal" 2012). However, by far the most enlightening finding from the post-mortem examination was that no bath salts were detected in the attacker's system (nor was he found to have recently consumed cocaine, LSD, amphetamines, heroin, PCP, or oxycodone). In fact, the only drug registered in the toxicology analysis was marijuana (Hiaasen and Green 2012).

Though the Miami cannibalism incident undoubtedly sparked a quick rise in media attention toward bath salts, news outlets had been periodically warning about synthetic cathinones for at least one or two years prior. For example, in January 2011, a *Washington Post* headline read, "Officials Fear Bath Salts Becoming the Next Big Drug Menace." The article cited a variety of law enforcement agency officials who spoke about the role of bath salts in multiple violent incidents, including a suicide in Louisiana and a homicide in Tennessee. One former user said he still had psychological scars from his previous bath salt consumption (Byrd 2011). In April 2011, Mehmet Oz, of the nationally televised *Dr. Oz Show,* published an article in *Time* magazine titled "Bath Salts: Evil Lurking at Your Corner Store." In it, Oz (2011) wrote of the ease with which he purchased several kinds of bath salts at a local tobacco shop. "Kids everywhere are in danger from this substance, and the threat is legal, cheap and very deadly" (54). Two months later, the front page of the *New York Times* quoted the Louisiana poison control center director who described bath salts by stating, "If you take the worst attributes of meth, coke, PCP, LSD and ecstasy and put them together . . . that's what we're seeing sometimes" (Goodnough and Zezima 2011, A1). In the same article, a police chief from Illinois said, "I have never seen a drug that took off as fast as this one," while an officer from Pennsylvania relayed his own experience: "We had two instances in particular where [users of bath salts] were acting out in a very violent manner and they were Tasered and it had no effect. . . . One was only a small female, but it took four officers to hold her down, along with two orderlies. That's how out of control she was" (Goodnough and Zezima 2011, A1).

Much like the ice panic of 1989 and the more recent crystal meth scare, some media coverage of bath salts has incorporated the novelty theme. For example, an article in *The Economist* emphasized that "public health and law authorities are sounding an alarm about new drugs" ("The Synthetic Scare" 2012, 30), the *St. Paul Pioneer Press* warned of a "new wave of untested synthetic drugs" (Horner 2011), and the headline of the previously cited article by Abby Goodnough and Katie Zezima (2011) declared bath salts "An Alarming New Stimulant" (A1).

Claims that bath salts are "new" should be qualified. While evidence from poison control centers and hospitals certainly suggests that the use of synthetic cathinones in the United States has grown since about 2010 (NDIC 2011b), many of the drugs marketed as bath salts have existed for some time, while others are closely related derivatives of old drugs. Cathinone is the psychoactive stimulant found in the *Catha edulis* (khat) plant. Though members of many East African and Middle Eastern cultures have chewed khat leaves for centuries, the first synthetic versions were invented in the late 1920s (C. Brooke 1960; Prosser and Nelson 2012), during the pharmacological revolution that followed the Harrison Act's prohibition of cocaine. Bupropion—marketed as Wellbutrin to treat depression and Zyban to treat nicotine addiction—is one of only three synthetic cathinones with accepted medical use in the United States (NDIC 2011b; Prosser and Nelson 2012).

Frenzied media coverage of synthetic cathinones is also not new. In the early 1990s, methcathinone, then popularly referred to as "cat," became the subject of a brief drug scare when a series of clandestine labs were discovered in the upper Midwest (Jenkins 1999). Like methamphetamine, cat can be synthesized using ephedrine and pseudoephedrine precursors. Also as with meth, news attention toward cat was panicky in nature, as reports claimed the drug was spreading across the Midwest, was "worse than cocaine" (Jenkins 1999, 126), and was presenting considerable challenges to law enforcement and local ecologies. Much like the ice age, the "cat attack" ended almost as suddenly as it began (Jenkins 1999, 117).

Methylenedioxypyrovalerone (MDPV), mephedrone, and methylone were the most commonly abused synthetic cathinones of the early 2010s (Wieland, Halter, and Levine 2012). Though each bath salt chemical is molecularly unique, in general their effects have been described as similar to those of cocaine, methamphetamine, and MDMA (i.e., ecstasy). In other words, synthetic cathinones are psychomotor stimulants that increase energy, alertness, blood pressure, and heartbeat; some also have hallucinogenic effects (Winstock et al. 2011; Prosser and Nelson 2012; Wieland, Halter, and Levine 2012; DEA 2013d).

Bath salts surfaced in several European nations before making waves in the United States (Bossong, Van Dijk, and Niesink 2005). Researchers explain their popularity growth in the United Kingdom and the Netherlands as a consequence of legal restrictions and decreased availability of cocaine and ecstasy (Schifano et al. 2011; Freeman et al. 2012; Prosser and Nelson 2012). Given its history in Europe, it is reasonable to suppose that bath salt consumption increased in the United States due to similar forces. Indeed, citing the US emergence of MDPV, mephedrone, and methylone, the head of the DEA, Michele Leonhart, stated these substances were "being perceived as 'legal' alternatives to cocaine, methamphetamine, and MDMA" (Leonhart 2011, 74), a sentiment that has been echoed in several criminal justice agency publications (e.g., NDIC 2010b, 2011b). For these reasons, we might appropriately add "cultivating the rise of synthetic cathinones" to the list of unintended consequences (e.g., smokable meth, smurfing) of contemporary US policies designed to interdict methamphetamine and other stimulant drugs.

Although the cat scare prompted the DEA to list methcathinone as a Schedule I drug in 1992 (Jenkins 1999), MDPV, mephedrone, methylone, and many other synthetic cathinones have been available without a prescription or age requirement from the Internet, tobacco shops, and convenience stores. Manufacturers and distributors took advantage of a loophole in the Federal Analog Act of 1986, which prohibits the use of substance analogs, defined as chemicals "substantially similar" in structure or pharmacology to Schedule I or II drugs (Prosser and Nelson

2012). Essentially, this law made selling many synthetic cathinones (some of which had not even been synthesized when the 1986 act was passed) illegal, but only if they are marketed as drugs (Hogshire 1999; Prosser and Nelson 2012). The loophole has allowed these products to be sold as long as they are not promoted for human consumption. Hence, advertising them as "bath salts" (or "plant food," in some cases) was legal in the United States up until late 2011 (Prosser and Nelson 2012).

In response to the growing concerns over the more recently popular synthetic cathinones, the DEA invoked an emergency classification of mephedrone, MDPV, and methylone into Schedule I on October 21, 2011 (Leonhart 2011). In July 2012, President Barack Obama signed the FDA Safety and Innovation Act. Part of this act includes a bill that permanently establishes the Schedule I classification of mephedrone, MDPV, nine synthetic hallucinogens, and twenty forms of synthetic marijuana (Schumer 2012).[1] According to one source, the law also closed the loophole that would have allowed manufacturers to market yet-invented analogs as "not for human consumption." "When new compounds (which have most likely already been created by drug designers) hit the market, drug enforcement agents will be able to crack down on them under the same law, without the need for new legislation" (Haggin 2012).

Given the historical evolution of speed in the United States, that this most recent piece of legislation will stop the use of bath salts or other stimulants is doubtful. Some reports indicate that newly synthesized cathinones subsequently emerged as replacements for the ones prohibited by the 2012 law (see Baumann, Partilla, and Lehner 2013). If legitimate manufacturers do not continue to find ways around newer restrictions, a black market will possibly develop to take on the bulk of the manufacturing and trafficking of synthetic cathinones. Or perhaps the heightened law enforcement scrutiny of bath salts will permit greater availability and reduced cost of methamphetamine, cocaine, ecstasy, or all of the above.

Considering the crystal meth "epidemic" had become passé by decade's end, the bath salts minipanic of 2011 to 2012 seemed to have fulfilled some of the demand for drug scares exhibited by news media, audiences, and drug enforcement agencies alike. This discussion is not meant to convey the notion that synthetic cathinones are safe to consume. While no evidence suggests that use of bath salts has been widespread in the United States, the medical literature indicates serious physiological harms from these drugs (e.g., Ross, Watson, and Goldberger

2011; Kasick, McKnight, and Kilsovic 2012). But what can the brief social history of synthetic cathinones, or the longer history of US stimulant scares, offer to those seeking a more comprehensive appreciation of the relationship between drugs and society? Though there are many answers to this question, I believe several lessons can be learned from, of all places, the fictional television show *Breaking Bad*.

Repeating the Past

In a scene from the first season of AMC's award-winning drama, Walter White, a former high school chemistry teacher turned rogue clandestine meth cook, is enjoying a cocktail and Cuban cigar courtesy of his brother-in-law Hank Schrader, an Albuquerque-based DEA agent who is unaware of Walter's dealings. After Hank brushes off Walt's inquiry about the illegality of Cuban cigars, Walt offers a subtly subversive challenge by commenting, "It's funny, isn't it? How we draw that line . . . [between] what's legal [and] what's illegal. You know, Cuban cigars, alcohol. If we were drinking this in 1930, we'd be breaking the law. Another year, we'd be OK. Who knows what will be legal next year?" (P. Gould 2008). Hank exhibits slight agitation over this proposition, to which Walt responds, "I'm just saying, it's arbitrary." Hank replies, "Well, you oughtta visit lockup. You hear a lot of guys talking like that. . . . Shit, buddy. It don't only go one way either. Sometimes there's stuff that's legal, that shouldn't be. I mean, friggin' meth used to be legal. Used to sell it over every counter at every pharmacy across America. Thank God they came to their senses on that one, huh?" (P. Gould 2008).

This exchange between two of *Breaking Bad*'s main characters is insightful for at least two reasons. First, Walter White's observation about "how we draw that line" is an acknowledgment that the boundaries separating licit and illicit substances are socially constructed. Indeed, part of the story of methamphetamine in the United States is a story about the human tendency toward classification. Cultural classification systems serve the purpose of creating black-and-white distinctions out of a gray reality. In "an inevitably arbitrary act," classification systems break up objects from the external world "into discrete islands of meaning" (Zerubavel 2002, 227). Language, the central ingredient in the "social construction of discontinuity," provides us with the category labels (in the form of words) we use to classify ambiguities from the real world into discernible pieces of information, infused with culturally bestowed meaning (Zerubavel 2002, 227). What else could better explain why methamphetamine hydrochloride obtained from a pharmacy is legally and socially considered a therapeutic "medicine," while the same chemical purchased from a local clandestine meth maker is perceived as a deadly and dangerous "drug"?

Claims-making crusades that have periodically captured the public's imagination with synthetic stimulants over the past eighty years have ultimately constructed such rigid boundaries between meth the medicine and meth the drug that public discourse over the latter virtually never acknowledges the existence of pharmaceutical speed. Surely it is no secret that millions of US residents legally and responsibly use stimulants every day (although many people are surprised to learn that meth is available via prescription). But public debates over prescription medicines are generally made separate from controversies over illicit drugs such that little to no connections are drawn between the two. The notion that methamphetamine can be helpful in some contexts and hurtful in others challenges the socially constructed boundaries demarcating "medicines" from "drugs," and threatens to illuminate a major contradiction in US drug policy and practice (see DeGrandpre 2006). And while a discourse of fear and hysteria, largely communicated through the mass media, is likely a chief explanation for American culture's apparent lack of a collective "vocabulary with which people can speak about drugs in this more complicated, qualified way" (Reinarman and Levine 1997a, 9), perhaps it is also simply more convenient for individuals to think of the world of chemical substances in terms of the deeply ingrained, socially defined categories that help clearly distinguish medicines from drugs, right from wrong, and good from evil.[2]

A second insight into Walter and Hank's conversation concerns Hank's assertion that "they" (lawmakers, presumably) "came to their senses" by prohibiting OTC sales of methamphetamine.[3] The majority of persons in society would probably not support lifting the current restrictions on synthetic stimulants for fear that doing so would only worsen extant hazards from meth. Many people who study drug issues—including some of those who argue for completely legalizing all drugs—agree that legalization would likely result in an increase in use, at least in the short term. Yet the important question that many legalization advocates ask is, Would the anticipated increase in use be offset by a reduction in drug-related harms that exist because of current prohibitions? Of course, this question will remain fully unanswered unless complete legalization takes place, a prospect difficult to envision even in the distant future.[4]

But Hank's comment—like the sentiments conveyed by the majority of successful claims makers involved in the social construction of the United States' multiple methamphetamine scares—indicates a lack of appreciation for historical fact. The old adage "If people don't know or understand history, they're doomed to repeat past mistakes" is relevant in this context.

In the early 1900s, some people experienced problems from using cocaine. The legislative solution, in the form of the Harrison Act, was to forbid manufacturers and doctors from supplying the drug and punish people for using it. The Harrison Act of 1914 directly facilitated the discovery and mass production of amphetamines by pharmaceutical companies. As speed's popularity grew, some people experienced problems from their use of amphetamines.

Government and industry measures to control the amphetamine supply created new problems. Restrictions on Benzedrine inhalers gave rise to the popularity of Benzedrine tablets. When the Durham-Humphrey Amendment of 1951 mandated a doctor's prescription for amphetamine tablets, resulting difficulties in securing speed in pill form encouraged some to resort to methamphetamine inhalers. When manufacturers introduced devices or denaturants to their inhalers to prevent oral abuse, users learned to extract speed in liquid form and administer it intravenously. In adapting to these various controls, some users experienced problems from their evolved use of amphetamines.

After drugstore sales of pharmaceutically manufactured Methedrine ampoules ceased in the 1960s, clandestine meth labs were born. When the DEA exercised its discretionary power to reclassify all amphetamines as Schedule II drugs and impose tight production quotas on licit manufacturers, the black market for meth fully transformed, and cocaine consumption skyrocketed.

As domestic meth labs began to create problems for some manufacturers, users, and communities, Congress reacted by imposing restrictions on P2P. When clandestine chemists switched to ephedrine, Congress imposed restrictions on it. When clandestine chemists switched to pseudoephedrine, lawmakers responded with more supply restrictions. Mexican DTOs stepped up as a major supplier of meth and, in doing so, more consistently provided US addicts with a smokable, more potent form of the drug. As US and Mexican government regulations attempted to disrupt this new supply chain, Mexican DTOs turned to other countries for precursors, relocated some of their operations to the United States, came to rely more upon "pre-precursors," and mastered the synthesis of smokable d-methamphetamine by reverting back to the old P2P production method. Concurrently, domestic meth makers adapted by developing smurfing networks and quicker synthesis techniques, and some users have taken up bath salts.

This historical escalation in stimulant-related harms can be seen largely as a consequence of successful crusades against stimulants communicated via mass media. The regulations implemented in response to each campaign eventually fostered a new series of harms that would be symbolically claimed and restructured by subsequent campaigns. And as the harms associated with methamphetamine markets and forms evolved over the years, so too did public perceptions of the drug. The medical framework through which methamphetamine was initially constructed as a miracle cure for depression, obesity, lethargy, and asthma was eliminated by the Methedrine scare of the late 1960s and early 1970s. The image of meth as a white, domestic problem began to be challenged during the brief ice age of 1989–1990, when claims makers communicated threats about Asian traffickers. These definitions fully transformed during the crystal meth scare of the late 1990s and early 2000s, as depictions of meth as a homegrown menace affecting poor rural whites were replaced with constructions of innocent users and nonusers victimized by merciless Mexican gangs and drug runners. The third methamphetamine scare also succeeded in constructing hedonistic sexual desires of homosexual men as a popular motivation for using the drug, an image that challenged traditional portrayals of meth as a workplace performance enhancement tool through which people could increase their chances of achieving the American Dream.

This series of temporal reconstructions of methamphetamine, from medicine to drug, white to brown, domestic to foreign, marginalized to mainstream, and instrumental to sinful, was made possible in part by the identification and renunciation of folk devils. Speed freaks, tweakers, gays, Asians, and Hispanics hell-bent on violence and sexual deviance were singled out for their destruction of innocence. Atrocity tales provided much of the foundation on which claims makers communicated the essence of methamphetamine's dangers. Constructing the worst cases of meth use as characteristic of the experiences of all users permitted only a limited range of viable solutions.

The extreme levels of media and political hysteria broadcast throughout much of the United States' three methamphetamine scares stifled any chance for prolonged sober discourse. Each new press report on the latest series of meth-related problems was accompanied by powerful, structurally connected claims makers calling for more restrictions, tighter controls, and stiffer penalties. Upon enactment, each new major piece of legislation functioned to symbolically expunge speed freaks, tweakers, and other folk devils from society.

Methamphetamine has had and continues to have detrimental effects on users and nonusers, children, the environment, law enforcement agents, and communities. Yet to truly understand the myriad harms caused by drugs, to understand the damage caused at the *chemical level,* we must exercise a sociological imagination (see Mills [1959] 2000) by tracing molecular structures back to historical decisions made by human beings vying for attention, resources, and power. Methamphetamine was nonexistent in the United States until the prohibition of cocaine. Meth labs did not originate until OTC sales of amphetamines were banned. Smokable meth was generally unheard of prior to the series of precursor regulations that began in 1980. Given these facts about the mutation of the synthetic stimulant problem in the United States, the "get-tough" approach to drug problems, as exemplified in the aforementioned *Breaking Bad* scene in which Hank says that lawmakers "came to their senses" by favoring supply-side solutions, makes little sense at all.

New Directions

As I have argued throughout, much of the explanation for contemporary stimulant problems lies in a history of policy that has generally discount-ed the population's demand for stimulation. To be fair, claims makers from a variety of occupational fields, including law enforcement, recog-nize that demand reduction is an important component of well-rounded, sensible drug policy. This perspective was evident in media coverage of the crystal meth scare, as representatives of the medical and drug treat-ment industries received some airtime to argue for more resources to reduce methamphetamine dependence. And while I found calls for methamphetamine treatment were secondary to demands for additional law enforcement resources, penalties, and precursor laws, media presen-tations of meth were more likely to embody a public health perspective on drug problems than presentations of crack cocaine, according to one content analysis of major US newspapers (Cobbina 2008). Uncertain, however, is whether this ostensibly emerging shift in sentiment actually indicates a growing resistance to criminal justice approaches to drug issues, or whether it is more a response to differences in racial portrayals of stereotypical methamphetamine and crack users.[5]

Still, the potential shift in public sentiment toward acknowledging the demand side of drug problems is further illustrated in statements issued by

Gil Kerlikowske, director of the ONDCP under President Obama. In a speech delivered at the 2009 International Association of Chiefs of Police Conference, Kerlikowske repeatedly called for federal drug control policies designed to reduce both the supply and demand for drugs in the United States: "It's time to rethink our strategy. . . . It's time to recognize drug abuse and addiction for what it is—not just a law enforcement and criminal justice issue, but also a very complex and dynamic public health challenge, one that demands a systematic, comprehensive, and evidence-based approach if we are going to be equal to the task" (Kerlikowske 2009, 2). More recently, Obama's drug czar has maintained this stance. Testifying in Congress during a hearing specifically focused on methamphetamine, Kerlikowske (2012) asserted, "We need to change the conversation in this country to emphasize the importance and effectiveness of treatment and recovery" (2).

The more comprehensive approach advocated by Kerlikowske indicates a toning down of traditional war-on-drugs rhetoric by government leaders and should be encouraging. Yet an analysis of the ONDCP's budget tells a slightly different story. Of the $25.4 billion proposed in the 2014 budget request, 42 percent is designated for demand reduction programs, and 58 percent is allocated for supply reduction and interdiction efforts (ONDCP 2013). These percentages are virtually identical to 2002 allotments of 59.3 percent and 40.7 percent, respectively (Kutinsky 2011). While the ONDCP's total budget has more than doubled over the past ten years, the consistent concentration of resources devoted to law enforcement, interdiction, and international supply reduction efforts (e.g., crop eradication) suggests the federal government remains heavily committed to a criminal justice approach to drug problems.

Little Demand for Demand Reduction

The relatively peripheral focus on demand reduction, common since at least the 1970s, is not surprising for a number of reasons. For one, politicians have made careers touting "Just Say No" and advocating stiffer penalties for drug users and dealers. In reference to marijuana specifically, Ethan Nadelmann (2004) notes that many "police, prosecutors, judges, and politicians . . . *quietly agree*" that criminalization policies create more problems than they solve (1; emphasis added). A get-tough ideology has become so ingrained in US discourse over the past forty years that many of those in elected positions likely fear that talking about drugs from the standpoint of public health would result in being labeled "soft on crime."[6]

A second likely reason why US policies tend to favor a supply-side approach to drugs lies in the historical dominance of drug agents and other law enforcement groups as primary claims makers defining drugs and drug issues. Portrayals of law enforcement officials as heroic, besieged, frontline defenders against evil outsiders help construct the war on drugs as a patriotic endeavor and reinforce the image of *illicit* drug use as anti-American. The regular close proximity of criminal justice organizations to the news media ultimately allows drug issues to be defined and communicated primarily as crime problems that can only be solved with more criminal justice resources, more prison cells, and more drug prohibitions.

Perhaps the most overlooked explanation for the relative shortage of consideration of policies and programs that aim to reduce demand relates to the extent to which drug problems derive from social forces. Unemployment, income inequality, family disruption, urban and rural poverty, the historical decline of the manufacturing industry, and a failing public education system are several of many sociological factors that directly or indirectly influence people's decisions to use, deal, or manufacture illicit drugs. Because quick fixes for these structural correlates of demand do not exist, virtually no claims makers—regardless of goals, political affiliations, or organizational interests—consider addressing the sociological bases for drug problems as one potential way to diminish the collective desire for consciousness alteration. A cultural emphasis on the value of individualism encourages faith in pharmacological determinism and fits with the apparent lack of sociological imagination through which drugs and drug users are viewed by those in power and the public at large.

Harm Reduction?

Although a great deal of research finds that the demand for altered states of mind can be reduced through carefully designed prevention and treatment programs, a quick inspection of every past and present human civilization suggests that drug use among some segments of the population will never be fully eliminated. This historical and contemporary truth has led some to favor a harm reduction approach to drug problems. Harm reduction's basic premise is that in recognition of the fact that some persons will always use drugs, policymakers and citizens alike should encourage initiatives that lessen the problems associated with drug use. Drawing an analogy with sexual behavior, Nadelmann (2012) contends, "Abstinence from drugs is the best way to avoid trouble, but one always needs a fallback strategy for those who can't or won't refrain. 'Zero tolerance' policies deter some people, but they also dramatically increase the harms and costs for those who don't resist. Drugs become more potent, drug use becomes more hazardous, and people who use drugs are marginalized in ways that serve no one" (387). Needle exchanges, safe-use sites, and methadone maintenance are several effective, albeit anti-Puritanical harm reduction strategies.

Nadelmann (2012) also argues that legalization may be the best form of harm reduction due to the myriad harms that exist as a direct consequence of drug prohibitions. While I agree that legalizing methamphetamine should at the very least be subject to honest open discourse, two middle-ground solutions based on harm reduction principles might include providing easier access to prescription amphetamines and reducing restrictions on cocaine.

Though certainly not the only nation, the United States clearly has a need for speed. While a hard-core using minority actively seeks out the hallucinations and delirium that accompany a weeklong crystal meth binge, many people get involved with the drug because they are looking for an edge in work, school, or sport. Ours is a competitive society, where personal value is often measured by occupational prestige and financial success. These forces propel some people into illegal drugs, and many of them get caught up in the myriad negative consequences endemic to the illicit marketplace. Nicholas Rasmussen (2008a) identifies historical and contemporary practices of the pharmaceutical industry as major reasons for US amphetamine abuse, and while his criticisms are persuasive, when legitimate drug companies dominated the synthetic speed scene, prices were relatively low, meth labs and lawless DTOs did not exist, products were generally sterile and of known dosage, and most users did not smoke methamphetamine. Although their controversial commentary in *Nature* did not center on reducing black-market harms, Henry Greely and colleagues (2008) argue for recognizing the "growing demand for cognitive enhancement" in modern society (702). Surely, new problems will arise if a wider spectrum of the population is allowed easy, legal access to prescription amphetamines or other non-amphetamine stimulants. At the same time, such changes would also likely facilitate decentralization of the illicit market and a corresponding decrease in its associated harms.

Most of the contemporary black-market harms stemming from methamphetamine were also nonexistent when cocaine was legal, and all things being equal, cocaine appears to be a safer stimulant than meth. The high from cocaine lasts for a shorter period of time than the high from amphetamines, and cocaine is much more similar in chemical structure to endogenous brain chemicals. Because methamphetamine and other synthetics are "drugs that nature never thought of," cocaine and many other nature-based drugs "interact more smoothly with the body's own chemistry" (Weil and Rosen 2004, 34). Since meth and cocaine provide the same general physiological sensations, reducing or eliminating the criminal penalties for minor cocaine possession, particularly in its original plant form (see Weil and Rosen 2004), might provide a safer alternative for persons seeking to fulfill their demand for stimulation. Additionally, cocaine's status as a Schedule II drug means that prescriptions are legal (albeit rare, and virtually impossible to fill at any pharmacy). While increasing prescription availability of cocaine is unlikely for a number of reasons, a return to effective nature-based stimulants should be considered as another form of harm reduction.[7]

* * *

Recounting an experience from a professional meeting on drug use held in 1992, Jock Young, the British sociologist who first employed the term *moral panic* to refer to public reactions to drug taking, described a conference lecture delivered by a drug enforcement official. The police officer's presentation included a tragic story and photograph depicting an "unbearably disfigured" woman who accidentally died when the cocaine-filled condom she swallowed had split open inside her stomach. Young (2011) states,

> "This," [the officer] informed us, "is what we are up against, this is the sort of tragedy that drugs create and which policing works to prevent." When my turn came [to deliver my conference presentation,] I had to point out the irony of the situation. No one swallows condoms of cocaine for the fun of it; the condoms were employed because of the situation of illegality, indeed the high price of cocaine in the marketplace was a direct result of policing. . . . The problem was socially constructed creating secondary harm much greater than the primary harm of the drug itself. (251)

The administration of high doses of methamphetamine, especially when injected or smoked, can lead to very negative health consequences among users. But the majority of the other problems associated with contemporary US meth use exist because of legislative decisions and law enforcement efforts guided more by morality and panic than by rational and reasoned deliberation (see Johns and Borrero 1991).

Repeatedly communicated via the mass media, many of these harms are constructed in a sociological and historical vacuum. Instead of acknowledging that the damages caused by clandestine labs, meth trafficking, bath salts, and so forth ultimately stem from a punitive, interdiction-based approach to stimulants, the same old tired drug war rhetoric continues, the black market adapts accordingly, and new, often worse harms are generated.

One of the nonchemical components of drug addiction is the feeling of relief the user experiences from the routines and traditions accompanying drug use. The repetitive act of going outside to smoke a cigarette, for example, provides a therapeutic and positive reinforcement beyond the physical pleasure one receives from administering nicotine. Persons who have become dependent on drugs are often encouraged to find the strength to "break the cycle of addiction," a cycle that consists partly of the comfort afforded by the routines associated with drug use. In a similar vein, but on a societal level, policymakers, claims makers, and audiences in the United States have grown comfortable with the standard of sensationalizing drug problems and with the tradition of the knee-jerk, lock-'em-up reactions that routinely follow. If we genuinely seek to limit the amount of societal harm inflicted by drugs, much like the individual drug addict, we must strive to break the cycle of familiarity to which we have been accustomed to think and talk about drugs.

Notes

1. Although methylone was left out of the 2012 law, it has remained in Schedule I by order of the DEA. On April 12, 2013, the DEA exercised its authority to permanently list methylone as a Schedule I drug ("Schedule of Controlled" 2013).

2. Hank's comment that "friggin' meth used to be legal" implies it is now illegal. This choice of language subtly illuminates the depth to which cultural classification systems facilitate the social construction of meaning and ultimately influence the ways in which we perceive reality. In the vast majority of discursive exchanges on this subject, including many in which I have participated, statements that "meth is illegal" are made with an a priori understanding that "meth" refers to the illicit street version of the drug. Of course, manufacture, distribution, and consumption of methamphetamine are legal in some contexts. Yet taken-for-granted cultural rules and language systems prevent any ambiguity resulting from statements that "meth used to be legal," even among individuals who are aware that use of Desoxyn is lawful with a doctor's prescription.

3. In another interpretation, Hank's support of early legislative action to restrict methamphetamine could be explained by the fact that he might not be employed by the DEA if speed were still available OTC.

4. Observation of the experiences other countries have had with shifting their drug policies from a punitive model that treats drug use as a criminal problem to a medical perspective that views drugs as a public health issue might shed some light on what might happen should the United States revert to a pre–Harrison Act era in which all drugs were legally and readily accessible. For a brief overview of the evolution of Portugal's drug problems following 2001 legislation that decriminalized simple possession of all illicit drugs, see the work of Caitlin Elizabeth Hughes and Alex Stevens (2010).

5. Certainly, an either/or explanation is not necessary here. It is quite possible that today's media and citizenry are more open to exploring public health approaches to drug problems because the failures of the modern drug war have become more apparent *and* because members of relatively powerful social groups (e.g., middle-class whites) are better able to empathize with methamphetamine addicts, a group that came to be portrayed as middle-class whites in the early 2000s.

6. The reluctance of government officials to seriously challenge the status quo may be shifting, as evidenced, for example, by an increase in political leaders across party lines denouncing criminal justice approaches to drug problems (e.g., Senator Rand Paul, Representative Jared Polis, former New Mexico governor and presidential candidate Gary Johnson) and the rise in popularity of anti–drug war interest groups in positions of legal authority (e.g., Law Enforcement Against Prohibition).

7. Of course, cocaine is unlikely to become obtainable in prescription form due to fears of increased rates of consumption, addiction, cocaine-related violence, and the like. Beyond these explanations, the fact that cocaine derives from nature means that it cannot be patented. In addition to being unable to earn large profits from nonpatentable natural drugs, pharmaceutical companies—particularly those who manufacture patent-protected synthetic stimulants—would likely perceive an increase in the prescription availability of cocaine as a threat to their business interests.

Appendix:
Methodology Note

Chapter 3

Discussions of media coverage of amphetamine in Chapter 3 are based largely on reports published in *Time* magazine, the *New York Times,* and many regional US newspapers. To find amphetamine-related newspaper and newsmagazine articles, common search terms used were "amphetamine*," "Benzedrine," and "ephedrine." Articles from *Time* were obtained from the magazine's website at www.time.com, which provides archived issues from 1923 (the first year of publication) to the present. Old issues of the *New York Times* were searched using ProQuest's historical newspaper database at www.proquest.com, unless otherwise noted in the References. In addition, the search engine EBSCOhost was used to locate articles in the *Saturday Evening Post*. Finally, old issues of regional and local newspapers were searched using the website www.newspaper archive.com. According to its website the NewspaperARCHIVE provides access to over 1 billion articles, published in 3,304 newspapers, spanning 241 years of coverage. While it does not provide comprehensive coverage of all regional newspapers for all time periods, it is a great resource for obtaining newspaper articles published during the early years of US amphetamine use.

Chapter 4

Media coverage of methamphetamine presented in Chapter 4 comes mainly from stories published in *Time* magazine, the *New York Times,* and many regional US newspapers. To find methamphetamine-related news-paper articles, common search terms used were "methamphetamine*," "Methedrine," and "Desoxyn." Articles from *Time* magazine were obtained from the magazine's website at www.time.com. Past issues of the *New York Times* were searched using ProQuest's historical newspapers database at www.proquest.com. Regional newspapers, including the *Oakland Tribune,* were searched using the website www.newspaper archive.com. The *Oakland Tribune* was used as a source of news coverage about methamphetamine because it was the only San Francisco Bay Area newspaper to which I could gain electronic access to articles published over the 1960s and 1970s.

Data on articles appearing in *Time* magazine, the *New York Times,* and the *Oakland Tribune,* as reported in Figure 4.1, are based on raw counts of articles containing "methamphetamine*" or "Methedrine" or "Desoxyn" (very few articles containing the word *Desoxyn* appeared in these publications from 1961 to 1977, for it was a much less popular brand-name methamphetamine than Methedrine).

Chapters 5–7

Search Commands

Methamphetamine data presented in Figures 5.1, 5.5, 6.1, 6.2, and 7.4 were compiled using the following Boolean search command: metham-phetamine* OR "crystal meth*" OR "methedrine" OR "desoxyn."

Crack cocaine data presented in Figures 5.5 and 7.4 were compiled using the following Boolean search command: "crack cocaine*."

Since some news stories included discussions of both methampheta-mine and crack cocaine, duplicate counts appear in Figures 5.5 and 7.4.

The search terms utilized for data presented in Figure 7.3 were sim-ply "gay marriage," "illegal immigration," and "global warming."

Sources

Time magazine articles were located at www.time.com/time/archive. In the early 2000s, *Time* began publishing multiple versions, including *Time Asia* and *Time Europe.* In recent years, *Time* has published "daily" articles on its website, in addition to stories that appear in its weekly magazine. Counts reported in Figures 6.1 and 7.4 were limited to domestic, weekly issues of *Time* magazine. Articles from *Newsweek* and

US News and World Report come from print issues only and were located using the LexisNexis Academic search engine at www.lexisnexis .com/en-us/Home.page. In the late 1990s, *Newsweek* began publishing multiple editions, including *Newsweek Atlantic* and *Newsweek International*. Counts in Figures 6.1 and 7.4 come from articles published in the US edition only. Also, *US News and World Report* reduced from weekly to biweekly print issues in mid-2008 and monthly print issues in 2009. *US News* converted to a solely online publication in December 2010 (which is why no 2011–2012 data from this publication appear in Figure 6.1).

Newspaper data presented in Figures 5.1, 5.5, and 6.2 come from www.proquest.com. Since multiple editions for many of these newspapers are available (especially for recent years), searches were limited to the "main" edition of each newspaper. In addition, attempts were made to exclude technical reports in the form of police blotters, in order to focus on substantive articles only. ProQuest only offers eastern editions of the *New York Times* and *Wall Street Journal*. While both publications are rather national in scope since, historically, methamphetamine has been more common in the West, caution must be exercised when attempting to make interpretations of national concerns over methamphetamine from eastern editions.

All figures presenting counts of television news segments were created with data located through the Vanderbilt Television News Archive, at http://tvnews.vanderbilt.edu/. Vanderbilt University defines this data source as "the world's most extensive and complete archive of television news. We have been recording, preserving and providing access to television news broadcasts of the national networks since August 5, 1968" ("Vanderbilt Television" 2012). Data on television news coverage presented in all relevant figures include only those nationally televised nightly news programs broadcast on ABC, NBC, and CBS. Results from "Commercials" and "Specials" were excluded. Most in-text excerpts of television news reports come from segment abstracts provided by Vanderbilt University. I occasionally consulted LexisNexis Academic for full transcripts, which are available for more recently broadcast news segments.

Acronyms

ADAM	Arrestee Drug Abuse Monitoring Program
ADD	attention-deficit disorder
ADHD	attention-deficit/hyperactivity disorder
AIDS	acquired immune deficiency syndrome
AMA	American Medical Association
APhA	American Pharmaceutical Association
BNDD	Bureau of Narcotics and Dangerous Drugs
CMEA	Combat Methamphetamine Epidemic Act
CSA	Controlled Substances Act
DAWN	Drug Abuse Warning Network
DEA	Drug Enforcement Administration
DMT	dimethyltryptamine
DTO	drug-trafficking organization
ED	emergency department
EGCG	epigallocatechin gallate
EPIC	El Paso Intelligence Center
FBN	Federal Bureau of Narcotics
FDA	Food and Drug Administration
HIV	human immunodeficiency virus
LSD	lysergic acid diethylamide
MDMA	methylenedioxymethamphetamine (i.e., "ecstasy")
MDPV	methylenedioxypyrovalerone
MMP	Montana Meth Project
MTF	Monitoring the Future
NACo	National Association of Counties
NDIC	National Drug Intelligence Center

NIDA   National Institute on Drug Abuse
NSDUH   National Survey on Drug Use and Health
ONDCP   Office of National Drug Control Policy
OTC   over the counter
P2P   phenyl-2-propanone
PCP   phencyclidine
R-DAS   Restricted-Use Data Analysis System
SAMHSA   Substance Abuse and Mental Health Services
            Administration
SKF   Smith, Kline, and French
STRIDE   System to Retrieve Information from Drug Evidence
TEDS   Treatment Episode Data Set
UNICRI   United Nations Interregional Crime and Justice Research
            Institute
WHO   World Health Organization

References

Abood, Richard. 2005. *Pharmacy Practice and the Law.* 4th ed. Boston: Jones and Bartlett.

Abourashed, Ehab A., Abir T. El-Alfy, Ikhlas A. Khan, and Larry Walker. 2003. "Ephedra in Perspective: A Current Review." *Phytotherapy Research* 17:703–712.

ADAM (Arrestee Drug Abuse Monitoring Program). 2000. *Arrestee Drug Abuse Monitoring (ADAM) Program in the United States, 2000* (computer file). ICPSR version. Washington, DC: US Department of Justice, National Institute of Justice (producer), 2001. Ann Arbor, MI: Inter-university Consortium for Political and Social Research (distributor), 2001.

———. 2001. *Arrestee Drug Abuse Monitoring (ADAM) Program in the United States, 2001* (computer file). ICPSR version. Washington, DC: US Department of Justice, National Institute of Justice (producer), 2003. Ann Arbor, MI: Inter-university Consortium for Political and Social Research (distributor), 2003.

———. 2002. *Arrestee Drug Abuse Monitoring (ADAM) Program in the United States, 2002* (computer file). ICPSR version. Washington, DC: US Department of Justice, National Institute of Justice (producer), 2004. Ann Arbor, MI: Inter-university Consortium for Political and Social Research (distributor), 2004.

———. 2003. *Arrestee Drug Abuse Monitoring (ADAM) Program in the United States, 2003* (computer file). ICPSR version. Washington, DC: US Department of Justice, National Institute of Justice (producer), 2004. Ann Arbor, MI: Inter-university Consortium for Political and Social Research (distributor), 2004.

ADAM II (Arrestee Drug Abuse Monitoring Program II). 2011. "2010 Annual Report." Arrestee Drug Abuse Monitoring Program II, Office of National Drug Control Policy, May.

———. 2012. "2011 Annual Report." Arrestee Drug Abuse Monitoring Program II, Office of National Drug Control Policy, May.

Adams, Cecil. 2009. "How Would I Go About Laundering Money?" Retrieved September 1, 2012, from www.thestraightdope.com.

Adams, Samuel Hopkins. 1905. "The Great American Fraud." *Collier's*, October 7, pp. 14–15.

Adler, Patricia A., and Peter Adler. 2012. "Constructing Deviance." In *Constructions of Deviance: Social Power, Context, and Interaction,* 7th ed., edited by Patricia A. Adler and Peter Adler, 149–157. Belmont, CA: Thomson/Wadsworth.

"Agents Crack Drug Source, Seize Osteopath." 1963. *Fresno Bee,* February 5, p. 1.

"The Aim and Future of Natural Science." 1890. *Science: A Weekly Newspaper of All the Arts and Sciences* 16 (404): 239–244.

Altheide, David L. 1997. "The News Media, the Problem Frame, and the Production of Fear." *Sociological Quarterly* 38:647–668.

Altheide, David L., and R. Sam Michalowski. 1999. "Fear in the News: A Discourse of Control." *Sociological Quarterly* 40:475–503.

"American Agenda (Drugs: Made in US)." 1989. *ABC Evening News,* January 24.

American Journal of Nursing. 1951. 51 (6): 29.

———. 1952. 52 (1): 23.

"America's Homeless Children." 2004. *The National Center on Family Homelessness.* Retrieved December 22, 2008, from www.familyhomelessness.org.

"Amphetamine Kicks." 1959. *Time,* February 2. Retrieved June 12, 2008, from www.time.com.

"Ancient Drug in New Role." 1926. *New York Times,* May 20, p. 29.

Anderson, D. Mark. 2010. "Does Information Matter? The Effect of the Meth Project on Meth Use Among Youths." *Journal of Health Economics* 29:732–742.

Anglin, M. Douglas, Cynthia Burke, Brian Perrochet, Ewa Stamper, and Samia Dawud-Noursi. 2000. "History of the Methamphetamine Problem." *Journal of Psychoactive Drugs* 32:137–141.

Anti-Drug Abuse Act of 1986. Pub. L. No. 99-570. 100 Stat. 3207 (1986).

Archibold, Randal C. 2004. "Edwards Calls for Drug Crackdown in Rural Areas." *New York Times,* October 12, p. A22.

Armstrong, Edward G. 2007. "Moral Panic over Meth." *Contemporary Justice Review* 10:427–442.

Ashton, Florence L. 1906. "The Alleviation of Discomforts Following Anaesthesia." *American Journal of Nursing* 6:865–870.

Asnis, Stephen F., and Roger C. Smith. 1979. "Amphetamine Abuse and Violence." In *Amphetamine Use, Misuse, and Abuse,* edited by David E. Smith, 205–217. Boston: G. K. Hall.

Bai, Matt. 1997. "White Storm Warning." *Newsweek,* March 31, p. 66.

Baker, James N., et al. 1989. "The Newest Drug War." *Newsweek,* April 3, p. 20.

Ballentine, Carol. 1981. "Taste of Raspberries, Taste of Death: The 1937 Elixir Sulfanilamide Incident." *FDA Consumer Magazine,* June. Retrieved August 27, 2012, from www.fda.gov/oc/history/elixir.html.

Barak, Gregg. 1994. "Media, Society, and Criminology." In *Media, Process, and the Social Construction of Crime,* edited by Gregg Barak, 3–45. New York: Garland.

Barden, Connie. 2012. "New Drug Risk." *Miami Herald,* June 4. Retrieved September 1, 2012, from www.miamiherald.com.

Barlow, Mellissa Hickman. 1998. "Race and the Problem of Crime in *Time* and *Newsweek* Cover Stories, 1946 to 1995." *Social Justice* 25:149–183.

Barmack, Joseph E. 1938. "The Effect of Benzedrine Sulfate (Benzyl Methyl Carbinamine) upon the Report of Boredom and Other Factors." *Journal of Psychology* 5:125–132.

Baumann, Michael H., John S. Partilla, and Kurt R. Lehner. 2013. "Psychoactive 'Bath Salts': Not So Soothing." *European Journal of Pharmacology* 698:1–5.

"Be-bop Be-bopped." 1946. *Time,* March 25. Retrieved June 12, 2008, from www.time.com.

Becker, Howard S. 1963. *Outsiders: Studies in the Sociology of Deviance.* New York: The Free Press.

Beiser, Vince. 2002. "The Dark Side of the Boom." *US News and World Report,* March 19, p. 34.

Benbow, Dana Hunsinger. 2012. "Cleaning Up Mess Left by Meth Labs a Profitable Niche." *Indianapolis Star*, March 25. Retrieved August 4, 2013, from www.usatoday.com.

"Bennies the Menace." 1954. *Time*, June 14. Retrieved June 12, 2008, from www.time.com.

"Benny Is My Co-Pilot." 1956. *Time*, June 11. Retrieved June 12, 2008, from www.time.com.

"Benzedrine Alerts." 1944. *Time*, February 21. Retrieved June 12, 2008, from www.time.com.

Berggren, Sven, and Lennart Soderberg. 1938. "The Effect of Phenylisopropylamine (Benzedrine) on Cardiac Output and Basal Metabolism in Man." *Acta Physiologica* 79:115–120.

Bertram, Eva, Morris Blachman, Kenneth Sharpe, and Peter Andreas. 1996. *Drug War Politics: The Price of Denial*. Berkeley: University of California Press.

Best, Joel. 1990. *Threatened Children: Rhetoric and Concern About Child-Victims*. Chicago: University of Chicago Press.

———. 2008. *Social Problems*. New York: W. W. Norton.

Best, Joel, and Scott R. Harris. 2013. *Making Sense of Social Problems*. Boulder, CO: Lynne Rienner.

Best, Joel, and David F. Luckenbill. 1994. *Organizing Deviance*. 2nd ed. Englewood Cliffs, NJ: Prentice Hall.

Bickel, Warren K., and Richard J. DeGrandpre. 1996. *Drug Policy and Human Nature: Psychological Perspectives on the Prevention, Management, and Treatment of Illicit Drug Abuse*. New York: Plenum.

Bigart, Homer. 1964. "1,100 Police Get Narcotics Duty in Drive to Curb Rise in Addicts." *New York Times*, September 10, p. 1.

Bishop, Katherine. 1989. "Fear Grows over Effects of a New Smokable Drug." *New York Times*, September 16, p. A1.

Blendon, Robert J., and John T. Young. 1998. "The Public and the War on Illicit Drugs." *Journal of the American Medical Association* 279:827–832.

Blumenson, Eric, and Eva Nilsen. 1998. "Policing for Profit: The Drug War's Hidden Economic Agenda." *University of Chicago Law Review* 65:35–114.

Boorstein, Michelle. 2004. "In Va., Narcotic Makes an Isolated Rise; By Large Margin, Shenandoah Valley Has Region's Heaviest Methamphetamine Traffic." *Washington Post*, August 22, p. C8.

Borders, Tyrone F., Brenda M. Booth, Xiaotong Han, Patricia Wright, Carl Leukefeld, Russel S. Falck, and Robert G. Carlson. 2008. "Longitudinal Changes in Methamphetamine and Cocaine Use in Untreated Rural Stimulant Users: Racial Differences and the Impact of Methamphetamine Legislation." *Addiction* 103:800–808.

Bossong, M. G., J. P. Van Dijk, and R. J. M. Niesink. 2005. "Methylone and mCPP, Two New Drugs of Abuse?" *Addiction Biology* 10:321–323.

Bottel, Helen. 1967. "Helen Help Us!" *Lebanon Daily News*, October 24, p. 15.

Bouffard, Jeffrey A., and Katie A. Richardson. 2007. "The Effectiveness of Drug Court Programming for Specific Kinds of Offenders: Methamphetamine and DWI Offenders Versus Other Drug-Involved Offenders." *Criminal Justice Policy Review* 18:274–293.

Bradley, Charles. 1937. "The Behavior of Children Receiving Benzedrine." *American Journal of Psychiatry* 94:577–585.

Brecher, Edward M. 1972. *Licit and Illicit Drugs: The Consumers Union Report on Narcotics, Stimulants, Depressants, Inhalants, Hallucinogens, and Marijuana— Including Caffeine, Nicotine, and Alcohol*. Mount Vernon, NY: Consumers Union.

Brody, Jane E. 1967. "Trips with a One-Way Ticket." *New York Times*, October 22, p. 210, http://select.nytimes.com/gst/abstract.html?res=F50816F83A55107A93C0AB178BD 95F438685F9.

Brooke, Clarke. 1960. "Khat (*Catha edulis*): Its Production and Trade in the Middle East." *The Geographical Journal* 126:52–59.

Brooke, James. 2003. "North Korea, Protesting New Ship Inspections, Suspends Its Passenger Ferry Link with Japan." *New York Times*, June 9, p. A8.

Brown, David. 2005. "Scope of Unusual HIV Strain Is Unknown, Experts Say." *Washington Post*, February 13, p. A16.

Brownstein, Henry H. 2000. *The Social Reality of Crime*. Boston: Allyn and Bacon.

Burton, Brent T. 1991. "Heavy Metals and Organic Contaminants Associated with Illicit Methamphetamine Production." In *Methamphetamine Abuse: Epidemiologic Issues and Implications*, NIDA Research Monograph 115, edited by Marissa A. Miller and Nicholas J. Kozel, 47–59. Washington, DC: US Government Printing Office.

Bush, George H. W. 1989. "Address to the Nation on the National Drug Control Strategy," September 5. *The American Presidency Project,* online, by Gerhard Peters and John T. Woolley. Retrieved February 12, 2013, from www.presidency.ucsb.edu.

Butterfield, Fox. 2002. "As Drug Use Drops in Big Cities, Small Towns Confront Upsurge." *New York Times*, February 11, p. A1.

———. 2004a. "Home Drug-Making Laboratories Expose Children to Toxic Fallout." *New York Times*, February 23, p. A1.

———. 2004b. "Across Rural America, Drug Casts a Grim Shadow." *New York Times*, January 4, p. A10.

Byker, Carl (writer). 2006. "The Meth Epidemic." *PBS: Frontline*, season 24, episode 3, aired February 14, 2006, DVD.

Byles, Daniel W. 1968. "Abuse Control Laws and the Drug Industry." In *Amphetamine Abuse*, edited by J. Robert Russo, 39–50. Springfield, IL: Charles C. Thomas.

Byrd, Sheila. 2011. "Officials Fear Bath Salts Becoming the Next Big Drug Menace." *Washington Post*, January 23, p. A7.

"California / Methamphetamines / Explosion." 1995. *ABC Evening News*, December 27.

Carey, Frank. 1948. "FDA Reports Benzedrine Contents Eaten." *Corpus Christi Caller-Times*, February 15, p. 10B.

Carey, James T., and Jerry Mandel. 1968. "A San Francisco Bay Area 'Speed' Scene." *Journal of Health and Social Behavior* 9:164–174.

Carnevale, John. 2005. "Methamphetamine: What Do the Data Tell Us?" Presentation at the Second Methamphetamine Legislative and Policy Conference of the National Alliance for Model State Drug Law, December 2. Retrieved September 3, 2012, from www.namsdl.org/home.htm.

"*Catha edulis* (Khat): Some Introductory Remarks." 1980. United Nations Office on Drugs and Crime. Retrieved June 25, 2008, from www.unodc.org.

"Causeway Cannibal Had No Flesh in His Stomach." 2012. *CBS Miami*, June 9. Retrieved September 1, 2012, from http://miami.cbslocal.com.

Cha, Carol. 2013. "Drug Control: State Approaches Taken to Control Access to Key Methamphetamine Ingredient Show Varied Impact on Domestic Drug Labs." US Government Accountability Office. GAO-13-204. January. Retrieved May 8, 2013, from www.gao.gov.

Chambliss, William J. 1994. "Policing the Ghetto Underclass: The Politics of Law and Law Enforcement." *Social Problems* 41:177–194.

Charukamnoetkanok, Puwat, and Michael D. Wagoner. 2004. "Facial and Ocular Injuries Associated with Methamphetamine Production Accidents." *American Journal of Ophthalmology* 138:875–876.

Chen, Ko Kuei, and Carl Frederic Schmidt. 1930. *Ephedrine and Related Substances.* Baltimore: Williams and Wilkins.

Chermak, Steven. 1994. "Crime in the News Media: A Refined Understanding of How Crimes Become News." In *Media, Process, and the Social Construction of Crime*, edited by Gregg Barak, 95–129. New York: Garland.

Cho, Arthur K. 1990. "Ice: A New Dosage Form of an Old Drug." *Science* 249:631–634.

Cho, Arthur K., and William P. Melega. 2002. "Patterns of Methamphetamine Abuse and Their Consequences." *Journal of Addictive Diseases* 21:21–34.

Clement, Beverly A., Christina M. Goff, and T. David Forbes. 1998. "Toxic Amines and Alkaloids from *Acacia rigidula*." *Phytochemistry* 49:1377–1380.

Clinton, Bill. 1996. "Remarks on Signing the Comprehensive Methamphetamine Control Act of 1996." October 3. Retrieved June 5, 2008, from www.gpo.gov.

———. 1997. "Remarks by the President at US Conference of Mayors." May 21. Retrieved June 5, 2008, from http://tie.samhsa.gov/news/mayors.html.

"A Closer Look (Meth Crisis)." 2007. *ABC Evening News*, March 17.

Cobbina, Jennifer E. 2008. "Race and Class Differences in Print Media Portrayals of Crack Cocaine and Methamphetamine." *Journal of Criminal Justice and Popular Culture* 15:145–167.

Cohen, Stanley. [1972] 1980. *Folk Devils and Moral Panics: The Creation of the Mods and Rockers.* Oxford: Basil Blackwell.

"Company Announces New Anhydrous Ammonia Additive Designed to Deter Theft." 2004. *Microgram Bulletin* 37 (10): 183.

Congdon-Hohman, Joshua M. 2013. "The Lasting Effects of Crime: The Relationship of Discovered Methamphetamine Laboratories and Home Values." *Regional Science and Urban Economics* 43:31–41.

"Controlled Substances by CSA Schedule." 2013. US Department of Justice, Office of Diversion Control. Retrieved May 8, 2013, from www.deadiversion.usdoj.gov.

"Controls on Abuse of 2 Drugs Urged." 1963. *New York Times*, July 27, p. 46.

"Convicts Use Benzedrine Inhalers to Get Thrill." 1948. *Ackley World-Journal*, May 6, p. 3.

"Cooking Up Solutions to a Cooked Up Menace: Responses to Methamphetamine in a Federal System." 2006. *Harvard Law Review* 119:2508–2529.

Coontz, Stephanie. 1999. "How History and Sociology Can Help Today's Families." In *The Practice Skeptic: Readings in Sociology*, edited by Lisa J. McIntyre, 20–31. Mountain View, CA: Mayfield.

Copeland, Amy L., and James L. Sorensen. 2001. "Differences Between Methamphetamine Users and Cocaine Users in Treatment." *Drug and Alcohol Dependence* 62:91–95.

Copeland, Larry. 2005. "States Hope Laws Will Curtail Meth Labs." *USA Today*, April 26, p. 5A.

Cox, Carole, and Reginald G. Smart. 1970. "The Nature and Extent of Speed Use in North America." *Canadian Medical Association Journal* 102:724–729.

Critcher, Chas. 2000. "'Still Raving': Social Reaction to Ecstasy." *Leisure Studies* 19:145–162.

Crowley, Kathleen (executive producer). 2006. "World's Most Dangerous Drug," *National Geographic Explorer,* season 21, episode 5, directed by Cara Biega, aired October 18, 2006, DVD.

Cunningham, James K., Ietza Bojorquez, Octavio Campollo, Lon-Mu Liu, and Jane Carlisle Maxwell. 2010. "Mexico's Methamphetamine Precursor Chemical Interventions: Impacts on Drug Treatment Admissions." *Addiction* 105: 1973–1983.

Cunningham, James K., Lon-Mu Liu, and Myra Muramoto. 2008. "Methamphetamine Suppression and Route of Administration: Precursor Regulation Impacts on Snorting, Smoking, Swallowing, and Injecting." *Addiction* 103:1174–1186.

Cuomo, Chris, and Jon Scott. 1998. "Meth Madness." *Fox Files*, Fox News Network. LexisNexis Academic, Transcript no. 092401cb.255, September 24.

Dai, Serena. 2012. "Spending Money on the Drug War Really Isn't Lowering Drug Use." *Atlantic Wire,* October 24. Retrieved March 10, 2013, from atlanticwire.com.

Davey, Monika. 2005. "Grisly Effect of One Drug: 'Meth Mouth.'" *New York Times*, June 11, p. A1.

David, Matthew, Amanda Rohloff, Julian Petley, and Jason Hughes. 2011. "The Idea of Moral Panic—Ten Dimensions of Dispute." *Crime, Media, Culture* 7:215–228.

Davidson, Bill. 1965. "The Thrill-Pill Menace." *Saturday Evening Post*, December 3, pp. 23–27.

Davis, Robert. 1995. "'Meth' Use in the '90s: A Growing 'Epidemic.'" *USA Today*, September 7, p. 7A.

DAWN (Drug Abuse Warning Network). 2011. "Drug Abuse Warning Network, 2009: Methodology Report." Substance Abuse and Mental Health Services Administration, April, Rockville, MD.

———. 2012. "DAWN 2010 Emergency Department Excel Files—National Tables: National Estimates of Drug-Related Emergency Department Visits, 2004–2010— All Misuse and Abuse." Substance Abuse and Mental Health Services Administration. Retrieved September 3, 2012, from www.samhsa.gov.

Dayrit, Fabian M., and Morphy C. Dumlao. 2004. "Impurity Profiling of Methamphetamine Hydrochloride Drugs Seized in the Philippines." *Forensic Science International* 144:29–36.

DEA (Drug Enforcement Agency). 1994. "Clandestine Laboratory Seizures in the United States: 1993." *Drug Intelligence Report,* DEA-94080, US Department of Justice, December.

———. 2004. "State of Oklahoma Places Pseudoephedrine Tablets into Schedule V." US Department of Justice, June 10. Retrieved January 12, 2009, from www.usdoj.gov/dea.

———. 2008. "Maps of Methamphetamine Lab Seizures." US Department of Justice. Retrieved December 30, 2008, from www.usdoj.gov/dea.

———. 2013a. "DEA Staffing and Budget." US Department of Justice. Retrieved May 3, 2013, from www.justice.gov.

———. 2013b. "Drug Enforcement Administration (DEA): FY 2013 Budget at a Glance." US Department of Justice. Retrieved May 10, 2013, from www.justice.gov.

———. 2013c. "Methamphetamine Lab Incidents, 2004–2012." US Department of Justice. Retrieved April 12, 2013, from www.justice.gov.

———. 2013d. "3,4-Methylenedioxypyrovalerone (MDPV)." Office of Diversion Control, May. Retrieved May 5, 2013, from www.deadiversion.usdoj.gov.

DeGrandpre, Richard. 2006. *The Cult of Pharmacology: How America Became the World's Most Troubled Drug Culture.* Durham, NC: Duke University Press.

Derlet, Robert W. 1990. "Methamphetamine: Stimulant of the 1990s?" *Western Journal of Medicine* 153:625–628.

DIB (Drug Identification Bible). 2006. *Drug Identification Bible*. Grand Junction, CO: Amera-Chem.

————. 2012. *Drug Identification Bible*. Grand Junction, CO: Amera-Chem.

Dillon, Sam. 1995a. "Mexican Drug Dealer Pushes Speed, Helping Set Off an Epidemic in US." *New York Times*, December 27, p. A7.

————. 1995b. "Speed Catches Up with Crack." *New York Times*, December 31, p. D2.

Dittrich, Luke. 2007. "Tonight on *Dateline* This Man Will Die." *Esquire*, September. Retrieved June 17, 2008, from www.esquire.com.

Dobkin, Carlos, and Nancy Nicosia. 2009. "The War on Drugs: Methamphetamine, Public Health, and Crime." *American Economic Review* 99:324–349.

"Doctor-Angler Reels Out Pharmaceutical Fish Tale." 1949. *New York Times*, July 9, p. 15.

"Doctor Brady's Health Talks: Portrait of a Benzedrine Addict." 1939. *Nebraska State Journal*, November 23, p. 8.

Dodd, Thomas J. 1962. "'Kick Drugs'—Growing Teen-Age Menace." *Family Weekly* (in *Lowell Sun*), March 18, p. 59.

Dolak, Kevin. 2012. "Bath Salts: Use of Dangerous Drug Increasing Across US." *ABC News*, June 5. Retrieved September 1, 2012, from http://abcnews.go.com.

Doppelt, Jack C., and Peter M. Manikas. 1990. "Mass Media and Criminal Justice Decision Making." In *The Media and Criminal Justice Policy*, edited by Ray Surette, 129–142. Springfield, IL: Charles C. Thomas.

Dowler, Kenneth. 2003. "Media Consumption and Public Attitudes Toward Crime and Justice: The Relationship Between Fear of Crime, Punitive Attitudes, and Perceived Police Effectiveness." *Journal of Criminal Justice and Popular Culture* 10:109–126.

"Drug Abuse / Crank." 1989. *CBS Evening News*, February 28.

"Drug Abuse / Rural Meth Labs." 2004. *NBC Evening News*, March 10.

"Drug Fact Sheet: Methamphetamine." 2012. Drug Enforcement Administration, US Department of Justice. Retrieved September 2, 2012, from www.justice.gov/dea.

"Drug Held Cure for Alcoholism." 1938. *New York Times,* December 28. Retrieved March 10, 2013, from www.nytimes.com.

"Drug Ring Probe Shifts to Druggists." 1962. *San Mateo Times and Daily News Leader*, November 28, p. 7.

"Drugs / Meth Ice." 2006. *FOX Evening News*, February 25.

"Drugs / Meth Wars." 2005. *ABC Evening News*, July 5.

"Drugs / The Meth Crisis." 2006. *NBC Evening News*, March 18.

Duggan, Paul, and Ernesto Londo. 2007. "Not Your Average Drug Bust; Suspect Wanted in Mexico Found in Wheaton Restaurant." *Washington Post*, July 25, p. A1.

D'Ulisse, Ronald J. 2013. "Ronald J. D'Ulisse." Retrieved April 15, 2013, from www.cecity.com/ncpa/tampa_2008/pharmacy_crime/dulisse.htm.

"Efficiency of Brain Held Due to Its 'Fuel'; Cells Found Speeded Up by Synthetic Drug." 1937. *New York Times*, April 10, p. 6.

Egan, Timothy. 2002. "Meth Building Its Hell's Kitchen in Rural America." *New York Times*, February 6, p. A14.

Eggen, Dan. 2005. "400 Arrested in US Methamphetamine Raids." *Washington Post*, August 31, p. A2.

Epstein, Edward Jay. 1990. *Agency of Fear: Opiates and Political Power in America*. Rev. ed. London: Verso.

Erceg-Hurn, David M. 2008. "Drugs, Money, and Graphic Ads: A Critical Review of the Montana Meth Project." *Prevention Science* 9:256–263.

Erikson, Kai T. [1966] 2006. "On the Sociology of Deviance." In *Constructions of Deviance: Social Power, Context, and Interaction,* 5th ed., edited by Patricia A. Adler and Peter Adler, 13–20. Belmont, CA: Thomson/Wadsworth.

Essoyan, Susan. 1989. "Use of Highly Addictive 'Ice' Growing in Hawaii Drugs." *Los Angeles Times*, October 16, p. 17.

Farah, Douglas. 1997. "100 Arrested, 3 Labs Closed in Methamphetamine Probe." *Washington Post*, December 6, p. A01.

Farber, M. A. 1973. "Opinion Remains Divided over Effect of State's New Drug Law." *New York Times*, August 31, p. 16.

Faupel, Charles, Alan Horowitz, and Greg Weaver. 2004. *The Sociology of American Drug Use*. New York: McGraw Hill.

FBI (Federal Bureau of Investigation). 2013a. "Table 1. Crime in the United States, by Volume and Rate per 100,000 Inhabitants, 1992–2011." Uniform Crime Reports, Federal Bureau of Investigation. Retrieved March 5, 2013, from www.fbi.gov.

———. 2013b. "Persons Arrested. Arrests Table. Arrests for Drug Abuse Violations, Percent Distribution by Region, 2011." Uniform Crime Reports, Federal Bureau of Investigation. Retrieved March 5, 2013, from www.fbi.gov.

"Federal Crack Cocaine Sentencing." 2010. *The Sentencing Project*, October. Retrieved September 1, 2012, from http://sentencingproject.org/template/index.cfm.

Field, Bryan. 1941. "Aonbarr Is First in Bowie Feature." *New York Times*, November 23, p. S1.

"Find Drug That Will Keep Sleepy Persons Wide Awake." 1935. *The Science News-Letter* 28:403. December 28.

Fine, Gary Alan. 1985. "The Goliath Effect: Corporate Dominance and Mercantile Legends." *Journal of American Folklore* 98:63–84.

Fiore, Faye. 1989. "Drug 'Cooks' Leave Health Hazards Behind Toxics." *Los Angeles Times*, November 19, p. 1.

Fish, Jefferson M. 2006. "Five Drug Policy Fallacies." In *Drugs and Society: US Public Policy*, edited by Jefferson M. Fish, 79–96. Lanham, MD: Rowman and Littlefield.

Fitzgerald, John L., and Terry Threadgold. 2004. "Fear of Sense in the Street Heroin Market." *International Journal of Drug Policy* 15:407–417.

"Focus: Methamphetamines." 2001. *NBC Evening News*, August 5.

Fort, Joel. 1964. "The Problem of Barbiturates in the United States of America." *UNODC Bulletin on Narcotics* 1:17–35.

"42 Ordered in 'Lift Pill' Sale." 1955. *New York Times*, October 26, p. 13.

"4 Seized in Illegal Drug Lab Raid." 1963. *Oakland Tribune*, January 13, p. 1.

Franco, Celinda. 2007. "Methamphetamine: Background, Prevalence, and Federal Drug Control Policies." Congressional Research Service, CRS Report for Congress, January 24.

Frank, R. S. 1983. "The Clandestine Drug Laboratory Situation in the United States." *Journal of Forensic Sciences* 28:18–31.

Freeman, Tom P., Celia J. A. Morgan, James Vaughn-Jones, Nahida Hussain, Kash Karimi, and H. Valerie Curran. 2012. "Cognitive and Subjective Effects of Mephedrone and Factors Influencing Use of a 'New Legal High.'" *Addiction* 107:792–800.

Frontline. 2006. "The Meth Epidemic." Public Broadcasting Corporation. Retrieved April 1, 2007, from www.pbs.org.

Gahlinger, Paul. 2004. *Illegal Drugs: A Complete Guide to Their History, Chemistry, Use, and Abuse*. New York: Plume.

Gambrell, Jon. 2007. "New Threat: Fruit-Flavored Meth." *Seattle Times*, May 2. Retrieved January 5, 2009, from www.seattletimes.com.

Garland, David. 1996. "The Limits of the Sovereign State: Strategies of Crime Control in Contemporary Society." *British Journal of Criminology* 36:445–471.

Gfroerer, Joseph. 2002. "Introduction." In *Redesigning an Ongoing National Household Survey: Methodological Issues*, edited by J. Gfroerer, J. Eyerman, and J. Chromy, 1–8. DHHS Publication No. SMA 03-3768. Rockville, MD: Substance Abuse and Mental Health Services Administration, Office of Applied Studies.

Gfroerer, Joseph, and Marc Brodsky. 1992. "The Incidence of Illicit Drug Use in the United States, 1962–1989." *British Journal of Addiction* 87:1345–1351.

Gfroerer, Joseph, et al. 2004. "Estimating Trends in Substance Use Based on Reports of Prior Use in a Cross-Sectional Survey." In *Eighth Conference on Health Survey Research Methods*, edited by S. B. Cohen and J. M. Lepkowski, 29–34. Hyattsville, MD: National Center for Health Statistics.

Gieringer, Dale. 2006. "Anniversary of the Opium Exclusion Act." *Free Internet Press*, February 9. Retrieved October 10, 2008, from www.freeinternetpress.com.

Gillespie, Nick. 2005. "Meth Still Driving People Nuts." *Reason Online*. Retrieved May 2, 2013, from www.reason.com.

"Girl Held for 'Pills.'" 1962. *San Mateo Times and Daily News Leader*, December 11, sec. 2, p. 21.

Gizzi, Michael C. 2011. "Methamphetamine and Its Impact on the Criminal Justice System: A Three-Year Examination of Felony Drug Filings." *Journal of Crime and Justice* 34:103–123.

Goddard, Terry. 2005. "Crying Wolf About Meth Abuse?" *New York Times*, August 11, p. A22.

Goetz, Andrew C. 2007. "One Stop, No Stop, Two Stop, Terry Stop: Reasonable Suspicion and Pseudoephedrine Purchases by Suspected Methamphetamine Manufacturers." *Michigan Law Review* 105:1573–1595.

Goldberg, Carey. 1997. "Way Out West and Under the Influence." *New York Times*, March 16, p. E16.

Golden, Tim. 2002. "Mexican Drug Dealers Turning US Towns into Major Depots." *New York Times*, November 16, p. A1.

Goldstein, Paul. 1985. "The Drugs/Violence Nexus: A Tripartite Conceptual Framework." *Journal of Drug Issues* 15:493–506.

Goode, Erich, and Nachman Ben-Yehuda. 1994a. *Moral Panics: The Social Construction of Deviance*. Oxford: Blackwell.

———. 1994b. "Moral Panics: Culture, Politics, and Social Construction." *Annual Review of Sociology* 20:149–171.

Goodnough, Abby, and Katie Zezima. 2011. "An Alarming New Stimulant, Legal in Many States." *New York Times*, July 16, p. A1.

Gould, Peter (writer). 2008. "A No-Rough-Stuff-Type Deal," *Breaking Bad,* season 1, episode 7, directed by Tim Hunter, Sony Pictures Home Entertainment, aired March 9, 2008, DVD.

Gould, Whitney. 1969. "Ex–Drug Users Share 'Bad Trips' with East Students." *Capital Times*, April 16, p. 43.

Graber, Doris A. 1980. *Crime News and the Public*. New York: Praeger.

Graham, James M. 1972. "Amphetamine Politics on Capitol Hill." In *Muckraking Sociology: Research as Social Criticism*, edited by Gary T. Marx, 177–205. New Brunswick, NJ: Transaction.

Greely, Henry, Barbara Sahakian, John Harris, Ronald C. Kessler, Michael Gazzaniga, Philip Campbell, and Martha J. Farah. 2008. "Towards Responsible Use of Cognitive-Enhancing Drugs by the Healthy." *Nature* 456:702–705.

Grinspoon, Lester, and James B. Bakalar. 1979. "The Amphetamines: Medical Uses and Health Hazards." In *Amphetamine Use, Misuse, and Abuse*, edited by David E. Smith, 18–34. Boston: G. K. Hall.

Grinspoon, Lester, and Peter Hedblom. 1975. *The Speed Culture: Amphetamine Use and Abuse in America*. Cambridge, MA: Harvard University Press.

Gross, Jane. 1988. "Speed's Gain in Use Could Rival Crack, Drug Experts Warn." *New York Times*, November 27, p. A1.

Gusfield, Joseph R. 1996. *Contested Meanings: The Construction of Alcohol Problems*. Madison: University of Wisconsin Press.

Guzman, Daniela, and Julie K. Brown. 2012. "Naked Man Killed by Police Near MacArthur Causeway Was 'Eating' Face off Victim." *Miami Herald*, May 27. Retrieved September 1, 2012, from www.miamiherald.com.

Haggin, Patience. 2012. "Obama Signs Federal Ban on 'Bath Salt' Drugs." *Time Newsfeed*, July 10. Retrieved September 1, 2012, from www.newsfeed.time.com.

"Haight-Ashbury Now a City of Fear." 1968. *Kingsport Times*, November 29, p. 5C.

Halbach, H. 1972. "Medical Aspects of the Chewing of Khat Leaves." *Bulletin of the World Health Organization* 47:21–29.

Hall, Wayne, Shane Darke, Michael Ross, and Alex Wodak. 1993. "Patterns of Drug Use and Risk-Taking Among Injecting Amphetamine and Opioid Drug Users in Sydney, Australia." *Addiction* 88:509–516.

Hamilton, Keegan. 2010. "Methology 101: Old-School Meth Labs Give Way to 'Shake and Bake.'" *Riverfront Times*, May 19. Retrieved September 1, 2012, from www.riverfronttimes.com.

"Harmless Drug Will Make You Life of Party." 1937. *Lima News*, September 19, p. 5.

Harrison Act of 1914. Pub. L. No. 63-223, 38 Stat. 785 (1914).

Hartung, Walter H. 1931. "Epenephrine and Related Compounds: Influence of Structure on Physiological Activity." *Chemical Reviews* 9:389–465.

Hartung, Walter H., and J. C. Munch. 1929. "Amino Alcohols. I. Phenylpropanolamine and Para-Tolylpropanolamine." *Journal of the American Chemical Society* 51:2262–2266.

Hatsukami, D. K., and M. W. Fischman. 1996. "Crack Cocaine and Cocaine Hydrochloride: Are the Differences Myth or Reality?" *Journal of the American Medical Association* 276:1580–1588.

"Hawaii / Drugs / Ice." 1989. *CBS Evening News*, September 6.

Heffernan, Virginia. 2006. "An Illegal Drug from Labs That Can't Be Shut Down." *New York Times*, February 14, p. E8.

Hein, Fred V. 1968. "Drug Abuse and the Role of Education." In *Amphetamine Abuse*, edited by J. Robert Russo, 98–110. Springfield, IL: Charles C. Thomas.

"Hell's Angels." 1979. *Time*, July 2. Retrieved November 27, 2007, from www.time.com.

Hiaasen, Scott, and Nadege Green. 2012. "No Bath Salts Detected." *Miami Herald*, June 27. Retrieved September 1, 2012, from www.miamiherald.com.

Hickman, Holly. 2004. "County Officials Fight Ravages of Methamphetamine." *Washington Post*, April 4, p. A14.

Hobbs, Frank, and Nicole Stoops. 2002. "Demographic Trends in the 20th Century: Census 2000 Special Reports." *US Bureau of the Census*, Series CENSR-4. Retrieved February 7, 2009, from www.census.gov.

Hogshire, Jim. 1999. *Pills-a-go-go: A Fiendish Investigation into Pill Marketing, Art, History and Consumption*. Venice, CA: Feral House.

Holden, Stephen. 2007. "Rock Bottom." *New York Times*, March 2, p. E10.

Holtz, Jeff. 2006. "A Stiff Proposal for Cold Medicines." *New York Times*, February 26, p. 14CN2.

Horner, Sarah. 2011. "New Wave of Untested Synthetic Drugs: Easy to Get, Deceptively Dangerous." *St. Paul Pioneer Press*, April 16. LexisNexis Academic.

Horwitz, Sari. 1989. "US Anti-Drug Effort Called Wrong for DC." *Washington Post*, December 16, p. A1.

Howlett, Debbie. 1997. "Meth: 'Drug of Choice in Midwest.' Easy-to-Concoct Drug Often Makes Users Turn Violent." *USA Today*, September 10, p. 1A.

———. 1998. "Murder Spree Suspect Talks of Methamphetamine Binge." *USA Today*, April 14, p. 3A.

Hoxie, R. F. 1913. "The Truth About the I.W.W." *Journal of the Political Economy* 21:785–797.

Hudson, Kenneth, Jean Stockard, and Zach Ramberg. 2007. "The Impact of Socioeconomic Status and Race-Ethnicity on Dental Health." *Sociological Perspectives* 50:7–25.

Hughes, Caitlin Elizabeth, and Alex Stevens. 2010. "What Can We Learn from the Portuguese Decriminalization of Illicit Drugs?" *British Journal of Criminology* 50:999–1022.

Hughes, Joe. 1995. "Tank Thief Scripted Rampage, DA Says." *San Diego Union-Tribune*, June 28, p. B1.

Hunt, Dana, Sarah Kuck, and Linda Truitt. 2006. "Methamphetamine Use: Lessons Learned." Contract No. 99-C-008. Cambridge, MA: Abt Associates. Retrieved April 10, 2013, from ncjrs.gov.

Hyman, Albert Salisbury. 1960. "Use of Drugs in Sports." *New York Times*, September 12, p. 28.

"'Hypo' Party Is Raided." 1962. *San Mateo Times and Daily News Leader*, November 20, p. 2.

"In Depth (Ice Meth)." 2007. *NBC Evening News*, March 29.

"In San Diego, an Old Drug Comes Back." 1996. *New York Times*, February 22, p. A19.

Inciardi, James A. 2002. *The War on Drugs III: The Continuing Saga of the Mysteries and Miseries of Intoxication, Addiction, Crime, and Public Policy*. Boston: Allyn and Bacon.

Inoue, Hiroyuki, Yuko T. Iwata, and Kenji Kuwayama. 2008. "Characterization and Profiling of Methamphetamine Seizures." *Journal of Health Science* 54:615–622.

Irvine, Gary D., and Ling Chin. 1991. "The Environmental Impact and Adverse Health Effects of the Clandestine Manufacture of Methamphetamine." In *Methamphetamine Abuse: Epidemiologic Issues and Implications*, NIDA Research Monograph 115, edited by Marissa A. Miller and Nicholas J. Kozel, 33–46. Washington, DC: US Government Printing Office.

Irvine, Martha. 2005. "Teenagers Lured into Meth's Net." *Washington Post*, July 24, p. A5.

Iversen, Leslie. 2006. *Speed, Ecstasy, Ritalin: The Science of Amphetamines*. New York: Oxford University Press.

Jackson, Charles O. 1979. "The Amphetamine Inhaler: A Case Study of Medical Abuse." In *Amphetamine Use, Misuse, and Abuse*, edited by David E. Smith, 33–45. Boston: G. K. Hall.

Jackson, Robert L. 2000. "Clinton Urges FDA Role on Tobacco." *Los Angeles Times*, March 26, p. A11.

Jacobs, Andrew. 2002. "In Clubs, a Potent Drug Stirs Fear of an Epidemic." *New York Times*, January 29, p. B1.

———. 2004. "The Beast in the Bathhouse." *New York Times*, January 12, p. B1.

———. 2006. "Battling H.I.V. Where Sex Meets Crystal Meth." *New York Times*, February 21, p. B1.

James, Sara. 1998. "Methamphetamine Use on the Rise in Many Cities." *NBC Nightly News*, July 12. LexisNexis Academic.

Jefferson, David J., et al. 2005a. "America's Most Dangerous Drug." *Newsweek*, August 8, pp. 41–48.

———. 2005b. "Party, Play—and Pay." *Newsweek*, February 28, p. 38.

Jenkins, Philip. 1992. "Narcotics Trafficking and the American Mafia: The Myth of Internal Prohibition." *Crime, Law, and Social Change* 18:303–318.

———. 1994. "'The Ice Age': The Social Construction of a Drug Panic." *Justice Quarterly* 11:7–31.

———. 1999. *Synthetic Panics: The Symbolic Power of Designer Drugs*. New York: New York University Press.

Johns, Christina Jacqueline, and Jose Maria Borrero. 1991. "The War on Drugs: Nothing Succeeds Like Failure." In *Crimes by the Capitalist State: An Introduction to State Criminality*, edited by Gregg Barak, 67–100. Albany: State University of New York Press.

Johnson, Akilah. 2003. "The Region; Studies Help Police Follow Meth Culture." *Los Angeles Times*, May 12, p. B4.

Johnson, Dirk. 1996. "Good People Go Bad in Iowa, and a Drug Is Being Blamed." *New York Times*, February 22, p. A1.

———. 2004. "Policing a Rural Plague." *Newsweek*, March 8, p. 41.

Johnson, Kevin. 2001. "Drug Labs Poisoning Forests." *USA Today*, January 30, p. 3A.

Johnson, Kirk. 2006. "Puzzling Killing of 3 Students Leaves Wyoming City on Edge." *New York Times*, July 19, p. A19.

Johnston, Lloyd D., et al. 2012. "Monitoring the Future National Survey Results on Drug Use, 1975–2011: Volume I, Secondary School Students." Ann Arbor: Institute for Social Research, University of Michigan.

Join Together Staff. 2007. "Meth Ado About Nothing? Flavored Meth and Cheese Heroin Stories Smack of Fearmongering." Partnership at Drugfree.org, June 22. Retrieved September 3, 2012, from www.drugfree.org.

Jones, Charisse. 2005. "Ore. May Set Precedent on Meth Laws." *USA Today*, July 22, p. 3A.

Joseph, Miriam. 2000. *Speed: Its History and Lore*. London: Carlton.

"Juvenile Thrill Seekers Big Dope Users, Police Say." 1962. *Oakland Tribune*, May 17, p. 12.

Kalant, Harold, and Oriana Josseau Kalant. 1979. "Death in Amphetamine Users: Causes and Rates." In *Amphetamine Use, Misuse, and Abuse*, edited by David E. Smith, 169–188. Boston: G. K. Hall.

Karch, Steven B. 2001. *Karch's Pathology of Drug Abuse*. 3rd ed. Boca Raton, FL: CRC.

———. 2002. "Amphetamines." In *Performance-Enhancing Substances in Sport and Exercise*, edited by Michael S. Bahrke and Charles E. Yesalis, 257–266. Champaign, IL: Human Kinetics.

Kasick, David P., Curtis A. McKnight, and Eleonora Klisovic. 2012. "'Bath Salt' Ingestion Leading to Severe Intoxication Delirium: Two Cases and a Brief Review of the Emergence of Mephedrone Use." *American Journal of Drug and Alcohol Abuse* 38:176–180.

Kasinsky, Renée G. 1994. "Patrolling the Facts: Media, Cops, and Crime." In *Media, Process, and the Social Construction of Crime*, edited by Gregg Barak, 203–234. New York: Garland.

Kaufman, Joshua, James R. Allen, and Louis J. West. 1969. "Runaways, Hippies, and Marihuana." *American Journal of Psychiatry* 126:717–720.

Keen, Judy. 2006. "Meth Labs Abundant This Hunting Season." *USA Today*, December 11, p. 3A.

Kerlikowske, R. Gil. 2009. "Statement of R. Gil Kerlikowske." Speech delivered at 2009 International Association of Chiefs of Police Annual Conference, Denver, Colorado. Retrieved August 28, 2012, from http://dadonfire.files.wordpress.com /2009/10/100309_iacp.pdf.

———. 2012. "Meth Revisited: Review of State and Federal Efforts to Solve the Domestic Methamphetamine Production Resurgence." Testimony delivered July 24 to Committee on Oversight and Government Reform Subcommittee on Health Care, District of Columbia, Census and the National Archives. US House of Representatives. Retrieved August 28, 2012, from http://oversight.house.gov.

"Key to Success (Montana Meth Project) Part I." 2007. *ABC Evening News*, October 1.

Kifner, John. 1967a. "Even Hippies Worried About Methedrine Use." *Albuquerque Tribune*, October 18, p. A4.

———. 1967b. "Violence Pursues the Flower People." *New York Times*, October 15, p. 197.

———. 1967c. "Methedrine Use Is Growing." *New York Times*, October 17, p. 1.

King, Rufus. 1972. *The Drug Hang-Up: America's Fifty Year Folly*. Springfield, IL: Charles C. Thomas. Retrieved December 20, 2008, from www.druglibrary.org /special/king/dhu/dhumenu.htm.

King, Ryan. 2006. "The Next Big Thing? Methamphetamine in the United States." *The Sentencing Project*, June. Retrieved January 12, 2007, from www.sentencing project.org.

Kirn, Walter. 1998. "Crank." *Time*, June 22. Retrieved November 27, 2007, from www.time.com.

Klasser, G. D., and J. Epstein. 2005. "Methamphetamine and Its Impact on Dental Care." *Journal of the Canadian Dental Association* 71:759–762.

Klee, H. 2001. "Amphetamine Use: Crystal Gazing into the New Millennium: Part One—What Is Driving the Demand?" *Journal of Substance Use* 6:22–35.

Klemesrud, Judy. 1967. "Helping Young People Overcome 'Pills, Pot, and Psychedelics.'" *New York Times*, March 22, p. 34.

Konnor, Delbert D. 2006. *Pharmacy Law Desk Reference*. New York: Haworth.

Korcok, Milan. 1978. "The Medical Applications of Marihuana and Heroin: High Time the Laws Were Changed." *Canadian Medical Association Journal* 119:374–380.

Kram, T. C. 1977. "Analysis of Impurities in Illicit Methamphetamine Exhibits. III: Determination of Methamphetamine and Methylamine Adulterant by Nuclear Magnetic Resonance Spectroscopy." *Journal of Forensic Sciences* 22:508–514.

Kramer, J. C., V. S. Fischman, and D. C. Littlefield. 1967. "Amphetamine Abuse: Pattern and Effects of High Doses Taken Intravenously." *Journal of the American Medical Association* 201:305–309.

Kurtis, Bill (executive producer). 1997. "Meth's Deadly High." Kurtis Productions, LTD and A&E Television Networks.

Kutinsky, Ethan. 2011. "Feds Don't Walk Their Talk in Drug Control Budget." *American Civil Liberties Union of Washington State*. Retrieved September 1, 2012, from www.aclu-wa.org/blog.

Kyle, Angelo D., and Bill Hansell. 2005. "The Meth Epidemic in America: Two Surveys of US Counties." National Association of Counties, July 5. Retrieved April 23, 2013, from www.naco.org.

Labi, Nadya. 1998. "Amiss Among the Amish." *Time*, July 6. Retrieved November 27, 2007, from www.time.com.

Lait, Matt. 1988. "California's New Role: Leading PCP Supplier." *Washington Post*, April 17, p. A01.

Lang, Gladys E., and Kurt Lang. 1983. *The Battle for Public Opinion*. New York: Columbia University Press.

Lauderback, David, and Dan Waldorf. 1993. "Whatever Happened to Ice? The Latest Drug Scare." *Journal of Drug Issues* 23:597–613.

Lavrakas, Paul J., Dennis P. Rosenbaum, and Arthur J. Lurigio. 1990. "Media Cooperation with Police: The Case of Crime Stoppers." In *The Media and Criminal Justice Policy*, edited by Ray Surette, 225–241. Springfield, IL: Charles C. Thomas.

Leinwand, Donna. 2005. "Counties Say Meth Is Top Drug Threat." *USA Today*, July 5, p. 3A.

———. 2006a. "States List Meth Offenders on Web." *USA Today*, August 23, p. 1A.

———. 2006b. "Backers Call Meth Registries a Safety Measure." *USA Today*, August 23, p. 3A.

———. 2007. "DEA Sees Flavored Meth Use; Trend May Be Effort to Lure Young Market." *USA Today*, March 26, p. 3A.

Lelyveld, Joseph. 1964. "Pharmacist Held in 'Pep-Pill' Sale." *New York Times*, August 22, p. 23.

Lendon, Brad. 2012. "Reports: Miami 'Zombie' Attacker May Have Been Using 'Bath Salts.'" CNN, May 29. Retrieved September 1, 2012, from http://news.blogs.cnn.com.

Leonhart, Michele M. 2011. "Scheduling Update." *Microgram Bulletin* 44 (11): 72–76.

Lerner, Michael A. 1988. "An Explosion of Drug Labs." *Newsweek*, April 25, p. 25.

———. 1989. "The Fire of 'Ice.'" *Newsweek*, November 27, p. 37.

Levine, Craig, and Harry Reinarman. 1991. "From Prohibition to Regulation: Lessons from Alcohol Policy for Drug Policy." *Milbank Quarterly* 69:461–494.

LexisNexis Academic. www.lexisnexis.com/en-us/Home.page.

Lind, Wilfred N. 1945. "With a B-29 over Japan: A Pilot's Story." *New York Times*, March 25, p. SM3.

Lindesmith, A. R. 1940a. "'Dope Fiend' Mythology." *Journal of Criminal Law, Criminology, and Police Science* 31:199–208.

———. 1940b. "The Drug Addict as a Psychopath." *American Sociological Review* 5:914–920.

Linnemann, Travis. 2010. "Mad Men, Meth Moms, Moral Panic: Gendering Meth Crimes in the Midwest." *Critical Criminology* 18:95–110.

"The Loco Weed." 1912. *The American Practitioner* 46:182–183.

Loseke, Donileen R. 2003. *Thinking About Social Problems*. 2nd ed. New Brunswick, NJ: Transaction.

Loseke, Donileen R., and Joel B. Best. 2003. *Social Problems: Constructionist Readings*. New York: Aldine de Gruyter.

Lukas, Scott E. 1985. *Amphetamines: Danger in the Fast Lane*. New York: Chelsea House.

MacNamara, Mark. 1989. "More Menacing Than Crack, 'Ice' Strikes." *USA Today*, September 7, p. 3A.

Maisto, Stephen A., Mark Galizio, and Gerard J. Connors. 2008. *Drug Use and Abuse*. 5th ed. Belmont, CA: Thomson/Wadsworth.

"The Malignant Enemy." 1965. *Time*, March 19. Retrieved June 12, 2008, from www.time.com.

"Man Shot Dead During Rampage in Stolen Tank." 1995. *Vancouver Sun*, May 19, p. A15.

Manges, Morris. 1900. "A Second Report on the Therapeutics of Heroin." *New York Medical Journal* 71:79–83.

Manning, Paul. 2006. "There's No Glamour in Glue: News and the Symbolic Framing of Substance Misuse." *Crime, Media, Culture* 2:49–66.

Marks, Harry M. 1995. "Revisiting the Origins of Compulsory Drug Prescriptions." *American Journal of Public Health* 85:109–115.

Matson, Charles. 2005. "Examining Methamphetamine." In *Medical-Legal Aspects of Abused Substances*, edited by Marcelline Burns and Thomas E. Page, 105–124. Tucson, AZ: Lawyers and Judges.

Mauer, Marc, and Ryan S. King. 2007. "A 25-Year Quagmire: The War on Drugs and Its Impact on American Society." *The Sentencing Project*. Retrieved June 12, 2008, from www.sentencingproject.org.

Maxwell, Jane Carlisle, and Mary-Lynn Brecht. 2011. "Methamphetamine: Here We Go Again?" *Addictive Behaviors* 36:1168–1173.

McBride, Duane C., Yvonne M. Terry-McElrath, Jamie F. Chriqui, Jean C. O'Connor, Curtis J. VanderWaal, and Karen L. Mattson. 2011. "State Methamphetamine Precursor Policies and Changes in Small Toxic Lab Methamphetamine Production." *Journal of Drug Issues* 41:253–282.

McCaffrey, Barry. 1998. *The National Drug Control Strategy, 1998: A Ten Year Plan.* Darby, PA: DIANE.

McDonagh, Marian S., Kim Peterson, Sujata Thakurta, and Allison Low. 2011. "Pharmacologic Treatments for Attention Deficit Hyperactivity Disorder, Final Update 4 Report." Portland: Oregon Health and Science University. Retrieved July 25, 2013, from www.ncbi.nlm.nih.gov.

McGraw, Dan, et al. 1999. "New Rules for Star Athletes." *US News and World Report*, March 22, p. 12.

McGraw, Dan, and Gordon Witkin. 1998. "The Iowan Connection." *US News and World Report*, March 2, p. 33.

McKenna, Terrence. 1991. *The Archaic Revival.* New York: HarperCollins.

McKetin, Rebecca. 2007. "Methamphetamine Precursor Regulation: Are We Controlling or Diverting the Drug Problem?" *Addiction* 103:521–523.

McKetin, Rebecca, Rachel Sutherland, David A. Bright, and Melissa M. Norberg. 2011. "A Systematic Review of Methamphetamine Precursor Regulations." *Addiction* 106:1911–1924.

Meddis, Sam. 1990. "US Drug Users Steer Clear of 'Ice.'" *USA Today*, April 6, p. 3A.

Melnikova, Natalia, Wanda Lizak Welles, Rebecca E. Wilburn, Nancy Rice, Jennifer Wu, and Martha Stanbury. 2011. "Hazards of Illicit Methamphetamine Production and Efforts at Reduction: Data from the Hazardous Substances Emergency Events Surveillance System." *Public Health Reports* 126:116–123.

Meredith, Charles W., Craig Jaffe, Kathleen Ang-Lee, and Andrew J. Saxon. 2005. "Implications of Chronic Methamphetamine Use: A Literature Review." *Harvard Review of Psychiatry* 13:141–154.

"The Merida Initative: Expanding the US/Mexico Partnership." 2012. US Department of State, Bureau of Western Hemisphere Affairs, March 29. Retrieved May 3, 2013, from www.state.gov.

"Meth Crisis." 2005. *CBS Evening News*, April 29.

"The Meth Crisis: Danger at Home (Part II)." 2005. *NBC Evening News*, August 9.

"The Meth Crisis: Danger at Home (Part IV)." 2005. *NBC Evening News*, August 11.

"Meth Labs." 2010. *The Police Chief*, February, p. 91.

"The Meth Project." 2013. Meth Project, The Partnership at Drugfree.org. Retrieved July 28, 2013, from www.methproject.org/about/.

Mikkelson, Barbara. 2012. "Quick Start," February 27. Retrieved September 3, 2012, from www.snopes.com.

Miller, Iona. 2013. "Pineal Gland, DMT and Altered States of Consciousness." *Journal of Consciousness Exploration and Research* 4:214–233.

Miller, Marissa A. 1997. "History and Epidemiology of Amphetamine Abuse in the United States." In *Amphetamine Misuse: International Perspectives on Current Trends*, edited by Hilary Klee, 113–134. Amsterdam: Harwood Academic.

Mills, C. Wright. [1959] 2000. *The Sociological Imagination*. Oxford: Oxford University Press.

Molotch, Harvey, and Marilyn Lester. 1974. "News as Purposive Behavior: On the Strategic Use of Routine Events, Accidents, and Scandals." *American Sociological Review* 39:101–112.

———. 1975. "Accidental News: The Great Oil Spill as Local Occurrence and National Event." *American Journal of Sociology* 81:235–260.

Monroe, Russell R., and Hyman J. Drell. 1947. "Oral Use of Stimulants Obtained from Inhalers." *Journal of the American Medical Association* 135:909–915.

Morgan, H. Wayne. 1981. *Drugs in America: A Social History, 1800–1980*. Syracuse, NY: Syracuse University Press.

Morgan, John P. 1979. "The Clinical Pharmacology of Amphetamine." In *Amphetamine Use, Misuse, and Abuse*, edited by David E. Smith, 3–10. Boston: G. K. Hall.

Morgan, John P., and Lynn Zimmer. 1997. "The Social Pharmacology of Smokeable Cocaine: Not All It's Cracked Up to Be." In *Crack in America: Demon Drugs and Social Justice,* edited by Craig Reinarman and Harry G. Levine, 131–170. Berkeley: University of California Press.

Morgan, Patricia, and Jerome E. Beck. 1997. "The Legacy and the Paradox: Hidden Contexts of Methamphetamine Use in the United States." In *Amphetamine Misuse: International Perspectives on Current Trends*, edited by Hilary Klee, 135–162. Amsterdam: Harwood Academic.

Morriss, John D. 1955. "Narcotics Traffic Faces New Curbs." *New York Times*, October 24, p. 29.

Mosher, Clayton J. 1985. "The Twentieth Century Marihuana Phenomenon in Canada." Master's thesis, School of Criminology, Simon Fraser University, Burnaby, British Columbia, Canada.

Mosher, Clayton J., and Scott Akins. 2007. *Drugs and Drug Policy: The Control of Consciousness Alteration*. Thousand Oaks, CA: Sage.

"Mosk Urges Addicts Be Forced to Report." 1962. *Independent*, October 25, p. 12.

"Mosk Urges Changes in Dope Laws." 1962. *Fresno Bee*, October 25, p. 6-C.

Murray, John B. 1998. "Psychophysiological Aspects of Amphetamine-Methamphetamine Abuse." *Journal of Psychology* 132:227–237.

Musto, David F. 1987. *The American Disease: Origins of Narcotic Control*. Expanded ed. New York: Oxford University Press.

"Mylan and Teva Settle Generic Provigil Dispute." 2012. Associated Press, June 8. Retrieved July 9, 2012, from www.businessweek.com.

NACo. (National Association of Counties). 2012. "About NACo." Retrieved September 3, 2012, from www.naco.org.

Nadelmann, Ethan A. 1989. "Drug Prohibition in the United States: Costs, Consequences, and Alternatives." *Science* 245:939–947.

———. 2004. "An End to Marijuana Prohibition." *National Review*, July 12, pp. 1–7.

———. 2012. "Think Again: Drugs." In *Drugs and the American Dream*, edited by Patricia A. Adler, Peter Adler, and Patrick K. O'Brien, 386–390. West Sussex, UK: Wiley-Blackwell.

"Narcotics Addicts Hunted in Newark." 1962. *New York Times*, July 16, p. 14.

"Nation: Hell's Angels." 1979. *Time*, July 2. Retrieved September 2, 2012, from www.time.com.

"Nazi Pep-Pills." 1942. *Time*, September 14. Retrieved June 12, 2008, from www.time.com.

NDIC (National Drug Intelligence Center). 2001. "Pennsylvania Drug Threat Assessment." National Drug Intelligence Center, US Department of Justice, June. Retrieved May 14, 2008, from www.usdoj.gov/ndic.

———. 2002. "Hawaii Drug Threat Assessment." National Drug Intelligence Center, US Department of Justice, May. Retrieved May 14, 2008, from www.usdoj.gov/ndic.

———. 2004. "National Drug Threat Assessment." National Drug Intelligence Center, US Department of Justice, April. Retrieved June 24, 2012, from www.justice.gov.

———. 2005. "Methamphetamine Drug Threat Assessment." National Drug Intelligence Center, US Department of Justice, March. Retrieved June 24, 2012, from www.justice.gov.

———. 2006. "National Methamphetamine Threat Assessment, 2007: OCDETF Regional Methamphetamine Summaries." National Drug Intelligence Center, US Department of Justice, November. Retrieved February 12, 2009, from www.usdoj.gov/ndic.

———. 2007a. "National Methamphetamine Threat Assessment, 2008." National Drug Intelligence Center, US Department of Justice, December. Retrieved June 24, 2012, from www.justice.gov/archive/ndic.

———. 2007b. "National Drug Threat Assessment, 2008." National Drug Intelligence Center, US Department of Justice, October. Retrieved February 12, 2009, from www.usdoj.gov/ndic.

———. 2008. "National Drug Threat Assessment, 2009." National Drug Intelligence Center, US Department of Justice, December. Retrieved February 12, 2009, from www.usdoj.gov/ndic.

———. 2009. "North Texas High Intensity Drug Trafficking Area Drug Market Analysis, 2009." National Drug Intelligence Center, US Department of Justice, April. Retrieved April 8, 2013, from www.justice.gov/archive.

———. 2010a. "National Drug Threat Assessment, 2010." National Drug Intelligence Center, US Department of Justice, February. Retrieved June 24, 2012, from www.justice.gov.

———. 2010b. "Drug Alert Watch: Increasing Abuse of Bath Salts." National Drug Intelligence Center, US Department of Justice, Sentry Management Team, EWS Report 000007, December 17. Retrieved June 24, 2012, from www.justice.gov/archive/ndic.

———. 2011a. "National Drug Threat Assessment, 2011." National Drug Intelligence Center, US Department of Justice, August. Retrieved June 24, 2012, from www.justice.gov.

———. 2011b. "Situation Report: Synthetic Cathinones (Bath Salts): An Emerging Domestic Threat." National Drug Intelligence Center, US Department of Justice, Product Number 2011-S0787-004, July. Retrieved June 24, 2012, from www.justice.gov.

"New Arrests Fight 'Pep' Pills Traffic." 1959. *New York Times*, December 30, p. 28.

"New Drug Is Found to Combat Suicide." 1936. *New York Times*, September 3, p. 16.

"New Gain Reported in Treating Colds." 1939. *New York Times*, September 13, p. 20.

NewspaperARCHIVE. Available at http://www.newspaperarchive.com.

Nicosia, Nancy, et al. 2009. "The Economic Cost of Methamphetamine Use in the United States, 2005." RAND Corporation, Drug Policy Research Center. Retrieved February 5, 2009, from www.rand.org.

NIDA (National Institute of Drug Abuse). 2010. "Epidemiologic Trends in Drug Abuse." *Proceedings of the Community Epidemiology Work Group, Volume I, Highlights and Executive Summary,* June 2009. US Department of Health and Human Services, National Institutes of Health, June. NIH Publication No. 10-7421.

Nonnemaker, James, Mark Engelen, and Daniel Shive. 2011. "Are Methamphetamine Precursor Control Laws Effective Tools to Fight the Methamphetamine Epidemic?" *Health Economics* 20:519–531.

"Notes on Science." 1947. *New York Times,* December 7, p. 127.

———. 1949. *New York Times,* August 7, p. E9.

O'Brien, Denes. 1969. "Lions Club Hears of Drug Abuse in County." *The News* (Frederick, MD), July 18, p. B14.

O'Connor, Matthew. 1968. "Law Enforcement and the Amphetamines." In *Amphetamine Abuse,* edited by J. Robert Russo, 88–97. Springfield, IL: Charles C. Thomas.

O'Donnell, John A., et al. 1976. *Young Men and Drugs: A Nationwide Survey.* NIDA Research Monograph 5. Rockville, MD: Department of Health, Education, and Welfare.

"Offerings to Buyers, Cont'd." 1945. *New York Times,* December 2, p. F6.

ONDCP (Office of National Drug Control Policy). 2012. "FY2013 Budget and Performance Summary." April. Retrieved May 3, 2013, from www.white house.gov.

———. 2013. "National Drug Control Budget: FY2014 Funding Highlights." April. Retrieved May 10, 2013, from www.whitehouse.gov.

Osborne, Duncan. 2005. *Suicide Tuesday: Gay Men and the Crystal Meth Scare.* New York: Carroll and Graf.

Owen, Frank. 2004. "No Man Is a Crystal Meth User unto Himself." *New York Times,* August 29, p. I1.

———. 2007. *No Speed Limit: The Highs and Lows of Meth.* New York: St. Martin's.

Oz, Mehmet. 2011. "'Bath Salts': Evil Lurking at Your Corner Store." *Time,* April 25, p. 54.

Packer, Lisa, et al. 2002. "Changes in NHSDA Measures of Substance Use Initiation." In *Redesigning an Ongoing National Household Survey: Methodological Issues,* edited by J. Gfroerer, J. Eyerman, and J. Chromy, 185–220. DHHS Publication No. SMA 03-3768. Rockville, MD: Substance Abuse and Mental Health Services Administration, Office of Applied Studies.

Padgett, Tim, and Elaine Shannon. 2001. "The Border Monsters." *Time,* June 11. Retrieved November 27, 2007, from www.time.com.

Paley, Amit R. 2006a. "The Next Crack Cocaine?" *Washington Post,* March 19, p. C1.

———. 2006b. "A Spring Break Road Trip to the Drugstore." *Washington Post,* April 4, p. B5.

Parsons, Nicholas L. 2012. "Fear of Crime and Fear of Drugs: The Role of Mass Media." In *Local Issues, Global Impact: Perspectives on Contemporary Social Issues,* edited by Michael J. Stern, 157–173. San Diego: Cognella.

"'Pep' Drug Found Useful in Relaxing the Eyes." 1937. *The Science News-Letter* 32 (October 30): 279.

"'Pep Pills' Keep Takers Awake 18 Hours." 1942. *New York Times,* December 24, p. 7.

"Pep-Pill Poisoning." 1937. *Time,* May 10. Retrieved September 6, 2008, from www.time.com.

Perlmutter, Emanuel. 1967. "Girl, Youth Slain in Village Cellar." *New York Times,* October 9, p. 1.

Peterson, Joel B. 1928. "Standardization of Ephedrine and Its Salts." *Industrial and Chemical Engineering* 20:388–391.

Peterson, Ruth D. 1985. "Discriminatory Decision Making at the Legislative Level: An Analysis of the Comprehensive Drug Abuse Prevention and Control Act of 1970." *Law and Human Behavior* 9:243–269.

Platts, Todd K. 2013. "Locating Zombies in the Sociology of Popular Culture." *Sociology Compass* 7:547–560.

Plumb, Robert K. 1959. "Pep Drugs Found to Spur Athletes." *New York Times*, May 29, p. 1.

"Police Arrest Woman, Man." 1962. *The Daily Review*, September 12, p. 21.

Pollack, Andrew. 2010. "A Drug's Second Act: Battling Jet Lag." *New York Times*, January 6, p. B1.

"Prescribing S.F. Nurse Arrested." 1962. *Oakland Tribune,* August 24, p. 9.

Pretti, John. 2011. "'Smurfing' for Extra Income During Hard Times." *Jackson County Floridian,* December 26. Retrieved September 1, 2012, from www.examiner.com /article/smurfing-for-extra-income-during-hard-times.

Pritchard, David. 1986. "Homicide and Bargained Justice: The Agenda-Setting Effect of Crime News on Prosecutors." *Public Opinion Quarterly* 50:143–159.

"Prosecutor Fighting Meth Using Law That Punishes Terrorism." 2003. *Citizen-Times,* July 16. Retrieved July 29, 2013, from www.amphetamines.com.

Prosser, Jane M., and Lewis S. Nelson. 2012. "The Toxicology of Bath Salts: A Review of Synthetic Cathinones." *Journal of Medical Toxicology* 8:33–42.

"Psychic Treatment Is Urged in Surgery." 1931. *New York Times*, October 14, p. 18.

Puder, Karoline S., Doreen V. Kagan, and John P. Morgan. 1988. "Illicit Methamphetamine: Analysis, Synthesis, and Availability." *American Journal of Drug and Alcohol Abuse* 14:463–473.

"Purpose and Design." 2012. *Monitoring the Future.* Retrieved September 2, 2012, from www.monitoringthefuture.org.

Rasmussen, Nicolas. 2006. "Making the First Anti-Depressant: Amphetamine in American Medicine, 1929–1950." *Journal of the History of Medicine and Allied Sciences* 61:288–323.

———. 2008a. *On Speed: The Many Lives of Amphetamine.* New York: New York University Press.

———. 2008b. "America's First Amphetamine Epidemic 1929–1971: A Quantitative and Qualitative Retrospective with Implications for the Present." *American Journal of Public Health* 98:974–985.

———. 2011. "Medical Science and the Military: The Allies' Use of Amphetamine During World War II." *Journal of Interdisciplinary History* 42 (2): 205–233.

Rawlin, John William. 1968. "Street Level Abuse of Amphetamines." In *Amphetamine Abuse*, edited by J. Robert Russo, 51–65. Springfield, IL: Charles C. Thomas.

Reagan, Ronald. 1986. "Proclamation 5537: National Drug Abuse Education and Prevention Week and National Drug Abuse Education Day, 1986." October 6. Retrieved June 18, 2008, from www.reagan.utexas.edu.

Reasons, Charles E. 1976. "Images of Crime and the Criminal: The Dope Fiend Mythology." *Journal of Research in Crime and Delinquency* 13:133–144.

Reding, Nick. 2009. *Methland.* New York: Bloomsbury.

Reeves, Jimmie L., and Richard Campbell. 1994. *Cracked Coverage.* Durham, NC: Duke University Press.

Reinarman, Craig. 2012. "The Social Construction of Drug Scares." In *Constructions of Deviance: Social Power, Context, and Interaction,* 7th ed., edited by Patricia A. Adler and Peter Adler, 159–170. Belmont, CA: Thomson/Wadsworth.

Reinarman, Craig, and Harry G. Levine. 1997a. "Crack in Context: America's Latest Demon Drug." In *Crack in America: Demon Drugs and Social Justice,* edited by Craig Reinarman and Harry G. Levine, 1–17. Berkeley: University of California Press.

———. 1997b. "The Crack Attack: Politics and Media in the Crack Scare." In *Crack in America: Demon Drugs and Social Justice,* edited by Craig Reinarman and Harry G. Levine, 18–51. Berkeley: University of California Press.

———, eds. 1997c. *Crack in America: Demon Drugs and Social Justice.* Berkeley: University of California Press.

———. 1997d. "Punitive Prohibition in America." In *Crack in America: Demon Drugs and Social Justice,* edited by Craig Reinarman and Harry G. Levine, 321–333. Berkeley: University of California Press.

Reinarman, Craig, et al. 1997. "The Contingent Call of the Pipe: Bingeing and Addiction Among Heavy Cocaine Smokers." In *Crack in America: Demon Drugs and Social Justice,* edited by Craig Reinarman and Harry G. Levine, 77–97. Berkeley: University of California Press.

Renshaw, Patrick. 1968. "The IWW and the Red Scare, 1917–24." *Journal of Contemporary History* 3:63–72.

Robinson, Linda. 1998. "Raising the Stakes in US-Mexico Drug Wars." *US News and World Report,* October 5, p. 35.

Robles, Frances. 2012. "Homeless Victim of Cannibal Attack: Stranger 'Just Ripped Me to Ribbons.'" *Miami Herald,* August 8. Retrieved September 1, 2012, from www.miamiherald.com.

Romer, Christina D. 1992. "What Ended the Great Depression?" *Journal of Economic History* 52:757–784.

Rose, Joseph. 2004. "The Faces of Meth." *Oregonian,* December 28, p. D1.

Ross, Edward A., Mary Watson, and Bruce Goldberger. 2011. "'Bath Salts' Intoxication." *New England Journal of Medicine* 365:967–968.

Rotella, Sebastian, and Chris Kraul. 1995. "Tank's Hijacker Troubled: Family, Drug Woes Haunted Man Slain During Rampage." *Los Angeles Times,* May 19, p. A1.

Rudgley, Richard. 1999. *The Encyclopaedia of Psychoactive Substances.* New York: St. Martin's.

Salter, Jim. 2012. "National Meth Lab Busts Up in 2011." *Washington Times,* February 22. Retrieved June 25, 2012, from www.washingtontimes.com.

SAMHSA (Substance Abuse and Mental Health Services Administration). 2003. "Results from the 2002 National Survey on Drug Use and Health: Detailed Tables," Tables 4.2A, 4.13A, 4.59B, and 4.70B. Substance Abuse and Mental Health Services Administration. Office of Applied Studies, NHSDA Series H-22, DHHS Publication No. SMA 03–3836. Rockville, MD. Retrieved September 2, 2012, from www.samhsa.gov.

———. 2006a. "National Survey on Drug Use and Health, 2002." US Department of Health and Human Services. Substance Abuse and Mental Health Services Administration. Office of Applied Studies. ICPSR03903-v3. Ann Arbor, MI: Inter-university Consortium for Political and Social Research (distributor), 2006-10-26. doi:10.3886/ICPSR03903.v3.

———. 2006b. "National Survey on Drug Use and Health, 2003." US Department of Health and Human Services. Substance Abuse and Mental Health Services Administration. Office of Applied Studies. ICPSR04138-v2. Ann Arbor, MI: Inter-university Consortium for Political and Social Research (distributor), 2006-10-17. doi:10.3886/ICPSR04138.v2.

———. 2006c. "National Survey on Drug Use and Health, 2004." US Department of Health and Human Services. Substance Abuse and Mental Health Services

Administration. Office of Applied Studies. ICPSR04373-v1. Ann Arbor, MI: Inter-university Consortium for Political and Social Research (distributor), 2006-05-12. doi:10.3886/ICPSR04373.v1.

———. 2009a. "National Survey on Drug Use and Health, 2005." US Department of Health and Human Services. Substance Abuse and Mental Health Services Administration. Office of Applied Studies. ICPSR04596-v2. Ann Arbor, MI: Inter-university Consortium for Political and Social Research (distributor), 2009-08-12. doi:10.3886/ICPSR04596.v2.

———. 2009b. "SAMHSA Portfolio of Programs and Activities." Substance Abuse and Mental Health Services Administration, US Department of Health and Human Services, October 8. Retrieved September 2, 2012, from www.samhsa.gov.

———. 2009c. "National Survey on Drug Use and Health, 2006." US Department of Health and Human Services. Substance Abuse and Mental Health Services Administration. Office of Applied Studies. ICPSR21240-v4. Ann Arbor, MI: Inter-university Consortium for Political and Social Research (distributor), 2009-08-12. doi:10.3886/ICPSR21240.v4.

———. 2009d. "National Survey on Drug Use and Health, 2007." US Department of Health and Human Services. Substance Abuse and Mental Health Services Administration. Office of Applied Studies. ICPSR23782-v2. Ann Arbor, MI: Inter-university Consortium for Political and Social Research (distributor), 2009-08-12. doi:10.3886/ICPSR23782.v2.

———. 2009e. "National Survey on Drug Use and Health, 2008." US Department of Health and Human Services. Substance Abuse and Mental Health Services Administration. Office of Applied Studies. ICPSR26701-v2. Ann Arbor, MI: Inter-university Consortium for Political and Social Research (distributor), 2009-12-16. doi:10.3886/ICPSR26701.v2.

———. 2011. "National Survey on Drug Use and Health, 2010." US Department of Health and Human Services. Substance Abuse and Mental Health Services Administration. Center for Behavioral Health Statistics and Quality. ICPSR32722-v1. Ann Arbor, MI: Inter-university Consortium for Political and Social Research (distributor), 2011-12-05. doi:10.3886/ICPSR32722.v1.

———. 2012a. "National Survey on Drug Use and Health, 2011." US Department of Health and Human Services. Substance Abuse and Mental Health Services Administration. Center for Behavioral Health Statistics and Quality. ICPSR34481-v1. Ann Arbor, MI: Inter-university Consortium for Political and Social Research (distributor), 2012-11-28. doi:10.3886/ICPSR34481.v1.

———. 2012b. "Results from the 2011 National Survey on Drug Use and Health: Summary of National Findings." Substance Abuse and Mental Health Services Administration, NSDUH Series H-44, HHS Publication No. (SMA) 12-4713. Rockville, MD, September. Retrieved May 10, 2013, from www.samhsa.gov.

———. 2012c. "National Survey on Drug Use and Health, 2009." US Department of Health and Human Services. Substance Abuse and Mental Health Services Administration. Office of Applied Studies. ICPSR29621-v2. Ann Arbor, MI: Inter-university Consortium for Political and Social Research (distributor), 2012-02-10. doi:10.3886/ICPSR29621.v2.

———. 2013a. "National Survey on Drug Use and Health: 2-Year R-DAS (2002 to 2003, 2004 to 2005, 2006 to 2007, 2008 to 2009, and 2010 to 2011)." Substance Abuse and Mental Health Services Administration. SDA 3.5: Tables. Retrieved on April 26, 2013, from www.icpsr.umich.edu.

———. 2013b. "National Survey on Drug Use and Health: 8-Year R-DAS (2002 to 2009)." SDA 3.5: Tables. Substance Abuse and Mental Health Services Administration. Retrieved April 26, 2013, from www.icpsr.umich.edu.

Sanchez, Rene. 2001. "Meth Production Reaches 'Epidemic' Level on Coast." *Washington Post*, August 25, p. A03.

"Schedule of Controlled Substances: Placement of Methylone into Schedule I; Final Rule." 2013. *Federal Register* 78 (71): 21818–21825. Docket No. DEA-357, 21 CFR Part 1308, April 12.

Schifano, Fabrizio, Antonio Albanese, Suzanne Fergus, Jackie L. Stair, Paolo Deluca, Ornella Corazza, Zoe Davey, John Corkery, Holger Siemann, Norbert Scherbaum, Magi' Farre', Marta Torrens, Zsolt Demetrovics, and A. Hamid Ghodse. 2011. "Mephedrone (4-Methylmethcathinone; 'Meow Meow'): Chemical, Pharmacological and Clinical Issues." *Psychopharmacology* 214:593–602.

Schumer, Charles E. 2012. "Schumer Legislation Banning Bath Salts and 29 Other Deadly Synthetic Substances Signed into Law Today by President Obama." July 9. Retrieved September 1, 2012, from www.schumer.senate.gov.

Schwartz, Noaki. 2001. "Surge in Meth Use Takes Toll on Rural Children." *Los Angeles Times*, May 7, p. B1.

Scott, Michael S. 2002. "Clandestine Drug Labs." *Problem-Oriented Guides for Police Series,* No. 16. US Department of Justice, Office of Community Oriented Policing Services. Retrieved April 3, 2005, from www.cops.usdoj.gov.

Seevers, Maurice H. 1968. "Classification of Amphetamine and Amphetamine-Like Drugs." In *Amphetamine Abuse*, edited by J. Robert Russo, 116–118. Springfield, IL: Charles C. Thomas.

"S.F. Police Hunt Frantically for Dynamite 'Gifts' in Mail." 1968. *Independent Press Telegram*, March 6, p. 17.

Shanon, Benny. 2008. "Biblical Entheogens: A Speculative Hypothesis." *Time and Mind: The Journal of Archaeology Consciousness and Culture* 1:51–74.

Sheridan, Janie, et al. 2006. "Injury Associated with Methamphetamine Use: A Review of the Literature." *Harm Reduction Journal* 3:14. Retrieved January 15, 2009, from www.harmreductionjournal.com.

Shetty, Vivek, Larissa J. Mooney, Corwin M. Zigler, Thomas R. Belin, Debra Murphy, and Richard Rawson. 2010. "The Relationship Between Methamphetamine Use and Increased Dental Disease." *Journal of the American Dental Association* 141:307–318.

Shoblock, James R., Eric B. Sullivan, Isabelle M. Maisonneuve, and Stanley D. Glick. 2003. "Neurochemical and Behavioral Differences Between d-Methamphetamine and d-Amphetamine in Rats." *Psychopharmacology* 165:359–369.

Shulgin, Alexander T. 1976. "Abuse of the Term 'Amphetamines.'" *Clinical Toxicology* 9:351–352.

Siegel, Ronald K. 1989. *Intoxication: Life in Pursuit of Artificial Paradise*. New York: Dutton.

Simon, Jonathan. 2007. *Governing Through Crime: How the War on Crime Transformed American Democracy and Created a Culture of Fear*. New York: Oxford University Press.

Singer, Thea. 2006. "Recipe for Disaster." *Washington Post*, January 15, p. W22.

Skipp, Catharine, and Arian Campo-Flores. 2006. "Addiction: A 'Meth Prison' Movement." *Newsweek*, April 24, p. 9.

Skogan, Wesley G., and Michael G. Maxfield. 1981. *Coping with Crime: Individual and Neighborhood Reactions*. Beverly Hills, CA: Sage.

Smith, Roger C. 1969a. "The Marketplace of Speed: Compulsive Methamphetamine Abuse and Violence." Doctoral dissertation, University of California, Berkeley. Ann Arbor: University Microfilms.

————. 1969b. "The World of the Haight Ashbury Speed Freak." *Journal of Psychedelic Drugs* 3:172–188.

Soroka, Stuart N. 2002. "Number of Responses and the Most Important Problem." Nuffield College Politics Working Paper, 2002-W34 (unpublished). Retrieved December 22, 2008, from www.nuffield.ox.ac.uk.

"Speed Demons." 1984. *Time*, April 2. Retrieved September 2, 2012, from www.time.com.

"Speed Kills." 1967. *Time*, October 27. Retrieved October 20, 2008, from www.time.com.

"S.S.F. Woman Cracks Ring." 1963. *San Mateo Times and Daily News Leader*, February 6, p. II:15.

Staley, Sam. 1992. *Drug Policy and the Decline of American Cities*. New Brunswick, NJ: Transaction.

"State Estimates of Past Year Methamphetamine Use." 2006. *The NSDUH Report*, no. 37. Retrieved September 3, 2012, from www.oas.samhsa.gov.

Stewart, Sally Ann. 1989. "'Poor Man's Cocaine' Hits West." *USA Today*, July 26, p. 3A.

Stix, Gary. 2011. "Meth Hype Could Undermine Good Medicine." *Scientific American*, December 27. Retrieved July 27, 2013, from www.scientificamerican.com.

Stomberg, Christopher, and Arun Sharma. 2012. "Making Cold Medicine Rx Only Did Not Reduce Meth Use." Portland, OR: Cascade Policy Institute. Retrieved May 3, 2013, from cascadepolicy.org.

"Story of Girl Hippy Slain in 'Village' Arouses Wide Concern." 1967. *New York Times*, October 29, p. 57.

Strand, Robert. 1968. "'Speed' Drugs Bring Hate, Horror to Hippies' Haight-Ashbury Mecca." *Bridgeport Sunday Post*, September 8, p. C19.

Strang, John, Jenny Bearn, Michael Farrell, Emily Finch, Michael Gossop, Paul Griffiths, John Marsden, and Kim Wolff. 1998. "Route of Drug Use and Its Implications for Drug Effect, Risk of Dependence and Health Consequences." *Drug and Alcohol Review* 17:197–211.

Stuart, David M. 1962. "To Depress the Craving for Food." *American Journal of Nursing* 62:88–92.

"Students Warned Not to Use Pep Pills." 1937. *El Paso Herald-Post*, June 3, p. 9.

Suo, Steve. 2004a. "Shelved Solution: Achilles' Heel." *Oregonian*, October 6, p. A1.

————. 2004b. "Lobbyists and Loopholes." *Oregonian*, October 4, p. A1.

Surette, Ray. 1990. "Criminal Justice Policy and the Media." In *The Media and Criminal Justice Policy*, edited by Ray Surette, 3–21. Springfield, IL: Charles C. Thomas.

————. 1994. "Predator Criminals as Media Icons." In *Media, Process, and the Social Construction of Crime*, edited by Gregg Barak, 131–158. New York: Garland.

Suro, Robert. 1997. "Other Drugs Supplanting Cocaine Use; Methamphetamine, Heroin on the Rise, White House Reports." *Washington Post*, June 25, p. A01.

Suwaki, Hiroshi, Susumu Fukui, and Kyohei Konuma. 1997. "Methamphetamine Abuse in Japan: Its 45 Year History and Current Situation." In *Amphetamine Misuse: International Perspectives on Current Trends*, edited by Hilary Klee, 199–214. Amsterdam: Harwood Academic.

Swann, John P. 1994. "FDA and the Practice of Pharmacy: Prescription Drug Regulation Before the Durham-Humphrey Amendment of 1951." *Pharmacy in History* 36:55–70.

"The Synthetic Scare; Bath Salts." 2012. *Economist*, August 4, p. 30.

Szasz, Thomas. 1974. *Ceremonial Chemistry*. Garden City, NY: Anchor/Doubleday.

TEDS (Treatment Episode Data Set). 2010. "Treatment Episode Data Set—Admissions (TEDS-A)—Concatenated, 1992 to 2010. Codebook: 2005 to 2009."

Substance Abuse and Mental Health Services Administration. Office of Applied
    Studies, United States Department of Health and Human Services. ICPSR 25221.
    Ann Arbor, MI: Inter-university Consortium for Political and Social Research.

————. 2012. "Treatment Episode Data Set—Admissions (TEDS-A)—Concatenated,
    1992 to 2010." Substance Abuse and Mental Health Services Administration.
    Office of Applied Studies, US Department of Health and Human Services.
    ICPSR 25221-v5. Ann Arbor, MI: Inter-university Consortium for Political and
    Social Research (distributor), 2012-07-25. doi:10.3886/ICPSR25221.v5.

Terry, Don. 1989. "Raw and Bawdy, 42d St. Awaits a Big Change." *New York Times*,
    December 11, p. A1.

"Thinks Nazis Had Drug." 1940. *New York Times*, August 4, p. 21.

Thompson, Cheryl W. 2002. "Drug Ring Investigation Nets Arrests in 12 Cities."
    Washington Post, January 11, p. A3.

Thompson, Hunter S. [1966] 1999. *Hell's Angels: A Strange and Terrible Saga*. New
    York: Modern Library.

————. 1967. "The 'Hashbury' Is the Capital of the Hippies." *New York Times*, May
    14, p. SM14.

Thompson, Larry. 1989. "Ice: New, Smokable Form of Speed." *Washington Post*,
    November 21, p. Z11.

Thornton, Mark. 1998. "Perfect Drug Legalization." In *How to Legalize Drugs*, edited
    by Jefferson M. Fish, 638–660. Northvale, NJ: Jason Aronson.

Toufexis, Anastasia. 1996. "There Is No Safe Speed." *Time*, January 8. Retrieved
    November 27, 2007, from www.time.com.

Trapasso, Claire. 2012. "Dead Men Walkin'." *New York Daily News*, June 10, p. 20.

"Trends in US Corrections." 2012. *The Sentencing Project*, May. Retrieved September
    1, 2012, from www.sentencingproject.org.

"Trial and Error." 1936. *Time*, September 14. Retrieved June 22, 2008, from
    www.time.com.

"Typist Jailed on Dope Charge." 1962. *San Mateo Times and Daily News Leader*,
    September 27, sec. 2, p. 25.

UNODC (United Nations Office on Drugs and Crime). 2011. "World Drug Report 2011."
    Vienna: United Nations. Retrieved February 20, 2012, from www.unodc.org.

"Unsafe at Any Speed." 1967. *Time*, October 27. Retrieved October 20, 2008, from
    www.time.com.

"Ups and Downs with Pills." 1957. *New York Times*, June 23, p. 162.

US Congress, House of Representatives. 1989. *The Reemergence of
    Methamphetamine: Hearing Before the Select Committee on Narcotics Abuse and
    Control*. 101st Congress, 1st session, October 24. Retrieved May 11, 2013, from
    babel.hathitrust.org.

US Congress, Senate. 1990. *Omnibus Crime Bill*. Amendment No. 1683, 101st
    Congress, 2nd session. *Congressional Record* 136 (June 28, 1990): S9038.
    Retrieved April 20, 2013, from thomas.loc.gov.

"US Drug Ring Tied to Aid for Hezbollah." 2002. *New York Times*, September 3, p.
    A16.

"Use of Drug at U.W. Denied by Clinic Chief." 1937. *Wisconsin State Journal*, May 9,
    p. 5.

"Vanderbilt Television News Archive." 2012. Vanderbilt University. Retrieved
    September 3, 2012, from http://tvnews.vanderbilt.edu.

Vasquez, Daniel. 1996. "'Cooks' Create Drug Nightmare." *Journal Star*, December
    30, p. A1.

Vaughne, Isabella A. 2010. *The Merida Initiative*. New York: Nova Science.

Verweij, Anthonie M. A. 1989. "Impurities in Illicit Drug Preparations: Amphetamine and Methamphetamine." *Forensic Science Review* 1:1–11.

"View Ads." 2013. Montana Meth Project. Retrieved April 22, 2013, from www.meth project.org/ads/tv.

Visser, S. N., R. H. Bitsko, M. L. Danielson, R. Perou, and S. J. Blumberg. 2010. "Increasing Prevalence of Parent-Reported Attention-Deficit/Hyperactivity Disorder Among Children—United States, 2003 and 2007." *Morbidity and Mortality Weekly Report* 59:1439–1443.

Volwiler, Ernest H. 1940. "Pharmaceutical Manufacture." *Industrial and Engineering Chemistry* 32:1179.

"The War Next Door (Part II)." 2006. *CBS Evening News*, May 19.

"War on Drugs / Hawaii / Ice." 1989. *ABC Evening News*, September 8.

Warfa, Nasir, Axel Klein, Kamaldeep Bhui, Gerard Leavey, Tom Craig, and Stephen Alfred Stansfeld. 2007. "Khat Use and Mental Illness: A Critical Review." *Social Science and Medicine* 65:309–318.

"Warn Students on Use of 'Pep Pills.'" 1937. *Brainerd Daily Dispatch*, June 3, p. 3.

Weber, Max. [1920] 2002. *The Protestant Ethic and the Spirit of Capitalism*. 3rd ed. Translation and Introduction by Stephen Kalberg. Los Angeles: Roxbury.

Weidner, Robert R. 2009. "Methamphetamine in Three Small Midwestern Cities: Evidence of a Moral Panic." *Journal of Psychoactive Drugs* 41:227–239.

Weil, Andrew, and Winifred Rosen. 2004. *From Chocolate to Morphine: Everything You Need to Know About Mind-Altering Drugs*. Rev. ed. Boston: Houghton Mifflin.

Weisheit, Ralph A., and L. Edward Wells. 2010. "Methamphetamine Laboratories: The Geography of Drug Production." *Western Criminology Review* 11 (2): 9–26.

Weisheit, Ralph A., and William L. White. 2009. *Methamphetamine: Its History, Pharmacology, and Treatment*. Center City, MN: Hazelden.

Welch, Michael, Melissa Fenwick, and Meredith Roberts. 1997. "Primary Definitions of Crime and Moral Panic: A Content Analysis of Experts' Quotes in Feature Newspaper Articles on Crime." *Journal of Research in Crime and Delinquency* 34:474–494.

"Where Have All the Flowers Gone?" 1967. *Time*, October 13. Retrieved October 20, 2008, from www.time.com.

Whitaker, Mark. 2005. "The Editor's Desk." *Newsweek*, August 8, p. 4.

Wieland, Diane M., Margaret J. Halter, and Ciara Levine. 2012. "Bath Salts: They Are Not What You Think." *Journal of Psychosocial Nursing* 50 (2): 17–21.

Will, George F. 1996. "Wilder Living Through Chemistry." *Washington Post*, September 19, p. A31.

Willers-Russo, Lynn J. 1999. "Three Fatalities Involving Phosphine Gas, Produced as a Result of Methamphetamine Manufacturing." *Journal of Forensic Sciences* 44:647–652.

Williams, Edward H. 1914. *The Question of Alcohol*. New York: Goodhue.

Winstock, Adam, Luke Mitcheson, John Ramsey, Susannah Davies, Malgorzata Puchnarewicz, and John Marsden. 2011. "Mephedrone: Use, Subjective Effects, and Health Risks." *Addiction* 106:1991–1996.

Witkin, Gordon. 1989. "The New Midnight Dumpers." *US News and World Report*, January 9, p. 57.

———. 1995. "A New Drug Gallops Through the West." *US News and World Report*, November 13, p. 50.

Wren, Christopher. 1996. "Sharp Rise in Use of Methamphetamines Generates Concern." *New York Times*, February 14, p. A16.

———. 1997. "The Illegal Home Business: 'Speed' Manufacture." *New York Times*, July 8, p. A8.

Young, Jock. 1971. *The Drugtakers*. London: MacGibbon and Kee.

———. 2011. "Moral Panics and the Transgressive Other." *Crime, Media, Culture* 7:245–258.

Zernike, Kate. 2005a. "A Drug Scourge Creates Its Own Form of Orphan." *New York Times*, July 11, p. A1.

———. 2005b. "Officials Across US Describe Drug Woes." *New York Times*, July 6, p. A12.

Zerubavel, Eviatar. 2002. "The Fine Line: Making Distinctions in Everyday Life." In *Cultural Sociology*, edited by Lyn Spillman, 223–232. Oxford: Blackwell.

Zinberg, Norman E. 1984. *Drug, Set, and Setting*. New Haven, CT: Yale University Press.

Index

Abbott Laboratories, 19, 48, 49, 76, 91
Acquired immune deficiency syndrome (AIDS), 136–137
ADAM. *See* Arrestee Drug Abuse Monitoring Program
ADD. *See* attention-deficit/hyperactivity disorder
Adderall, 3, 19, 73, 92
Addiction. *See* dependence
ADHD. *See* attention-deficit/hyperactivity disorder
Adrenaline, 7, 47
Adulterants, 8, 39, 104–105
African Americans: and cocaine (powder), 33, 36, 38; and crack, 18, 112, 113, 148; jazz musicians, 54–55, 61; and methamphetamine, 159, 165
Agassi, Andre, 184
AIDS. *See* acquired immune deficiency syndrome
Akaka, Daniel, 116–117
Alcohol, 31, 64, 80; and amphetamines, 88, 132, 154, 184; and cocaine, 33; moral panic over, 15, 21
Alien others, 84–86
Alles, Gordon, 48–49
AMA. *See* American Medical Association
Ambien, 90
American Dream, 59, 193
American Medical Association (AMA): Harrison Act, role in, 34–35, 37; and stimulants, 46, 47, 54, 65, 67

American Pharmaceutical Association (APhA), 34
Amphetamines: black market for, 64–65, 67–69, 75, 99, 104; and cocaine, 41, 46, 197–198; and crime, 55–56, 65–67; and CSA, 91–92; and cultural values, 58–59, 61–62; and death, 88; demand for, 60–63; effects of, 2, 7, 41, 45, 47; and ephedrine, 47–49, 101; government control of, 59–60, 65–69, 192; historical context of, 56–65; media coverage of, 51, 54–56, 65–66; medical forms of, 2, 3, 19; medical indications of, 49–51, 69; and methamphetamine, 2, 49–50, 73, 91–92; military use of, 53–54, 58, 69, 70, 74; pharmaceutical production and sales of, 50, 60, 62, 68, 197; and physicians, 51, 54, 55, 63–64, 74–75; and popular culture, 51–52, 61–62; supply of, 63–65; synthesis of, 46; United States, introduction into, 41–42, 48–54; usage data on, 98; users, 51–53, 61. *See also specific amphetamines;* inhalers
Anhydrous ammonia, 140
Anslinger, Harry, 57–58
APhA. *See* American Pharmaceutical Association
Apidex, 3
Arrestee Drug Abuse Monitoring Program (ADAM), 160–161, 164–165, 181–182, 183

About the Book

Ice. Methedrine. Crank. Crystal. Whatever its guise, the social and political contexts of methamphetamine share a certain uniqueness. Nicholas Parsons chronicles the history and mythology of methamphetamine in the United States from the 1940s—when it was hailed as a wonder drug—to the present. In an intriguing analysis, he also makes an important contribution to our understanding of the social construction of social problems.

Nicholas L. Parsons is assistant professor of sociology at Eastern Connecticut State University.

Social Problems, Social Constructions

Joel Best and Scott R. Harris, series editors

What Is Constructionism?
Navigating Its Use in Sociology
Scott R. Harris

Judging Victims: Why We Stigmatize Survivors,
and How They Reclaim Respect
Jennifer L. Dunn

The Paradox of Youth Violence
J. William Spencer

Confronting Homelessness:
Poverty, Politics, and the Failure of Social Policy
David Wagner, with Jennifer Barton Gilman

Making Sense of Social Problems:
New Images, New Issues
edited by Joel Best and Scott R. Harris

Responding to School Violence:
Confronting the Columbine Effect
Glenn W. Muschert, Stuart Henry,
Nicole L. Bracy, and Anthony A. Peguero

Meth Mania: A History of Methamphetamine
Nicholas L. Parsons